HENRY BLOFELD

Ten to Win . . .
And the Last Man In

My Pick of Test Match Cliffhangers

HODDER &
STOUGHTON

First published in Great Britain in 2021 by Hodder & Stoughton
An Hachette UK company

This paperback edition published in 2022

1

A CIP catalogue record for this title is available from the British Library

Paperback ISBN 978 1 529 35998 5

Typeset in Adobe Caslon by Hewer Text UK Ltd, Edinburgh
Printed and bound in Great Britain by Clays Ltd, Elcograf S.p.A.

Hodder & Stoughton policy is to use papers that are natural, renewable
and recyclable products and made from wood grown in sustainable
forests. The logging and manufacturing processes are expected to
conform to the environmental regulations of the country of origin.

Hodder & Stoughton Ltd
Carmelite House
50 Victoria Embankment
London EC4Y 0DZ

www.hodder.co.uk

*To Valeria, the best of literary assistants,
with love and thanks.*

CONTENTS

At one match in ten thousand the ritual cricket equation of runs–wickets–time resolves itself into the pattern of complete drama. When that happens, it is not necessary to know cricket to correlate all this data, to feel that its ingredients, like the elements of the Greek drama, have compelled a balanced perfection of construction. It is in the air.

John Arlott

PREFACE

THE idea of this book came to me one day when I was poring over Henry Newbolt's 'Vitaï Lampada', which my father first read to me when I was only in single figures and in the early stages of discovering my passion for cricket. For me, it now begs the question: is there anything in sport to compare with the sustained excitement of a cricket match, especially a Test match, in which the advantage continually fluctuates one way and then the other, and when the match enters its last few minutes, all four results are still possible? I have been lucky to watch one or two of these myself from the commentary box and the press box, and even sitting in the stand as an ordinary spectator. Before I go on, I must say both strongly and apologetically that this is a personal collection and, of course, everyone who reads this book will have their own idea of the matches I should have come up with. This is the joy of mulling over cricket matches like this.

I have chosen twenty-four Test matches, all of which have seen extraordinary finishes, and four one-day internationals, where the drama at the end can be similarly breathtaking, even though without the same tantalising four-innings and five-day build-up. This comparison brings with it the thought that two-innings Test cricket is an examination, while the one-day game, for all its instant advantages of glamour and action, is an exhibition. I have not included any Twenty20 games and, at the time of writing, the new Hundred competition in England has not yet left the draw-ing board. Both of these newer forms of the game can and will be hugely exciting, but without answering the pertinent question: are they really cricket? Maybe, but as different as instant coffee is from that made from freshly ground beans. Or maybe as David Hockney and Jeff Koons are from Constable and Turner.

Not all of these Test matches have built up in the beguiling way I have suggested, and several have pottered along for three or four days before exploding at the end like an outrageous firework display. Of course, once you know the final outcome, the build-up may well assume a new and more vibrant perspective. In 1960–61, if Australia had decided to bat out the fifth day of what became the first ever tied Test match, at Brisbane, for a draw, the other ingredients, most notably Garry Sobers's 132 or Alan Davidson's remarkable all-round performance, would perhaps never have been appreciated as they deserved. The beauty of the construction work may only be fully understood when the building has been finished and the component parts can then be seen in relation to the beauty of the whole.

In spite of all I have said in these first three paragraphs, it is hard to deny that the World Cup final at Lord's in 2019 saw the most incredible finish there has ever been to a game of cricket. Ben Stokes and Jos Buttler retrieved England's fortunes in the main match, which was tied, and then took them to a position which led to that extraordinary match-winning tie in the second, the Super Over. Within the month, Stokes had done it again, in the Test match at Headingley, this time with left-arm, bespectacled spinner Jack Leach, a Harry Potter-like figure, as his unlikely partner when they put on 74 for the last wicket to beat Australia. The finishes to limited-overs matches are relentlessly and repetitiously exciting, but I can say with confidence that the climax to this World Cup final at Lord's, when those four (in)famous overthrows made the difference at the very end, will surely never be repeated, while the last two hours at Headingley will not come along too often. I cannot leave that Lord's final without paying tribute not only to the cricketing skills and know-how of the New

Zealand captain, Kane Williamson, but also to his and his team's supreme sportsmanship when they were deserted by Lady Luck in the cruellest of ways right at the end. England's women had set the standard two years earlier when, as you will see, Anya Shrubsole bowled the side to a remarkable last-minute victory.

In all the cricket I have watched, I have not sat through another match as exciting from first ball to last as the fifth Test in Georgetown, Guyana, in 1967–68, or such a nerve-wracking sixth and final day as we had in the same match. I was on the air in 1981 when Bob Willis removed Ray Bright's middle stump to give England an extraordinary victory in what has become known, a trifle unfairly to Willis (8–43 in Australia's second innings), as Botham's Match after his almost eponymous 149 not out. I was also commentating when Ian Botham removed Jeff Thomson by way of a catch, first dropped at second slip and then held by first slip, at Melbourne in 1982–83 which brought England victory by three runs. There is plenty to choose from.

I shall go to my grave hoping that if all then works out well for me, I shall somehow be in a position to watch Spofforth – his 'bunny' was no less a batsman than W.G. – taking 14 wickets at The Oval in 1882. This, I hope, will be followed by the last two Test matches in 1902, at Old Trafford and The Oval. Stanley Jackson's 128 in the first of those two must have been an amazing innings, as must Gilbert Jessop's remarkable 75-minute hundred in the second, before arguably the most famous last-wicket pair of all time, George Hirst and Wilfred Rhodes, did not resolve to get the 15 still needed in singles, but got them all the same. Another innings I would have loved to see was Kenneth Hutchings's 126 at Melbourne in 1907–08. Then there was Jack Crawford, who has become a hero of mine while writing this book. We see him as a young all-rounder, only four months out of school at Repton, in South Africa in 1905–06, and then, two years later, in Australia. He must have been a tricky chap, but he was a genius when it came to batting, and to bowling his quick off-breaks. And then there was the redoubtable Aubrey Faulkner, the South African who for me was relatively unknown when I began to write but by the end had become my joint favourite cricketer of all time along with Denis Compton, who we see adroitly steering England to a stirring victory in a low-scoring match on a wet pitch in Durban. Enjoy Aubrey Faulkner and lament his sad end.

I had as wonderful a time delving into these almost prehistoric Test matches as I did reliving those that I have actually watched. I also had a lot fun with the four 50-over matches which I could not possibly have left out. Having said that, the near-misses and leftovers would have made another pretty exciting book too.

There are two games I need to explain, although as soon as you read their story, I am sure you will agree that they more than deserve their inclusion. There is a great and happy romance in the story of Archie MacLaren's victory over the Australians at Eastbourne in 1921, and the deeds of Robert Fowler for Eton at Lord's in 1910 can only produce an amused bewilderment – even among Harrovians. The progress of Lieutenant Colonel C.P. Foley, who left the barber's chair in White's Club with his hair half cut and Harrow 21–6, before racing with Lord Brackley in a taxi to Lord's, was exciting. His Lordship even promised to pay the driver double fare if he did it in under fifteen minutes, and their adventure plays its part in showing what an absurdly irresist-ible game cricket can be.

Henry Blofeld
Norwich, June 2021

1
THE DEMON

England v Australia (Only Test)
28–29 August 1882; The Oval, London
Australia won by seven runs.

THE second Test match ever played in England was one of the most thrilling games of all time. It ended in two days, as the result of some of the most devastating bowling in the history of the game. The Australian fast bowler Frederick Spofforth, known appropriately as 'The Demon', took seven wickets in each England innings. He finished with 14–90 in a match which produced only 363 runs in four completed innings. The highest score was a hard-hit 55 by Australian opening batsman Hugh Massie. The Ashes came into being as a direct result of this match, which was the first England had lost at home, in England.

Before we get into the match itself, the story of the Ashes must once more be told. A day or two after England's defeat at The Oval, the *Sporting Times* published a mock obituary notice proclaiming the death of English cricket and ending by saying that the body would be cremated and the ashes taken to Australia. The following English winter, the Honourable Ivo Bligh took a side out to play a series of three official matches against Australia. The first two were played in Melbourne, Australia winning the first and England the second. On the Sunday after the second match, the England players were invited to lunch by the Clarke family in Sunbury. Two spirited ladies who were daughters of the house burnt a couple of bails and who knows what else, put the resulting ashes into an urn and presented it to Bligh, although at that point the series stood at one-all and it was therefore a romantic gesture.

England then won the third official Test, in Sydney, and a fourth match was then decided upon, also in Sydney, which Australia won, to level the series. For this match, they experimented by using a new pitch for each innings. In 1927, on the death of Bligh, who had by then become Lord Darnley, his family presented the urn as a gift to the MCC. It was not until England visited Australia in 1902–03 that it became generally accepted that the Ashes was what the two countries played for, even though they have remained permanently in England, first as the property of Lord Darnley and then of the Marylebone Cricket Club.

In 1880, England had beaten Australia by five wickets at The Oval principally, it seemed, because Spofforth had been unable to play because of an injured finger. Two years later, the Englishmen discovered how lucky they had been, for Spofforth was an extraordinary bowler. He had started his cricketing life as an underarm lob bowler. He had then watched the England players who visited Australia in 1863–64 and had been impressed by the fast bowling of George Tarrant and decided that was where his future lay. He was ideally built for the job, being a big man who stood six foot three inches tall. He was also slim, strong and extremely fit.

While Spofforth relied on sheer pace at the start of his fast-bowling career, it was not long before he revealed that his real genius lay in his ability to adapt his style and perfect subtle variations. One of his main strengths was his ability to change his pace without in any way altering his frenetic action. It was reckoned he could bowl at three very different speeds without signalling his intentions. He also bowled what were known in those days as break-backs, which later were called off-breaks. He could turn the ball the full width of the stumps given any help from the pitch. His accuracy was remarkable and he had an almost unplayable fast yorker. No other bowler has ever clean-bowled such a large proportion of his victims. From his short run-up – less than ten yards – he went into his delivery stride with a huge leap. The action itself was all whirling arms and legs and he had a long, straight follow-through which damaged the pitch on a good length at the bowler's end, although in those days no one worried too much about that. Spofforth was a fearsome spectacle.

He is described by a contemporary as having 'a swarthy complexion, black moustache and steely brown eyes which conveyed an unmistakable aura of hostility'. Another said he had a 'Mephistophelian cast of countenance and a catherine-wheel action which was all legs, arms and nose'. Spofforth had an impressive aquiline nose. In his introduction to Richard Daft's *Kings of Cricket*, Andrew Lang wrote of Spofforth's action, 'It has withal a something truculent and overbearing.'

In the late 1870s, Spofforth was reckoned to bowl as fast as anyone had ever done. It is surprising, therefore, to find that the first wicket he took for Australia, against England at Melbourne in 1876–77, the batsman, Alfred Shaw, was stumped, as were another 18 of his first-class victims. His principal victim, rather surprisingly, was W.G. Grace, whom he sent back 19 times in first-class matches. In that first match at The Oval when Spofforth was not playing, Grace had made 152. One of Spofforth's habits was to stare belligerently at batsmen as they walked out to bat and took guard. W.G. would not have enjoyed that.

At this distance in time, it seems strange that Billy Murdoch's side of 1882 should have come all the way from Australia for one solitary representative game against 'All England', in late August. They had begun their first game, against Oxford University, on 15 May and played 25 first-class matches before this all-important contest at The Oval. England, who had never been beaten at home, confidently expected to win a match scheduled to be played over three days. They were captained by Albert 'Monkey' Hornby, who also played rugby for his country. The Oval was full for the two days needed, with more than 20,000 people packed into the ground. Although with so few runs being scored, the pitch can hardly have been a batsman's paradise.

Murdoch won an important toss for Australia on a damp morning, for there had been much recent rain, and decided to bat. Amid great excitement, the start, which was delayed because of the weather, was made at ten past twelve. The Australian innings was then opened by Massie and Alick Bannerman – whose brother, Charles, had played an innings of 165 out of 245 in what eventually was considered to have been the first ever Test match, at Melbourne in March 1877. Those two had put on only six when a yorker from George Ulyett hit Massie's leg stump. The score had reached 21 when Murdoch played Edmund Peate's left-arm spin onto his wicket and one run later Richard Barlow removed George Bonnor's middle stump. W.G. Grace then held on to a pretty good one with his left hand low down at point when Bannerman cut at Peate. Australia had lurched to 26–4.

It was hard and there was a succession of maiden overs; Bannerman had batted more than an hour for nine, which says much for England's bowlers, but maybe not too much for the state of the rain-affected pitch. The crowd were loving every moment, for although it was generally expected that England would win the match, this was a brilliant start. And on it went. Four runs later, Tom Horan lost his leg stump to Barlow and, before another run had been added, George Giffen was bowled by Peate, who then had Tom Garrett well caught, much to the delight of the crowd, by Surrey's Maurice Read at long off. Soon after lunch, there was a short break for rain and then Peate and Barlow quickly finished off the innings. Australia had only themselves to blame for being bowled out for as little as 63 after 'The Demon' Spofforth had struck a solitary, but perhaps meaningful, four.

After this extraordinary start, an air of confidence settled round the ground as the crowd sat back to watch England, who were batting by 3.30 on this first day, take full control of the match.

This confidence soon proved to be misplaced. England had scored only 13 when Spofforth, much to his delight, got his bunny, yorking W.G. with a beauty. Five runs later Barlow was picked up by Bannerman at what, in those days, was called forward point, a sort of close cover point in front of square, and England were 18–2. The spectators were being made to realise that this was going to be a closely fought contest. Every ball now seemed threatening and as a result every run was enthusiastically cheered. For all the formal Victorian clothes and outfits, everyone in the crowd was now completely involved with what was going on in the middle. The atmosphere was electric. Alfred Lucas and George Ulyett played some exhilarating strokes, taking the score to 50 after only half an hour's play. Soon afterwards, Ulyett, known as 'Happy Jack', jumped out to drive Spofforth, yes Spofforth, and was easily stumped.

The amazing thing about this was that Spofforth must surely have started off by bowling fast, with Jack Blackham standing back. Now, after only half an hour's play, Spofforth had his wicket-keeper standing up close to the stumps. It is one thing to vary your pace, but quite another to alter your style of bowling, which Jack Blackham's position now suggests. Spofforth and Blackham were an important combination, just as Dennis Lillee and Rod Marsh were to become almost a hundred years later. Blackham had a hand in a great many of Spofforth's dismissals.

Two runs later, at 59, Lucas got a thin edge to Harry Boyle and Blackham was in business again. When Spofforth hit Charles Studd's bails one run later, England had lost half their wickets for 60 and were still three runs behind. With the scores level, Alfred Lyttelton pushed uncertainly outside the off stump, giving Blackham his third dismissal and Spofforth his fifth wicket. It was only an eighth-wicket stand of 26 between Maurice Read and Allan Steel that enabled England to reach three figures and a lead of 38 runs. Spofforth finished off the innings, getting rid of Hornby and Peate and taking, in all, 7–46 in 36 overs. England were all out for 101, five minutes before the close of play on the first day. It had been an amazing day's entertainment for the big crowd and what a match they now had on their hands. Another factor which makes this seem even more extraordinary for readers today is the fact that no fewer than 151.3 overs were bowled during a day on which 20 wickets fell.

It rained heavily during the night and again Australia did not begin their second innings until ten past midday, although in a book he later wrote, Dick Barlow said the pitch was not fit for play. The bowler's footholds were completely waterlogged. Massie and Bannerman took full advantage of the conditions as Massie went for his strokes while Bannerman made sure he stayed in at the other end, and for the first time in the match, the bat was in charge. After only 28 minutes' play, 30 runs were on the board and Hornby had already made two bowling changes. By 2.45, England's lead of 38 had been knocked off. They had put on 47 when William Barnes took over from Studd, and off his first ball, Lucas made a mess of a straightforward catch at long off from a lofted off drive which had not come quite out of the middle of the bat. Immediately after this, W.G. was seen to be pulling thoughtfully at his beard. Massie was then 38 and the 50 came up immediately afterwards in only 40 minutes. Massie played some thrilling strokes, much to the crowd's enjoyment. Sixteen runs later there was great jubilation when Massie hit across a straight half-volley from Steel and was bowled. He had made 55 out of 66 in 57 minutes, hitting nine fours in the most commanding and entertaining innings of the match. The crowd were generous in their appreciation.

Massie's place was taken by Bonnor and four runs later his middle stump was clinically removed by Ulyett. Bannerman's patient innings came to an end before another run had been scored. He drove Barnes to extra cover, having batted 70 minutes for his 13 runs. W.G. Grace soon picked up Horan with a good catch close in on the off side and when Giffen was immediately out in exactly the same way, Australia were 79–5, only 41 runs ahead. With the clouds gathering, Blackham now joined Murdoch. Without too much difficulty, they had taken the score to 99 when it began to rain and so lunch was taken.

A second shower delayed the restart until a quarter to three and before another run had been scored, Blackham was beautifully caught behind the wicket by his opposite number, Alfred Lyttelton. Sam Jones, who had gone in at number ten in the first innings, now came in eighth. He and Murdoch had taken the score to 114 when a most unfortunate incident involving W.G. Grace caused Jones to be run out. Murdoch had played a ball gently away to leg and Lyttelton, the wicketkeeper, set off in pursuit. He returned the ball to the stumps and Jones, having completed the easy single, imagined the ball was now dead and moved out of his crease to tap down a spot on the pitch. Grace, who was always a fierce competitor, happy to push the Laws to the limit and perhaps even to indulge in a spot of sharp practice, was holding the ball. Seeing that Jones was out of his crease, he immediately broke the wicket and appealed. Bob Thoms, an experienced umpire, was standing at square leg and had no option but to give Jones out. It may have been the letter of the Law, as W.G. will have known only too well, but it was certainly not the spirit.

Understandably, the Australians and most particularly Murdoch, who was playing a wonderfully patient and important captain's innings, were extremely upset. When the immediate high feelings had cooled down a little, one member of the Australian side, no doubt a diplomat at heart, which is not always a major attribute of his fellow countrymen, admitted that he would have done the same if he had been in Grace's place. One inhabitant of the pavilion was reported to have said, surely with his tongue in his cheek, 'Jones ought to thank the champion for teaching him something.' Spofforth, who now joined Billy Murdoch, was also visibly upset. I wonder if anyone else on the England side that day would have behaved as Grace had done.

Grace's reputation is such that I rather doubt it. Heavily bearded, of course, and supremely confident, he believed he could do almost anything and get away with it. He was an incomparable cricketer, but perhaps not an incomparable sportsman. These incidents leave a nasty taste.

Spofforth's middle stump soon became a lost cause and Murdoch's splendid defence was ended when he was run out by some smart fielding from Hornby, helped by Charles Studd and then Lyttelton. Boyle, the last man, soon perished to Steel and Australia were all out at 3.25 for 122. Edmund Peate, a Yorkshireman who had opened the bowling for England with his orthodox left-arm spin, had taken 4–40 in Australia's second innings to add to his 4–31 in the first. He had bowled beautifully and Lord Hawke, his county captain, said that he was blessed with the most perfect action one could ever wish to see.

England had been left to score 85 to win and they must have felt reasonably confident of getting them, even though it was far from being the best of pitches. No one could have foreseen the drama and the excitement that was to come. There was probably only one man in the ground who was certain England would not win and he was in the Australian dressing room. As the players were preparing to go out into the field, Spofforth spoke loud and clear when he said, 'Boys, this thing can be done.'

England began the final innings of the match at 3.45 when W.G. Grace went out with his captain, Hornby, who, curiously, had batted at number ten in the first innings. They put on 15 in the first 15 minutes before Hornby, who had made nine of them, had his off stump knocked over by Spofforth, whose hostility and determination was easy to see. Barlow took Hornby's place and his first ball beat him for pace and bowled him. Some excitingly adventurous strokeplay from both Grace and Ulyett took the score to 51, when Spofforth changed ends. Ulyett played for a break-back and when the ball went straight on, it took the edge and he was brilliantly caught by Blackham behind the stumps.

England now needed 34 with seven wickets in hand. Surely they could not lose. This brought in Lucas and, after tucking a ball neatly away for two, Grace drove at Boyle without getting to the pitch of the ball and Bannerman held a simple catch at mid off. Lyttelton now joined Lucas and adopted a purely defensive role while his bustling partner made more of an attempt to keep the score moving. Even so, the game came almost to a standstill and 12 successive maiden overs – four balls each – were bowled by Spofforth and Boyle. Spofforth now hatched a plot with Boyle and arranged a piece of deliberate misfielding by Bannerman at mid off which allowed the batsmen to take a single and change ends. This meant both the bowlers had a different batsman to work on. The tactic worked. After four more maiden overs, Spofforth took his fourth wicket when he bowled Lyttelton and England were 66–5, needing only 19 more to win, with five wickets left.

The cricket was as tense and exciting as anyone on the ground could remember. The crowd cheered every run to the echo, but the force was with the Australian bowlers, led by the incomparable Spofforth. Lucas hit a four, but Steel fell to Spofforth's slower ball, which was almost impossible to spot. He would let his slower ball go with seemingly the same speed of arm action he used to bowl his fastest deliveries. Steel played too soon and spooned up an easy return catch to the bowler who, in anticipation, had run far across to the leg side to take the catch. The whole ground now vibrated with excitement, but, before another run had been scored, Spofforth, bowling maybe with much the same determination as Bob Willis showed all those years later at Headingley, blasted one through Lucas's defence and spreadeagled his stumps. This brought in Barnes, who scored a somewhat fortunate two. Then came three byes which were greeted with thunderous cheers, as they took the score to 75. Ten were now needed. The tension had been such that already one poor, unfortunate spectator had died from a heart attack. Another was busily chewing his way through what must have been a highly indigestible umbrella handle.

Lucas had been in a long time for his five and was doing the important job for England of making one end safe. Suddenly, and for no obvious reason, he played Spofforth, against whom he had been defending with some ease, into his stumps. Moments later, with Studd as his new partner, Barnes gave a simple catch to Murdoch off his glove, which made it 75–9. Peate, who was the last man, turned Boyle to square leg for two before being comprehensively bowled by the next ball. Australia had won an astonishing game of cricket by seven runs in less than two days. It was hugely appropriate that such a dramatically exciting game as this should have led directly to the founding of the Ashes. The urn could not have been given a more inspirational baptism. Maybe it was also appropriate, in view of the result of this match, that the urn which carries the Ashes should have then come from Australia.

ENGLAND v AUSTRALIA (Only Test)

At The Oval, London, on 28–29 August 1882 (three-day match).

Australia

A.C. Bannerman c Grace b Peate	9		c Studd b Barnes	13
H.H. Massie b Ulyett	1		b Steel	55
*W.L. Murdoch b Peate	13	(4)	run out	29
G.J. Bonnor b Barlow	1	(3)	b Ulyett	2
T.P. Horan b Barlow	3		c Grace b Peate	2
G. Giffen b Peate	2		c Grace b Peate	0
†J.M. Blackham c Grace b Barlow	17		c Lyttelton b Peate	7
T.W. Garrett c Read b Peate	10	(10)	not out	2
H.F. Boyle b Barlow	2	(11)	b Steel	0
S.P. Jones c Barnes b Barlow	0	(8)	run out	6
F.R. Spofforth not out	4	(9)	b Peate	0
Extras (1 b)	1		(6 b)	6
Total (all out, 80 overs)	**63**		(all out, 63 overs)	**122**

1–6 2–21 3–22 4–26 5–30 6–30 7–48 8–53 9–59 10–63

1–66 2–70 3–70 4–79 5–79 6–99 7–114 8–117 9–122 10–122

Bowling, *1st innings*: Peate 38–24–31–4; Ulyett 9–5–11–1; Barlow 31–22–19–5; Steel 2–1–1–0. *2nd innings*: Barlow 13–5–27–0; Ulyett 6–2–10–1; Peate 21–9–40–4; Studd 4–1–9–0; Barnes 12–5–15–1; Steel 7–0–15–2.

England

R.G. Barlow c Bannerman b Spofforth	11	(3)	b Spofforth	0
W.G. Grace b Spofforth	4	(1)	c Bannerman b Boyle	32
G. Ulyett st Blackham b Spofforth	26	(4)	c Blackham b Spofforth	11
A.P. Lucas c Blackham b Boyle	9	(5)	b Spofforth	5
†A. Lyttelton c Blackham b Spofforth	2	(6)	b Spofforth	12
C.T. Studd b Spofforth	0	(10)	not out	0
J.M. Read not out	19	(8)	b Spofforth	0
W. Barnes b Boyle	5	(9)	c Murdoch b Boyle	2
A.G. Steel b Garrett	14	(7)	c and b Spofforth	0
*A.N. Hornby b Spofforth	2	(2)	b Spofforth	9
E. Peate c Boyle b Spofforth	0		b Boyle	2
Extras (6 b, 2 lb, 1 nb)	9		(3 b, 1 nb)	4
Total (all out, 71.3 overs)	**101**		(all out, 55 overs)	**77**

1–13 2–18 3–57 4–59 5–60 6–63 7–70 8–96 9–101 10–101.

1–15 2–15 3–51 4–53 5–66 6–70 7–70 8–75 9–75 10–77.

Bowling, *1st innings*: Spofforth 36.3–18–46–7; Garrett 16–7–22–1; Boyle 19–7–24–2. *2nd innings*: Spofforth 28–15–44–7; Garrett 7–2–10–0; Boyle 20–11–19–3.

Close of play, *day 1*: England (1) 101 all out.

Toss: Australia. Balls per over: Four. Last-innings target: 85 runs.
Umpires: L. Greenwood (Eng), R.A. Thoms (Eng).

AUSTRALIA won by seven runs.

2

FRED TATE'S LAST STAND

England v Australia (4th Test)
24–26 July 1902; Old Trafford, Manchester
Australia won by three runs.

THE Golden Age of cricket which stretched from 1890 to 1914 had nothing finer to offer than the last two Test matches on Australia's tour of England in 1902. They remain as two of the most exciting games ever to have been played in an Ashes series. Australia won the first at Old Trafford by three runs, making sure they retained the Ashes, and England won the second, at The Oval, by one wicket. The cast list was incomparable: Archie MacLaren, F.S. Jackson, Gilbert Jessop, K.S. Ranjitsinhji, C.B. Fry, George Hirst and Wilfred Rhodes were among those who did battle for England, while Australia's ranks included Victor Trumper, Clem Hill, Hugh Trumble, Joe Darling and Monty Noble. No two players defined the Golden Age more than Trumper and Ranji.

The teams arrived in Manchester after rain had prevented England winning at Edgbaston in the first Test of the series and almost completely washed out the next game, at Lord's. Australia had then convincingly won the only Test match ever played at Bramall Lane in Sheffield, and so were one up in the series when the teams met at Old Trafford.

It is amusing to realise that the selection of the England side for this fourth Test caused huge criticism, and at this distance in time the final selections still seem inexplicable. The main reason for this may have been that the England captain, MacLaren, had fallen out with Lord Hawke, who was the formidable chairman of the selectors. George Hirst, Sydney Barnes, Jessop and Fry had been dropped after England had lost at Bramall Lane and they were replaced by Lionel Palairet, Ranji, who had recovered from a leg injury, Bill Lockwood and, most surprisingly, Fred Tate, who was having a successful season for Sussex. Barnes had taken 6–49 in Australia's first innings in the previous match and was now replaced by Tate, who would effectively cost England the match. The decision not to play Barnes was so strange that it looks as if Lord Hawke must have been trying to show MacLaren who was in control.

Australia won the toss and decided to bat. The ground was wet and to start with the slow pitch played so easily that Trumper, who was in the form of his life, became the first batsman ever to score a hundred before lunch in a Test match. On this tour, Trumper strode through the country in a way no other batsman has been able to imitate. In an unusually wet summer, he made 2,570 runs, with 11 centuries. These are the sort of figures associated with Don Bradman, but there the comparison ends. One difference between the two, according to his team-mate Monty Noble, was that whenever Trumper reached a hundred, he then felt it was somebody else's turn. Bradman could never be accused of allowing such a thought to enter his mind. There was something inevitable, almost prosaic, about an innings by Bradman, whereas every stroke Trumper played was a joint product of genius and imagination. Bradman's story was told mainly by the quantity of his runs; Trumper's by the natural quality of his strokeplay, coupled with his own joyful nature, which seemed untainted by conscious thought, let alone a coach's advice. It goes without saying that he saw the ball early and his unhurried footwork always left him perfectly placed to play whichever stroke he chose.

Trumper and Reggie Duff put on 135 for the first wicket in 80 minutes. At lunch Australia were 173–1, with Trumper and Clem

Hill in control. England were handicapped by the wet ground and the approach to the wicket was so damp that Bill Lockwood was unable to bowl at the start because of the state of the run-ups. One of the reasons the scoring was so rapid on this first morning was that Wilfred Rhodes (slow left arm) and Stanley Jackson, who was medium-paced, opened the bowling and so the over rate was excellent. In those days, the bowling was often opened by spinners. Trumper perished immediately after lunch, beaten in the air, perhaps, and caught behind off Rhodes. Clem Hill who, once he emerged from his ugly, crouching stance, was the most delightful strokemaker, in spite of holding his bat at the very bottom of the handle. As that suggests, he was a bottom-handed player and, like most left-handers, particularly strong off his legs. As he was a short man, he did not have quite the fluency of stroke-play the taller left-handers usually seem to have. He batted well for his 65 now and there was also a most determined knock of 51 from Darling.

The innings was finished off for England by Lockwood who, bowling with rhythm and pace, took the last five wickets, finishing with 6–48. Lockwood was a bad-tempered man who was by no means universally liked. He had a Machiavellian streak within him. There seemed also to be a deliberate viciousness to his bowling, which may have been, in part, the reflection of a confused and unhappy character. He was the fifth bowler MacLaren had turned to in this first innings, because of the state of those run-ups. When Lockwood eventually found his feet, he was too much for the Australians, who had a problem spotting his well-concealed slower ball. In spite of all this, it was the opinion of no less a person than C.B. Fry that Lockwood would top the polls for the best genuine fast bowler in the history of the game up to that time. Lockwood made one unsuccessful tour to Australia and, in all, took 43 wickets in his 12 Test matches

Australia were all out after tea for 299. On a pitch which was drier and had been roughed up by the England bowlers, the biting left-arm spin of Jack Saunders and the accuracy of the tall Hugh Trumble's off-spin soon proved to be devastating. By the close of play on this first night, England were struggling at 70–5, Saunders having taken three wickets and Trumble two. Stanley Jackson and Len Braund had by then added 26 anxious runs for the sixth wicket. The next morning the pitch played more easily, and in a wonderful session for England, these two put on another 115 with a fine display of strokes. Jackson's driving and cutting was particularly impressive. Then, just before lunch, Braund came forward to drive a ball from Noble wide of the off stump with his bat away from his body and it flew off the inside edge into his stumps. After the interval, Jackson did not get much support from the lower order, but with the last two batsmen in he set about the bowling with some magnificent strokes. Jackson had come in when England were 30–4 and was last out, after batting for four and a half hours for his 128. It was a great innings and the best of all that he played for his country.

Jackson was a man of many talents as well as being an extraordinary cricketer. As a schoolboy, he had played for three years in the XI at Harrow, where Winston Churchill had been his fag. When Jackson became a Member of Parliament, Churchill introduced him to future Prime Minister David Lloyd George, who said to him at once, 'I've been looking all my life for the man who gave Winston Churchill a hiding at school.' As captain of Cambridge University, Jackson had brought Ranjitsinhji into the side in the face of considerable opposition, for he was the first Indian to play for the university. After being elected to Parliament in 1915, Jackson spent 11 years as a member before being made Governor of Bengal. He was there for five years and in 1932, when making a speech at Calcutta University, he survived an assassination attempt. A girl who was a member of a revolutionary party fired five pistol shots at him at close range, but her aim was poor. Apparently Jackson's coolness under fire was impressive and when the immediate kerfuffle had died down, he continued his speech. He played in 20 Test matches, all of them against Australia, but never went on any tours because of his considerable business commitments.

At Old Trafford, Australia had a first-innings lead of 37. They began their second innings at four o'clock on the second afternoon and in no time they were 10–3. With the new ball, Lockwood was a nasty proposition, bowling at a good pace and still managing to bring the ball back sharply off the pitch in to the right-hander. His slower ball also caused problems and in his opening overs he sent back the formidable trio of Trumper, Duff and Hill. Six more runs had been scored when the captain, the left-handed Darling, a real fighter, was facing Braund, a leg-spinner, who had taken over from Tate. Braund wanted his Somerset colleague Lionel Palairet to come up to short leg, which was where he always fielded when Braund was bowling for his county. Palairet had been at deep square leg with his back to the railway line, and now MacLaren sent Tate, normally a close fielder, to take his place. Braund bowled short and Darling, with the score 16–3, swung the ball high to deep square leg. Tate hovered for a long time underneath the ball and dropped a catch he never looked like holding.

Darling and Gregory went on to add 54 in a stand which ultimately was responsible for Australia's victory. It was MacLaren who, as captain, had made the fateful decision on the first morning of the match to play Tate, a good, honest county cricketer, instead of Hirst, a player of an altogether different calibre – he obviously did not want Lord Hawke, the chairman and, like Hirst, a Yorkshireman, to have the last word. Darling went on to make 37, but if that catch had been held, Australia would have been hard-pressed to reach 50. As it was, they were 85–8 at the end of the second day and England still appeared to be winning the match. Tate's dropped catch had not yet assumed its ultimate importance. In retrospect, poor Tate at least had the satisfaction of taking two wickets for England when he had both Gregory and Trumble lbw.

The last two wickets fell the next morning for the addition of just one run after heavy overnight rain had delayed the start until midday. Lockwood finished with 5–28, which gave him the splendid match figures of 11–76. England had to make 124 to win, but on what was a drying pitch, their target now looked more difficult. In the 50 minutes of play before lunch, in sunny weather, MacLaren and Palairet got them off to a splendid start, scoring 36 without being separated. There was a full-house crowd and they will have enjoyed their lunch, although acute indigestion was only just round the corner.

By the time play restarted, the sun was getting to work on the pitch. Eight more runs had been scored when Saunders turned one a long way which curled past Palairet's outside edge and bowled him. Johnny Tyldesley joined MacLaren and, with the ball turning and lifting, the batting became more anxious, as if they realised they had to score the runs quickly before the sun made the surface even more difficult. Tyldesley made 16 in quick time before he drove at Saunders and was caught by Warwick Armstrong at slip. Four runs later, MacLaren was caught in the deep off Trumble and England were 72–3, with only 52 needed.

Numerically, there was no reason for undue anxiety, but in these last few minutes the game had undergone a sea-change. There were also two new batsmen at the crease, even if they were as experienced as Ranji and Bobby Abel. As in the first innings, Ranji looked out of both form and confidence and was hardly recognisable as the man who had made 154 against Australia at Old Trafford six years before. They took the score uneasily to 92, when Ranji, caught in two minds, was lbw to another medium-paced off-break from Trumble. It had become a thrilling and tense dogfight. By now, the crowd were more than aware that an England victory was by no means a foregone conclusion. They were most certainly on the edge of their seats.

Trumble was as understated as a man as he was as a bowler. He stood six foot five inches tall with a narrow face, a large nose and ears like bats' wings. He was the calmest of men, with the most equable temperament. Nothing would upset him and his was the perfect temperament for a spin bowler. If his face was anything to go by, he would have made a brilliant poker player. With a lovely high action, he bowled his off-breaks at a brisk medium pace. Monty Noble described his action as 'sidelong and insinuating, with his neck craned like a gigantic bird'. Although Trumble thrived most of all on the softer wickets in England, he was always a threat on the harder pitches in Australia as well. His control was impeccable and was allied to subtle variations of pace and flight. He took 141 wickets for Australia in 32 Test matches and now, at Old Trafford, he had 4–75 in England's first innings and would take 6–53 in the second. Trumble was the first of the great off-spinners.

Five more runs had been scored when he struck again. Abel came forward to drive and was beaten in the air and bowled; Jackson drove Saunders to Gregory at mid off; Braund came down the pitch to Trumble and was stumped. Trumble then took his fifth wicket when he bowled Lockwood for a duck. These last four had been dismissed for the addition of 17 runs, leaving England perilously placed at 109–8, still needing another 15. The new batsman was Rhodes – in the absence of Hirst, the ideal man to have coming in at such a point. The sight of Rhodes soothed the nerves and without any fuss he hit a four which was greeted by the crowd as if it was the match-winning stroke. His partner Dick Lilley now played two strokes which brought him a two and a single.

Eight were needed when Lilley faced Trumble. A terrific heave, accompanied by yells of joy from the crowd, and the ball soared away towards square leg for what must have seemed a certain four. Clem Hill was fielding at a wide long on and as soon as the ball began to climb into the air, he set off like a greyhound. Just when it looked as if he would not quite make it, he despairingly stuck out his right hand and held an unbelievable catch in front of the pavilion. To say the crowd was stunned would be an understatement. Neville Cardus's mythical parson in the half-crown stand summed it up to perfection: 'A sinful catch' was how he described it.

As poor Fred Tate made his way to the middle, the memory of that dropped catch will have been searing through his mind. He arrived at the non-striker's end and watched Rhodes defend the last three balls of Trumble's over. Now, as Tate was just about to take guard to face Saunders, heavy rain began to fall. The players scampered back to the pavilion, but they knew it would not be for too long. There was clear sky in the distance where the weather was coming from. Tate's anxious respite lasted for only 40 minutes before he and Rhodes followed the Australians back onto the field at six minutes to five.

Now, with eight runs needed for an England victory, Tate took guard. He poked at Saunders's first ball, which somehow found the inside edge of his bat and raced away to the fine-leg boundary accompanied by frenzied cheering which, in the circumstances, may not have done that much for Tate's peace of mind. The best way of describing Saunders's next two balls is to say that somehow, with defensive strokes which were themselves pretty sinful, Tate managed to survive them both. The next ball, which Saunders pushed through, was a shooter which left Tate stranded and crashed into his stumps. Australia had won by three runs and had made sure of the Ashes too, now being two matches up with one to play.

Tate's walk back to the pavilion was the final act in one of the more extraordinary Test careers. The family's reputation at this level of the game was to be left in the safe hands of his son, Maurice, who was himself to play in 39 Test matches for England.

ENGLAND v AUSTRALIA (4th Test)

At Old Trafford, Manchester, on 24–26 July 1902 (three-day match).

Australia

V.T. Trumper c Lilley b Rhodes	104		c Braund b Lockwood	4
R.A. Duff c Lilley b Lockwood	54		b Lockwood	3
C. Hill c Rhodes b Lockwood	65		b Lockwood	0
M.A. Noble c and b Rhodes	2	(6)	c Lilley b Lockwood	4
S.E. Gregory c Lilley b Rhodes	3		lbw b Tate	24
*J. Darling c MacLaren b Rhodes	51	(4)	c Palairet b Rhodes	37
A.J.Y. Hopkins c Palairet b Lockwood	0		c Tate b Lockwood	2
W.W. Armstrong b Lockwood	5		b Rhodes	3
†J.J. Kelly not out	4		not out	2
H. Trumble c Tate b Lockwood	0		lbw b Tate	4
J.V. Saunders b Lockwood	3		c Tyldesley b Rhodes	0
Extras (5 b, 2 lb, 1 w)	8		(1 b, 1 lb, 1 nb)	3

Total (all out, 76.1 overs) **299**
1–135 2–175 3–179 4–183 5–256 6–256
7–288 8–292 9–292 10–299

(all out, 47.4 overs) **86**
1–7 2–9 3–10 4–64 5–74 6–76
7–77 8–79 9–85 10–86

Bowling, *1st innings*: Rhodes 25–3–104–4; Jackson 11–0–58–0; Tate 11–1–44–0;
Braund 9–0–37–0; Lockwood 20.1–5–48–6. *2nd innings*: Lockwood 17–5–28–5;
Braund 11–3–22–0; Rhodes 14.4–5–26–3; Tate 5–3–7–2.

England

L.C.H. Palairet c Noble b Saunders	6		b Saunders	17
R. Abel c Armstrong b Saunders	6	(5)	b Trumble	21
J.T. Tyldesley c Hopkins b Saunders	22		c Armstrong b Saunders	16
*A.C. MacLaren b Trumble	1	(2)	c Duff b Trumble	35
K.S. Ranjitsinhji lbw b Trumble	2	(4)	lbw b Trumble	4
F.S. Jackson c Duff b Trumble	128		c Gregory b Saunders	7
L.C. Braund b Noble	65		st Kelly b Trumble	3
†A.F.A. Lilley b Noble	7		c Hill b Trumble	4
W.H. Lockwood run out	7		b Trumble	0
W. Rhodes c and b Trumble	5		not out	4
F.W. Tate not out	5		b Saunders	4
Extras (6 b, 2 lb)	8		(5 b)	5

Total (all out, 114 overs). **262**
1–12 2–13 3–14 4–30 5–44 6–185 7–203
8–214 9–235 10–262

(all out, 49.4 overs) **120**
1–44 2–68 3–72 4–92 5–97 6–107
7–109 8–109 9–116 10–120

Bowling, *1st innings*: Trumble 43–16–75–4; Saunders 34–5–104–3; Noble 24–8–47–2;
Trumper 6–4–6–0; Armstrong 5–2–19–0; Hopkins 2–0–3–0. *2nd innings*: Trumble 25–9–53–6;
Noble 5–3–10–0; Saunders 19.4–4–52–4.

Close of play, *day 1*: England (1) 70–5 (Jackson 16*, Braund 13*);
day 2: Australia (2) 85–8 (Kelly 1*, Trumble 4*).

Toss: Australia. Last-innings target: 124 runs.
Umpires: J. Moss (Eng), T. Mycroft (Eng).

AUSTRALIA won by three runs.

3
THE CROUCHER

England v Australia (5th Test)
11–13 August 1902; The Oval, London
England won by one wicket.

THE players had hardly got their breath back after the dramas and excitement of the Old Trafford Test when they came to The Oval two weeks later for another match which was, if anything, even more exciting. Needing 263 to win, they had slumped to 48–5 when Gilbert Jessop hit maybe the most amazing Test hundred of all. He was seventh out for 104 when the score was 187, with 76 runs still needed. It was the cool heads and straight bats of those two stalwart Yorkshiremen, George Hirst and Wilfred Rhodes, that eventually steered England home as they added the 15 needed for the last wicket. As Rhodes, the last man, came out to bat, the story has it that Hirst greeted him with 'We'll get 'em in singles.' Both of them later denied this was ever said, and in any case the runs were not all scored in singles.

The game could not help but start as something of an anti-climax. Australia's victory at Old Trafford had already enabled them to retain the Ashes, which had been in their hands since 1897–98. For all that, England's honour was at stake and at least a good showing, if not victory, was important. As at Old Trafford, and in the best traditions of a game which in those days assumed an important place in society at most levels, this match at The

Oval fluctuated intriguingly and ended up as probably the more exciting of the two matches.

The memory of this match is still very much alive, not least because as a 15-year-old, the playwright Ben Travers was among the spectators. In 1980, he wrote a book called *94 Declared* which included a description of the match from his own perspective and as his memory would allow. His mind was still amazingly sharp and this piece brings the game alive in an unusual and extremely gripping way, even though it is now just over 118 years ago. Travers came up with some details which were as fascinating as they were surprising and which after all this time had remained sharply etched in his mind. In June 1980, during the lunch interval on the Saturday of the Test against the West Indies, Travers had come into the *Test Match Special* commentary box at the top of the Pavilion 'primed with John Arlott's Moët' and talked to Brian Johnston about this Test at The Oval. The interview was so popular that Travers was persuaded to write a book about his memories of the match. He died at the age of 94 soon after finishing it.

Australia won the toss and inevitably decided to bat. Putting the other side in at The Oval has seldom been a profitable exercise. Not surprisingly, Australia stuck to the team that had won the previous Test while the England selectors – full of guilt, one hopes – brought back Hirst and Jessop for Tate, highly relieved to be back on duty with Sussex, and Ranji, while there was also a Surrey swap, with Tom Hayward taking Bobby Abel's place.

Apart from a brisk and attractive 42 from Victor Trumper, the main Australian batsmen were in all sorts of trouble against Hirst. After starting life as a fast-medium left-arm bowler who, from a lively run, gained pace off the pitch, he learned how to master the art of sharp and late inswing, sometimes being able to straighten the ball on pitching. It was this late swing which enabled him to pick up the first five Australian wickets on the first day. Hirst was also a most capable and resolute performer with the bat, as he would show in both innings at The Oval. Added to this, he had just about the safest pair of hands in the business. In his career he took 605 catches, mostly off hard drives when bowling or fielding at mid off. Quite short and almost chubby, he was the most delightful of men, with a lovely Yorkshire sense of humour. He was, too, a man who greatly encouraged the young, and after retiring spent 18 years as a hugely successful and popular coach at Eton. As a Test cricketer, he may not have been quite the equal of Rhodes, but there was not much in it. In 1906 he became the only man ever to score more than 2,000 runs and take over 200 wickets in the same season, a record that will never be equalled, let alone beaten.

After Hirst had accounted for the top half of the Australian batting, the last three wickets, led by Hugh Trumble, who made a painstaking 64 not out, put on 149. This irritated the 15-year-old Travers, who wrote that Trumble's 'pottering about' caused 'a good deal of lingering resentment and muffled snorting'. In other words, he did rather well for Australia. Their final tally of 324 was made to seem a more-than-useful score by Trumble, who bowled his off-breaks unchanged through both England innings and took 12–173 in the match. He bowled even better than he had done at Old Trafford, and again he found a sterling partner in Jack Saunders, until Jessop got after him on the last day. Trumble, who took five of the wickets himself, reduced England to 83–6 in their first innings and they had an anxious time scoring the 92 they needed to avoid the follow-on.

Travers says that he remembered one immaculate cover drive of Lionel Palairet's better than he was later to remember any individual drive by Walter Hammond or Len Hutton. Two apparently straightforward slip catches by MacLaren also stuck in his mind for the ease with which he took them before immediately tossing away the ball almost with disdain. Hirst led the way here with a splendidly solid innings of 43 and he received good support from Len Braund and Bill Lockwood. England finished with 183, which gave Australia a lead of 141.

England had a huge piece of luck when Australia went in again, immediately after Hirst, of all people, had dropped a sitter from Duff at mid off. He and Trumper had scored six when Trumper pushed a ball from Lockwood into the off side and began to run. At the other end, Duff was alarmed by Jessop racing in from cover point and, as he was about to pick the ball up, screamed at Trumper to get back. Trumper slipped as he turned and was sitting on the pitch as the throw thumped into Dick Lilley's gloves. It may not have been that risky a single, but Jessop's reputation as a fielder had made Duff refuse to run and so caused the run-out. The early dismissal of Trumper was always a big psychological blow for Australia. The England bowling was tight, the catching excellent and the Australian batsmen struggled. MacLaren took a brilliant catch in the slips to send back the left-handed Clem Hill, the only batsman to look comfortable, when he drove at Hirst. Another full-house crowd went happily home after Johnny Tyldesley had held a beauty in the deep to get rid of Saunders off the last ball of the day. Australia were then 114–8, 255 ahead.

The day had ended beneath a cloudless sky and if the weather should stay fine, England had an outside chance. But while the England players were having dinner that evening in their hotel, the rain started. They could hear the raindrops falling and it was Jessop who later said, 'Only chloroform could have dammed the sound of the falling torrents.' To cheer everyone up, Jessop, who disapproved of gambling, now offered odds of 10–1 against anyone scoring a fifty the next day, and 20–1 against a hundred.

It was sunny the next morning, but the pitch and the outfield were wet. Lockwood took the last two Australian wickets while seven more runs were scored and England had to make 263 to win, a surely impossible target in these conditions. It had become an even more remote possibility when, after 20 minutes' batting, England's score stood at 10–3, MacLaren, Tyldesley and Palairet having all been bowled by Saunders, who was making the ball turn and lift sharply under the sun. It was 28–3 when a sudden shower of rain sent the players off for 35 minutes. As soon as they restarted, Hayward, who had never been happy, was caught behind off Saunders. Braund was, somewhat unluckily, fifth out at 48. He pushed at Trumble and edged the ball, which went through James Kelly's gloves, hit his body and bounced up above his head. Kelly reacted quickly enough to hold on to the ball as he fell. Stanley Jackson, at the other end, was the only batsman who had been able to cope with the conditions. He was now joined by Jessop.

At Cambridge, Jessop had been a remarkable athlete and was in the Cambridge cricket XI for four years. He was a genuine all-rounder, taking 873 first-class wickets in addition to scoring more than 26,000 runs, most of them for Gloucestershire. He was only five feet seven inches tall and there was a slight pugilistic look about him which, considering his batting style, seemed appropriate. He was a congenial companion who, in 1916, when he was in his early forties, had the wretched luck to be severely damaged by treatment for severe lumbago which went badly wrong and brought his sporting life to a sad and sudden halt. He was then serving with the Lincolnshire Regiment. He left behind him a strong feeling that he might have done more for England in 18 Test matches than score 569 runs and take 10 wickets, even if he had hit one of the most incredible hundreds in the history of the game.

As he strode through the pavilion, MacLaren said in a loud voice, 'I bet you don't make a century.' Jessop spun round and in a firm voice said, 'Done.' This was an exchange overheard and enjoyed by some of the crowd.

Jessop took a single off his first ball and scored off each of his next four, and so started maybe the most remarkably destructive innings in the history of the game. Trumble was then driven into the pavilion – in those days a ball had to be hit out of the ground for it to be counted as a six – and the next ball bounced back off the pavilion railings. It was said that Jessop was more careful than usual, although Ben Travers was surprised by his 'undaunted, almost it seemed heedless, approach', and described him as 'jaunty'. But, for all that, Jessop religiously avoided swinging across the line of Trumble. And on he went. Saunders was driven for four. Then he went to drive the next ball, which kept low and he missed it. Behind him, the ball went through Kelly too, and the stumping chance was not taken, not that it worried Jessop. He slashed the next ball over Armstrong's head at cover. Soon afterwards another lofted drive went down the ground and Trumper, running flat out at long off, just got a hand to a fiendishly difficult catch, but could not hold on.

The players trooped into lunch with the score 87–5 and Travers recalls seeing a number of members picking up their things and leaving the ground. In the morning, that passionate cricket lover P.G. Wodehouse had been among the crowd of 18,000, but now he had to go to work. He later wrote in an autobiography that he decided to give up his job in a City bank because that afternoon he had been forced to return to work without even having time to buy a sandwich. Which begs the question as to what he was doing there in the first place. The general feeling was that, heroic though Jessop and Jackson had been, England were doomed.

After lunch, Jessop wasted no time in getting going. A late cut for four soon brought up the 100 after only 80 minutes, an extraordinary rate of scoring after such a start to the innings. Before lunch, Jackson had middled everything, but his touch now deserted him and he might have been caught behind off Saunders. A clever late cut to the Vauxhall End by Jessop off Trumble allowed the batsmen to run five. The Oval in those days was a bigger ground than it is now and all-run fives were commonplace. His fifty came in the same over and he took consecutive fours off Saunders, while Jackson survived a simple chance to Armstrong at slip, off Trumble. Jessop then took 17 in an over from Saunders, followed by two fours in an over off Armstrong's leg-spin. The score had reached 157 when a subtle change of pace by Trumble deceived Jackson, who was caught and bowled for 49. Travers still remembered Jackson thumping his pad in annoyance when the catch was held. Hirst now survived a confident lbw appeal before he had scored. Jessop's answer to this was twice to drive Trumble into the pavilion.

The moment before Jessop reached his hundred was etched sharply into Travers's mind. The roars of the crowd 'subsided and gave way to an awesome, aspiring hush ... Jessop crouched. The bowler started his run ... The bowler bowled. Bang. Uproar ... Dozens of straw boaters were sent sailing from the crowd like boomerangs. Unlike boomerangs they failed to return ... but who cared?'

Jessop had scored a hundred in 75 minutes off 76 balls. After one more boundary, he swept at Armstrong and was caught by Noble at square leg. He had made 104 in 79 balls and the runs had been scored out of 139. There had been one five, 17 fours, two threes, four twos and 17 singles. It was the only hundred he made for England and it will never be forgotten.

The match was still a long way from being over. At 187–7, England needed 76 more runs. The Australian bowlers were in disarray after this prolonged assault and the crowd, which had grown to 22,000, was baying in hope of victory. Hirst was joined by Lockwood and they brought up the 200. After a number of agonised appeals for lbw, Lockwood was eventually lbw to Trumble when they had put on 27. For a time Lilley, the new batsman, lived a charmed life. He almost played Saunders into his stumps and then Trumble dropped a difficult low return catch. Magnificent ground fielding saved important runs for Australia before a powerfully hit square cut by Hirst took the score to 230 and then Lilley drove Trumble for a handsome four. In trying to repeat the stroke, he did not quite get to the pitch of the ball and Darling judged the catch perfectly at deep mid off.

The score was now 248–9 and Wilfred Rhodes, who within ten years would be opening the England innings against Australia as Jack Hobbs's regular partner, walked out to join his fellow Yorkshireman, who also came from the village of Kirkheaton. At

Melbourne in the fourth Test in 1911–12, Hobbs and Rhodes would put on 323 for the first wicket, with Rhodes making 179 and Hobbs 178. At The Oval, England needed 15 to win and no two Yorkshiremen have ever put together a more important partnership than this one. A single off the first ball of the next over brought Hirst to his fifty and he knew there was no need to try and protect Rhodes from the bowling. The tension was unbelievable and it was at this point that one old gentleman was seen to be methodically folding his gloves and making a parcel of them in his scorecard.

Rhodes now snicked Saunders for four and later in the same over was almost caught in the slips by Armstrong, who lost his balance and could not hold on. In the following over, Hirst pushed for a single and Rhodes then almost gave Trumble a return catch. At this point Hirst spent time rearranging his pads before every ball, surely not done out of nervousness – old soldiers like Hirst do not suffer from those sort of nerves – but as an attempt to ruffle the Australians. There was an overthrow when a return hit Hirst on the shoulder and bounced away out of a fielder's reach, to the obvious delight and amusement of the two batsmen. Singles came more easily and soon only three were required.

By now the sun had disappeared and it was beginning to rain. Noble was bowling and after playing the first five balls quietly away in defence, Hirst took a single off the last. He faced Trumble and an easy single which levelled the scores came off the first ball. England could not lose and pandemonium broke out in the crowd. At this moment, a spectator whose arithmetic was not up to much came running out onto the ground, beside himself with joy. It was later discovered that he was a parson. He soon realised the error of his ways and with some encouragement hastily withdrew. It would have been amusing to have heard him doing his stuff from the pulpit the following Sunday.

It took a while for the crowd to quieten down and Rhodes then pushed the next three balls carefully away. When the ball was back with Trumble after the third, he rubbed it in the heap of sawdust behind him to help dry it, paused a moment and then ran in to bowl. The ball was pitched up invitingly on the leg stump, but Rhodes was not to be tempted. He pushed it quietly past mid on and ran . . . and kept on running until he reached the pavilion. Hirst, who had been running towards the Vauxhall End, had to cope with the exultant crowd which had invaded the ground.

Everyone was shouting, perfect strangers shook hands and the noise was extraordinary. The spectators caught up with Hirst and carried him away in triumph. Even the press let their hair down and no less a person than the editor of *Wisden* actually stood up in his seat and waved his hat. It was Trumble, having bowled his off-breaks unchanged throughout the match, who later summed it all up to perfection: 'The only man living who could beat us, beat us.' That man was Gilbert Jessop.

Ben Travers said, 78 years later, that when he got home that night, 'I felt a bit of a hero at having actually been there on Jessop's Day. I still do.'

ENGLAND v AUSTRALIA (5th Test)

At The Oval, London, on 11–13 August 1902 (three-day match).

Australia

V.T. Trumper b Hirst	42		run out	2
R.A. Duff c Lilley b Hirst	23		b Lockwood	6
C. Hill b Hirst	11		c MacLaren b Hirst	34
*J. Darling c Lilley b Hirst	3		c MacLaren b Lockwood	15
M.A. Noble c and b Jackson	52		b Braund	13
S.E. Gregory b Hirst	23		b Braund	9
W.W. Armstrong b Jackson	17		b Lockwood	21
A.J.Y. Hopkins c MacLaren b Lockwood	40		c Lilley b Lockwood	3
H. Trumble not out	64	(10)	not out	7
†J.J. Kelly c Rhodes b Braund	39	(11)	lbw b Lockwood	0
J.V. Saunders lbw b Braund	0	(9)	c Tyldesley b Rhodes	2
Extras (5 b, 3 lb, 2 nb)	10		(7 b, 2 lb)	9
Total (all out, 123.5 overs)	**324**		(all out, 60 overs)	**121**

1–47 2–63 3–69 4–82 5–126 6–174 7–175
8–256 9–324 10–324.

1–6 2–9 3–31 4–71 5–75 6–91
7–99 8–114 9–115 10–121.

Bowling, *1st innings*: Lockwood 24–2–85–1; Rhodes 28–9–46–0; Hirst 29–5–77–5;
Braund 16.5–5–29–2; Jackson 20–4–66–2; Jessop 6–2–11–0. *2nd innings*: Rhodes 22–7–38–1;
Lockwood 20–6–45–5; Jackson 4–3–7–0; Hirst 5–1–7–1; Braund 9–1–15–2.

England

*A.C. MacLaren c Armstrong b Trumble	10	b Saunders	2
L.C.H. Palairet b Trumble	20	b Saunders	6
J.T. Tyldesley b Trumble	33	b Saunders	0
T.W. Hayward b Trumble	0	c Kelly b Saunders	7
F.S. Jackson c Armstrong b Saunders	2	c and b Trumble	49
L.C. Braund c Hill b Trumble	22	c Kelly b Trumble	2
G.L. Jessop b Trumble	13	c Noble b Armstrong	104
G.H. Hirst c and b Trumble	43	not out	58
W.H. Lockwood c Noble b Saunders	25	lbw b Trumble	2
†A.F.A. Lilley c Trumper b Trumble	0	c Darling b Trumble	16
W. Rhodes not out	0	not out	6
Extras (13 b, 2 lb)	15	(5 b, 6 lb)	11
Total (all out, 61 overs)	**183**	(9 wkts, 66.5 overs)	**263**

1–31 2–36 3–62 4–67 5–67 6–83 7–137
8–179 9–183 10–183.

1–5 2–5 3–10 4–31 5–48 6–157
7–187 8–214 9–248.

Bowling, *1st innings*: Trumble 31–13–65–8; Saunders 23–7–79–2; Noble 7–3–24–0.
2nd innings: Trumble 33.5–4–108–4; Saunders 24–3–105–4; Armstrong 4–0–28–1;
Noble 5–0–11–0.

Close of play, *day 1*: Australia (1) 324 all out; *day 2*: Australia (2) 114–8 (Armstrong 21*).

Toss: Australia. Last-innings target: 263 runs.
Umpires: C.E. Richardson (Eng), A. White (Eng).

ENGLAND won by one wicket.

4
LEG-SPIN WINS
THE DAY

South Africa v England (1st Test)

2–4 January 1906; Old Wanderers, Johannesburg

South Africa won by one wicket.

SOUTH Africa's first victory in a Test match came at the twelfth attempt in 1906, when, amid scenes of frenzied excitement, they beat England in Johannesburg by one wicket. Needing to score 284 in the fourth innings, the ninth wicket had fallen at 239, bringing in Percy Sherwell, the captain, to join A.W. 'Dave' Nourse. Contemporary accounts say that at this moment the crowd were so disappointed 'the silence could be felt'. Forty-five more runs were needed and with increasing confidence these two saw South Africa home to the first of four victories in this series, which they won by four matches to one.

In those days, England did not take all their best players on tours to South Africa, a habit which continued until the 1950s, but under Pelham 'Plum' Warner's captaincy, this was still a more than respectable side. The batting foundered on the matting pitches, principally against South Africa's four leg-break and googly bowlers. After this, no country could afford to take on South Africa with anything but the greatest of respect, especially on their own pitches. There were 10,000 ecstatic people packed into the Old Wanderers ground in the middle of the city. They had waited a long time for this victory, as South Africa had played their first Test match in Port Elizabeth in 1889, against an England side captained by C. Aubrey Smith, who was playing in his only Test match and went on to become a well-known Hollywood film star, for which he was knighted.

South Africa's all-important quiver of four leg-spinners made an interesting contrast. Aubrey Faulkner, a formidable all-rounder, was probably the best of the bunch, although he only took 14 wickets in the series. He bowled at medium pace and his googly was difficult to spot. He was also able to bowl a fast yorker without any apparent change of action. Reggie Schwarz was unusual in that he only bowled googlies, which might appear to make him easier to play, but his variations, his control and the pace and bounce he got from the pitch made him as dangerous as any of them. Some considered Albert Vogler the best of all, although like Gordon White, the fourth member of the quartet, he was sparingly used in this series. Results show there was little need for them. In this first Test, Schwarz and Faulkner opened the bowling and Schwarz was able to swing the new ball appreciably as well as to spin it. The batsmen found his googly, which he turned a long way, difficult to read because in his approach to the wicket he did not show the ball, and therefore his grip, to the batsman. White also cleverly disguised his 'wrong 'un', as they called it in South Africa.

England won the toss at the Wanderers and with South Africa opening the bowling with the two leg-spinners, they were soon 15–3. The best innings, of 44, was played by 19-year-old Jack Crawford, a tall, off-spinning all-rounder. Six months earlier, he had still been playing for his school First XI, at Repton. In the end, in England's first innings, it was only sterling work by the last pair of Jack Board and Colin 'Charlie' Blythe, who put on 25, that they reached 184. These old players could be a confusing lot. Blythe had been christened Colin, but always answered to 'Charlie', while, on the South African side, Nourse, who had started out as Arthur William, became known as 'Dave'. His son,

Dudley Nourse, went on to captain South Africa for 15 Tests and to score 2,960 runs in 34 Tests at 53.81. We will see him doing battle against England in Durban in 1948–49. Dudley was born when his father was touring Australia with South Africa in 1910–11. 'Dave' had just made 201 against South Australia. Hearing this, the Governor General of Australia, the Earl of Dudley, asked 'Dave' to name his son after him.

South Africa's batsmen now found life even more difficult against the pace of Walter Lees, who, playing in his first Test match, took 5–34 in this first innings. Lees was on the sharp side of medium and the combination of his off-spin with his skilful variations of flight and pace disconcerted the South African batsmen. Lees was well backed up by the left-arm spin of Blythe and the medium-paced off-spin of Crawford, who we come across in greater detail two years later in Melbourne in Jack Hobbs's first Test match. To the great disappointment of the crowd now in Johannesburg, South Africa were bowled out for 91.

Lees was one of many county cricketers who have been born in Yorkshire and taken their talents elsewhere. He made his cricketing home at The Oval with Surrey and had a strange career which veered from one extreme to the other. His best season came in 1905, when he found the pitches at The Oval suited him perfectly. He took 193 wickets that season and was the country's leading wicket-taker, which won him a place on this tour to South Africa. For a long time at The Oval, Lees was in the shadow of William Lockwood and Tom Richardson. He was a great success in South Africa, taking 26 wickets in the five Tests, but on his return to England he suffered repeatedly from injury and did not play in another Test match. In 1911, he lost form completely and was released by Surrey. Although there is no evidence of this, I cannot help but wonder how well he fitted into the dressing room and whether or not Lees ticked all the boxes with other players.

When England batted again, there was a painstaking innings from Warner, the captain, already setting out on a career which would lead to him becoming such an important figure in English cricket, first as a player and then as an administrator. He was supported by David Denton, and again the most impressive innings was played by Crawford, who made 43, and they enabled England to creep up to 190 at this second attempt. South Africa were left to make 284 to win, which would be much the biggest total of the match, and England will have felt firmly in control.

With Lees taking three wickets, it was not all that long before South Africa were struggling at 105–6, when Nourse joined Gordon White. They made an interesting contrast. White, a right-hander, was usually looking to play his fluent array of strokes, especially on the off side. He now saw that in this situation, with South Africa in such a poor position, perishing to extravagant strokeplay was not sensible. As a result, he put his head down and fought it out for more than four hours for 81. At the other end, Nourse, a left-hander whose determination and doggedness were watchwords and whose principal concern was to make sure he did not get out, made an ideal partner. They defended stoutly against everything the bowlers delivered and gradually the score mounted, until they found they had taken South Africa to within reach of what had seemed a most unlikely victory. They had brought the crowd back to life too, and every run was now being almost hysterically cheered. The score was 226–6, their stand having reached 121, when Albert Relf, the off-spinner from Sussex, suddenly turned one through White's defence and bowled him. Then, in quick succession, Ernie Hayes bowled Vogler with a leg-break and Relf caught and bowled Schwarz and it looked all over.

At 239–9 South Africa still needed 45 to win as Percy Sherwell, an outstanding wicketkeeper, particularly to the leg-spinners, but not much of a batsman, as his position in the order suggested, came out to join Nourse. Sherwell, strangely, was captaining South Africa in his first Test match and, perhaps because he must have known that not much was expected of him as a batsman, he relaxed and began to play pretty well. Rather surprisingly, the bowlers, thinking they had done their job, seemed to lose concentration and made things easier than they should have done for the last pair. The three main bowlers, Lees, Blythe and Crawford, suddenly lost line and length and runs came quicker and much more easily than anyone could reasonably have expected. Of course, Nourse's experience was important, although he soon realised that Sherwell was better able to take care of himself than he had feared. Sherwell obviously relished the fight and also made good use of any scoring opportunities that came his way.

By now the crowd were delirious as South Africa moved towards an historic victory. They had watched most of the day from a sense of duty, but now they were well and truly caught up in the excitement of it all. With eight runs wanted, Crawford began another over to Sherwell, who came forward to the first ball and, to the immense delight of the crowd, snicked it between first and second slip for four. In the next over, Nourse turned Relf to fine leg for three and the scores were level. It was now Relf who blinked first, bowling a full toss to Sherwell who smote it gratefully to the square-leg boundary and South Africa had won their first Test match. The scenes of celebration and joy among the spectators had to be seen to be believed. Strict Victorian etiquette was momentarily forgotten as the ladies in their formal clothes made good use of their parasols as they celebrated a famous victory.

When 'Dave' Nourse left the field at the end of the game, at the top of the stairs leading to the dressing room, he bumped into George Kempis, a former Transvaal bowler whose brother Gus had played in South Africa's first ever Test match, against Aubrey Smith's side, in 1888–89. George had become a great benefactor for South African cricket and now he pressed a gold coin into Nourse's hand. Not to be outdone, the other exultant members sitting in the members' stand followed suit, plunging their hands into their pockets in search of gold. In the end, it was said that Nourse carried back 'a small little fortune' for his efforts. Having made 93 not out in more than four hours and taken South Africa to victory, I am sure no one would have begrudged him a single carat of his haul. Another jubilant spectator paid him a handsome sum for his bat, which to this day hangs in the Kent Park Taverners bar across the road and behind the New Wanderers ground.

'Dave' Nourse went on to become the grand old man of South African cricket. He was born in Croydon in London in 1879 and came out to South Africa in 1895 as a boy drummer with the West Riding Regiment. He survived the Boer War with the Durban Light Infantry and played his first game for South Africa in 1902 against Australia, who played three Tests on their way back from England. The first Test began Nourse's run of 45 successive Tests for South Africa, finishing at The Oval in 1924 when he was 46 years old. He carried on playing first-class cricket until 1935–36 when, at the age of 57, his last game was against Victor Richardson's Australian team.

SOUTH AFRICA v ENGLAND (1st Test)

At the Old Wanderers, Johannesburg, on 2–4 January 1906 (four-day match).

England

*P.F. Warner c Snooke b Schwarz	6	b Vogler	51
F.L. Fane c Schwarz b Faulkner	1	b Snooke	3
D. Denton c Faulkner b Schwarz	0	b Faulkner	34
E.G. Wynyard st Sherwell b Schwarz	29	b Vogler	0
E.G. Hayes c and b Vogler	20	c Schwarz b Snooke	3
J.N. Crawford c Nourse b Sinclair	44	b Nourse	43
A.E. Relf b White	8	c Sherwell b Faulkner	7
S. Haigh b Faulkner	23	lbw b Nourse	0
†J.H. Board	9	lbw b Faulkner	7
W.S. Lees st Sherwell b White	11	not out	1
C. Blythe b Sinclair	17	b Faulkner	0
Extras (6 b, 9 lb, 1 nb)	16	(23 b, 8 lb)	31
Total (all out, 63 overs)	**184**	(all out, 58.5 overs)	**190**

1–6 2–6 3–15 4–53 5–76 6–97 7–145
8–147 9–159 10–184

1–3 2–55 3–56 4–73 5–113 6–166
7–174 8–185 9–190 10–190

Bowling, *1st innings*: Schwarz 21–5–72–3; Faulkner 22–7–35–2; Sinclair 11–1–36–2; Vogler 3–0–10–1; White 5–1–13–2; Nourse 1–0–2–0. *2nd innings*: Snooke 12–4–38–2; Schwarz 8–1–24–0; Vogler 11–3–24–2; Faulkner 12.5–5–26–4; Sinclair 5–1–25–0; White 4–0–15–0; Nourse 6–4–7–2.

South Africa

L.J. Tancred c Board b Lees	3	c Warner b Blythe	10
W.A. Shalders c Haigh b Blythe	4	run out	38
C.M.H. Hathorn b Lees	5	c Crawford b Lees	4
G.C. White c Blythe b Lees	8	b Relf	81
S.J. Snooke c Board b Blythe	19	lbw b Lees	9
J.H. Sinclair c and b Lees	0	c Fane b Lees	5
G.A. Faulkner b Blythe	4	run out	6
A.W. Nourse not out	18	not out	93
A.E.E. Vogler b Crawford	14	b Hayes	2
R.O. Schwarz c Relf b Crawford	5	c and b Relf	2
*†P.W. Sherwell lbw b Lees	1	not out	22
Extras (9 b, 1 lb)	10	(6 b, 2 lb, 7 nb)	15
Total (all out, 46.1 overs)	**91**	(9 wkts, 112.5 overs)	**287**

1–5 2–11 3–13 4–35 5–39 6–43 7–44 8–62
9–82 10–91

1–11 2–22 3–68 4–81 5–89 6–105
7–226 8–230 9–239

Bowling, *1st innings*: Lees 23.1–10–34–5; Blythe 16–5–33–3; Crawford 7–1–14–2. *2nd innings*: Lees 33–10–74–3; Blythe 28–12–50–1; Crawford 17–4–49–0; Haigh 1–0–9–0; Relf 21.5–7–47–2; Wynyard 3–0–15–0; Hayes 9–1–28–1.

Close of play, *day 1*: South Africa (1) 71–8 (Nourse 2*, Schwarz 3*);
day 2: South Africa (2) 68–2 (Shalders 38*, White 16*).

Toss: England. Last-innings target: 284 runs.
Umpires: J. Phillips (Aus), F.E. Smith (Eng).

SOUTH AFRICA won by one wicket.

5

UNDER A SUMMER HEAVEN

Australia v England (2nd Test)

1–7 January 1908; Melbourne Cricket Ground

England won by one wicket.

I T is curious that the perverseness of history has caused the Test matches of 1902 at Old Trafford and The Oval to be far better remembered than England's extraordinary one-wicket victory at the Melbourne Cricket Ground (MCG) in the New Year of 1908. This match followed a scarcely less exciting contest in Sydney just before Christmas, when Australia won by two wickets. If Australia had not made a complete mess of a simple run-out chance right at the end, this Test in Melbourne would have become the first tied Test match. Although England lost the series 4–1, they were in a potentially strong position at the halfway stage of two of the remaining matches, and they could have won the first. It was a fascinating series and it is a mystery that it has been forgotten, as have a few of the main England players too.

This second Test also happened to be the 25-year-old Jack Hobbs's first Test match, in which he made 83 and 28. Nowadays, the New Year's Test match in Australia, which is played in Sydney, starts on 2 January, to give the players the chance to recover from the New Year's Eve festivities. No such licence was allowed in the old days.

Before play began, Hobbs was hitting a few balls in front of the pavilion when the famous Australian batsman Clem Hill came up to him.

'So you're playing this time, Jack,' he said.

'Yes, I'm going to have a shot,' Hobbs replied.

'Hearty congratulations, then, and good luck,' was Hill's answer.

This was a wonderfully dated exchange which one would have been unlikely to hear even in 1930 when Hobbs played his last Test match, let alone in the fevered atmosphere of modern international cricket.

England's selection was affected by illness and injury. The captain, Arthur Jones of Nottinghamshire, was in hospital with pneumonia and his vice-captain, Fred Fane, from Essex, took charge. Fane was the eighth Irish-born cricketer to play Test cricket and the first to score a century for England, in Johannesburg in 1905–06. There was then a long wait until Eoin Morgan became the second, against Pakistan at Trent Bridge in 2010. Colin Blythe was also recuperating from a bad cold and so the left-arm spin bowling was left to, one would have felt, a more than adequate substitute in Wilfred Rhodes, to whom Fane had given only 12 overs in the first Test in Sydney, prompting Rhodes to say, and maybe not entirely in jest, 'I am in the team because of my singing.'

There had been five inches of rain in Melbourne just before this match, which will not have made it easy for the groundsman, or curator, as they are known in Australia. It was not surprising that it was a lifeless pitch and when Monty Noble won the toss for Australia and decided to bat, they made a far from convincing start. England's bowling was opened by Pip Fielder of Kent, another whose name has been allowed to sink into obscurity, although at the other end, Sydney Barnes needs little introduction. Barnes took 24 wickets in the series, while Fielder, with whom he shared the new ball for four matches, claimed 25. Fielder was genuinely fast, with an outswinger which brought him most of his wickets. He also had the one which came back in to the bat, making him a more awkward proposition. Now, in the first over, his third ball, which was the one that nipped back, completely beat and almost bowled Victor Trumper. The next, which moved away, found the edge of Trumper's bat and George Gunn put down a straightforward catch in the slips. Gunn had not been selected for the tour but was in Australia for health reasons and Fane had decided to call him up for the first Test, in which he made 119 and 74.

Although Victor Trumper and Charlie Macartney may sound like a golden opening partnership, on this pitch at the MCG they found it difficult to play their strokes with safety. They were both dismissed by the quick off-spin of Crawford, notable scalps for the young bowler. Noble was the only batsman to pass 50 in Australia's first innings of 266 before perishing to the guile of Rhodes. In reply, England initially owed much to Hobbs who, in his first Test innings, batted with the calm maturity which was to serve England so well for the next 22 years. He made 83 out of 160 before being bowled by Tibby Cotter, who Hobbs, on his own 80th birthday, described as being the quickest bowler he ever faced: 'He was very fast indeed, he really was. He came bounding in with energy and slammed the ball down and it went by you just like a flash of lightning sometimes.'

Hobbs put on 99 for the third wicket with Kenneth Hutchings, who went on to make an extraordinary 126. Hutchings had an unusual ability as a batsman, but his batting brought to life the will-o'-the-wisp traits in his character. Those who saw him bat for Kent in 1906 would have agreed with *Wisden*, which proclaimed that, 'Batting so remarkable and individual as his, has not been seen since Ranjitsinhji and Trumper first delighted the cricket world.' Hutchings was a tall, slim right-hander and his batting was a sublime combination of grace and power. A.A. Thomson, a well-known cricket writer who was as objective and unemotional as most diehard Yorkshiremen, once wrote, 'I sometimes think that if one last fragment of cricket had to be preserved, as though in amber, it should be a glimpse of K.L. Hutchings cover-driving under a summer heaven.'

For all that, it was as if Hutchings's heart was never completely in it. There were long absences from the Kent side when other interests took over. The most surprising aspect of this innings in Melbourne, which was his only Test hundred, was the way in which he was able to play his strokes on a surface which confounded the efforts of all the others on both sides, including, most notably, Victor Trumper. One unusual statistic from this innings was that 106 of his runs, all but 20, came from boundaries – 25 fours and one six – and Melbourne has the longest boundary of any Test ground in the world. He reached his hundred in 128 minutes and his second fifty in only 43 minutes. Hutchings sadly perished in the Battle of the Somme in 1916, at the age of 33.

It was illustrative of the skill of Hutchings and also Hobbs that after they had been out, none of the remaining batsmen were at ease on this pitch, and England were all out for 382. While Cotter took five wickets, they cost 142 runs, which shows that although he may have been extremely fast, he was also erratic. Warwick Armstrong was, perhaps, the most important of their bowlers. He realised that his leg theory was ideally suited to this slow pitch. Bowling his leg-breaks, which did not turn much, from round the wicket at a brisk pace with a packed leg-side field, he made it almost impossible for the batsmen to score runs. In this innings, he had the interesting figures of 34.2–15–36–2. In those days Armstrong, later a huge man who became known as 'the Big Ship', was a more modest size, for his appetite had not yet taken over.

In Australia's second innings, Trumper, maybe stung by Hutchings's strokeplay, was at his best, while Noble, who had promoted himself to open, was more cautious at the other end. The temperature climbed to well over 100 degrees as the match went on and the facilities at the ground were appalling, with only three taps for drinking water. Fights broke out in the crushes as people fought to get to the taps and the police had a busy time. Meanwhile, Trumper and Noble had put on 126 in a most entertaining first-wicket stand, which took Australia back into the lead, before Trumper was lbw when caught on the crease by the off-spin of Jack Crawford, who got him out in both innings – and there were not many bowlers who were able to do that. Soon afterwards, Crawford dismissed Noble with a deliberate full toss bowled to try and persuade him to hole out to square leg – but, in fact, it bowled him. When Fielder bowled Clem Hill for the second time in the match, three wickets had fallen for ten runs and again the advantage had swung.

Crawford had been regarded as the best schoolboy cricketer in the country when at Repton and had then, as we have seen, made a name for himself on England's tour of South Africa in 1905–06. In addition to his fast off-breaks, he was also a considerable batsman who later did the double of scoring 1,000 runs and taking 100 wickets in successive seasons for Surrey. He was tall, thin, angular and usually cheerful, but with a confused personality which led to a much-travelled cricket career. After Surrey he played for South Australia and for Otago in New Zealand, before returning to Surrey briefly after the First World War. Crawford had made his England debut at the Old Wanderers in January 1906, when with his first ball in Test cricket he bowled Bert Vogler, who had himself bowled Ernie Hayes only the day before with his first ball in Test cricket in England's first innings. At 19 years and 32 days, Crawford was the youngest cricketer to have played for England until the 18-year-old Brian Close came into the side in 1949.

After Australia's good opening stand in the second innings, most of the batsmen, except Hill, contributed, with Macartney, Armstrong and wicketkeeper Hanson Carter, a most useful batsman to have coming in at number eight, passing 50. Barnes, who took five wickets, and Crawford were the most successful bowlers and the crowd were enthralled as the advantage kept changing hands. In the end, England were left to score 282 to win, a big task in the fourth innings on a worn pitch.

By now, the pitch was even slower and the Australians bowled with great discipline and scoring runs was never easy. Hobbs took 69 minutes over his 28 and the slowness of the pitch reduced even Cotter to near impotence. The fifty had just come up when Noble spun an off-break through Hobbs's defence and bowled him, and two balls later Gunn played across the line and was lbw. The crowd, sensing things were moving their way, became increasingly involved, while a combination of the pitch and the bowling effectively stifled Hutchings, who was unable to play his strokes as freely as he had done in the first innings. Runs came slowly against Armstrong and Noble, who were backed up by some brilliant fielding. It took Fred Fane two and a half hours to get to his fifty, but England reached 121 for the loss of only two wickets and the crowd was beginning to grow restless. Then, in quick succession, Armstrong bowled Fane and Hutchings mistimed an attacking stroke against Macartney and it was 131–4. Len Braund and Joe Hardstaff now put their heads down and took England quietly to 159–4 by the close of the fifth day, when 123 more were needed. Only 196 runs had been scored during the day and seven wickets had fallen, but the crowd had been spellbound by such a fascinating battle.

The sixth day got off to a dramatic start. Three more runs had been scored when Cotter bowled a short one to Hardstaff, who swivelled and hooked it out of the middle of the bat. Vernon Ransford, running flat out round the backward-square-leg boundary, held another splendid catch above his head and England were 162–5 – Ransford had taken a beauty in the first innings, at long off, to get rid of Crawford. Again, Armstrong was the shrewdest and most economical of the bowlers as he stuck to his leg-side line and it was almost impossible to score more than the odd single against him. The score had reached 196 when, cleverly varying his pace, Armstrong beat Braund in the air and bowled him. Two runs later, Rhodes, of all people, ran himself out, which, in these circumstances, is most unlikely behaviour for a Yorkshireman, especially at a time of crisis, and it reflected the pressure the batsmen were being put under by some excellent bowling. England were now 198–7 with all the main batsmen gone, but there was no accounting for Barnes, who took his place.

All his cricketing career, and beyond, Barnes was his own man. He was strongly opinionated, would never be shaken from his beliefs and constantly kept those in authority on their toes, whether they were cricket administrators or those who ran the Staffordshire County Council for whom he worked. There is no doubt he was a difficult old what-not, but he was the greatest of bowlers. Off a short, bounding run, his pace was a sharp medium as his long arm swung over and the ball was whipped down by a strong wrist and released from long fingers. It might be an outswinger, a leg-break or an off-break – or anything else, for his variety was great. In Barnes's obituary, that well-known writer Jim Swanton, talking about England's tour to Australia in 1911–12, described Barnes bowling out the great Victor Trumper, who was then at his best, 'with a ball swerving from the leg stump to the off and then breaking back to hit the leg. "It was the sort of ball," said Charlie Macartney, "that a man might see when he was tight."'

While bowling was how Barnes usually won cricket matches, now it was his batting which made the difference. He was a good enough batsman to have scored a fifty for the Players against the Gentlemen at Lord's. When Barnes put his mind to something, he did not consider failure. His initial partner, Jack Crawford, was the better batsman but, without Barnes's sense of discipline and devotion, he let the situation get to him. After a heave for six, he tried to do it again and skied into the huge and welcoming hands of Armstrong. It was 209–8 and, with 73 wanted, the crowd relaxed, for it was surely all over.

Joe Humphries, the wicketkeeper, took Crawford's place and Barnes will have had a word with him and he will have done his best to do as he had been told. They added seven to the score before lunch, but they began to bat with such purpose afterwards that the mood of both the match and the crowd again began to change. With Barnes looking more and more in control, Humphries was content to let him farm the bowling. They had put on 34 when Armstrong found a way past Humphries's defensive stroke, hit his pad and he was given out lbw. It was a decision which made Barnes angry. Barnes himself took up the story: 'I was convinced he had played the ball and I told the umpire so. I got a little annoyed and as Fielder ... came out from the pavilion, I went to meet him and told him what had happened, and said to him, "Come on, Pip, we'll knock 'em off now."'

Barnes told Fielder to push his bat straight down the wicket at everything, which is precisely what he did, while Barnes himself kept the scoreboard moving. The tension was terrific as the score slowly got nearer to the target. The next day the correspondent of the *Sydney Morning Herald* wrote, 'There were men round the ground so breathless that they could not speak.' In the England dressing room the players did not dare move in case it broke the luck. Then, just two were needed.

'Fielder played one to mid on.' Barnes again. 'It was a very risky run. But as we were both of one mind, we got home safely. Then I faced Armstrong. As was usual with him, all the fieldsmen, with the exception of two, were on the leg side [no leg-side restrictions in those days]. The ball came at my legs, and I drew away from the wicket and pushed the ball to the off. It was an easy run and as I played the ball I was off down the pitch expecting Fielder to do the same, but to my consternation, I saw he was still in his ground. "For God's sake, Pip, get off," I shouted.'

By this time the 19-year-old Hazlitt, at cover point, had gathered the ball but instead of tossing it to the wicketkeeper, Carter, he tried to throw down the stumps – and missed. So Fielder, who would have been run out by yards, got safely home and the match was won.

In the previous Test in Sydney, Gerry Hazlitt had made 34 out of an eighth-wicket stand of 56, to see Australia home by two wickets. If his nerve had held now in Melbourne and he had thrown gently to the wicketkeeper, Carter, this would have been the first Test match to end in a tie.

AUSTRALIA v ENGLAND (2nd Test)

At the MCG, Melbourne, on 1–7 January 1908 (timeless match).

Australia

V.T. Trumper c Humphries b Crawford	49	(2)	lbw b Crawford		63
C.G. Macartney b Crawford	37	(6)	c Humphries b Barnes		54
C. Hill b Fielder	16		b Fielder		3
*M.A. Noble c Braund b Rhodes	61	(1)	b Crawford		64
W.W. Armstrong c Hutchings b Crawford	31		b Barnes		77
P.A. McAlister run out	10	(4)	run out		15
V.S. Ransford run out	27		c Hutchings b Barnes		18
A. Cotter b Crawford	17	(9)	lbw b Crawford		27
†H. Carter not out	15	(8)	c Fane b Barnes		53
G.R. Hazlitt b Crawford	1		b Barnes		3
J.V. Saunders b Fielder	0		not out		0
Extras (1 lb, 1 w)	2		(12 b, 8 lb)		20
Total (all out, 100.5 overs)	**266**		(all out, 121.4 overs)		**397**

1–84 2–93 3–111 4–168 5–197 6–214
7–240 8–261 9–265 10–266

1–126 2–131 3–135 4–162 5–268
6–303 7–312 8–361 9–392 10–397

Bowling, *1st innings*: Fielder 27.5–4–77–2; Barnes 17–7–30–0; Rhodes 11–0–37–1; Braund 16–5–41–0; Crawford 29–1–79–5. *2nd innings*: Fielder 27–6–74–1; Crawford 33–6–125–3; Barnes 27.4–4–72–5; Braund 18–2–68–0; Rhodes 16–6–38–0.

England

*F.L. Fane b Armstrong	13	(2)	b Armstrong		50
J.B. Hobbs b Cotter	83	(1)	b Noble		28
G. Gunn lbw b Cotter	15		lbw b Noble		0
K.L. Hutchings b Cotter	126		c Cotter b Macartney		39
L.C. Braund b Cotter	49		b Armstrong		30
J. Hardstaff b Saunders	12		c Ransford b Cotter		19
W. Rhodes b Saunders	32		run out		15
J.N. Crawford c Ransford b Saunders	16		c Armstrong b Saunders		10
S.F. Barnes c Hill b Armstrong	14		not out		38
†J. Humphries b Cotter	6		lbw b Armstrong		16
A. Fielder not out	6		not out		18
Extras (3 b, 3 lb, 3 nb, 1 w)	10		(9 b, 7 lb, 2 nb, 1 w)		19
Total (all out, 135.2 overs)	**382**		(9 wkts, 121.4 overs)		**282**

1–27 2–61 3–160 4–268 5–287 6–325
7–353 8–360 9–369 10–382

1–54 2–54 3–121 4–131 5–162
6–196 7–198 8–209 9–243

Bowling, *1st innings*: Cotter 33–4–142–5; Saunders 34–7–100–3; Noble 9–3–26–0; Armstrong 34.2–15–36–2; Hazlitt 13–1–34–0; Macartney 12–2–34–0. *2nd innings*: Cotter 28–3–82–1; Saunders 30–9–58–1; Armstrong 30.4–10–53–3; Noble 22–7–41–2; Hazlitt 2–1–8–0; Macartney 9–3–21–1.

Close of play, *day 1*: Australia (1) 255–7 (Ransford 22*, Carter 10*); *day 2*: England (1) 246–3 (Hutchings 117*, Braund 15*); *day 3*: Australia (2) 96–0 (Noble 50*, Trumper 46*); *day 4*: Australia (2) 360–7 (Carter 22*, Cotter 27*); *day 5*: England (2) 159–4 (Braund 17*, Hardstaff 17*).

Toss: Australia. Last-innings target: 282 runs.
Umpires: P. Argall (Aus), R.M. Crockett (Aus).

ENGLAND won by one wicket.

6
FOWLER'S MATCH

Eton v Harrow

8–9 July 1910; Lord's Cricket Ground, London

Eton won by nine runs.

Here is a chance to leave Test cricket for perhaps the most remarkable game ever played – at Lord's, at any rate, even if the opponents were Eton and Harrow rather than England and Australia. For most of these two days in July 1910, this was an extremely one-sided contest. Eton, bowled out for 67, had followed on 165 runs behind Harrow's first-innings total and when their ninth second-innings wicket had fallen, they were only four runs ahead. In the end, Harrow were set to score 55 to win and, with the Eton captain, Robert Fowler, taking 8–23, they were bowled out for 45 and lost by nine runs.

After winning the toss, Harrow's first innings revolved round Tom Wilson, an adhesive opener, and Jack Hillyard, who came in at number seven and opened the bowling. Their total of 232 was made to seem much more impressive when Eton had been reduced to 40–5 by the close of play. The next morning they were bowled out for 67, with Fowler the only batsman to reach double figures. They were asked to follow on and things did not go much better in the second innings. Their first five wickets fell for 65 and Eton's main batsmen found it almost impossible to play their strokes on a lifeless pitch. Fowler was the main exception to this, with help from Denis Wigan and then William Boswell, who came in last in the first innings but was now promoted, and they put on 57, but in spite of their efforts Eton were only four runs ahead when Fowler was out. His 64 was the highest score of the match.

By now, the Harrow supporters were making a prodigious noise, while a number of Etonians, past and present, were leaving the ground with their umbrellas dragging along behind them in disgust. John Manners, who had made Fowler a good partner for the ninth wicket, will not yet have known that his father, a passionate Old Etonian, had already gone home and had shut himself in his library, telling his butler he was under no circumstances to be disturbed. Lieutenant-Colonel C.P. Foley, who wrote a memorable account of the closing stages of the match in his book *Autumn Foliage*, came to the conclusion that watching a massive Harrow victory was not the best way of passing the afternoon either, and took a taxi to White's Club to pick up his suitcase. When he arrived, he decided that before going on to spend the weekend at Coombe with General Sir Arthur Paget, he needed to have his hair cut and tottered in to see the club's barber.

While the Lieutenant-Colonel was on his travels, Manners was joined in the middle at Lord's by the last man, Kenelm Lister-Kaye, who had a good eye but little else as far as batting was concerned. Manners had the quick eye and movement of a rackets player, added to which he was fearless and enjoyed a crisis. In 23 rather surprising minutes they threw their bats at everything and got away with it, putting on 50 runs. Manners played a number of splendid drives off the fast bowling of Guy Earle and it took an acrobatic catch in the slips by Tom Jameson to get rid of Lister-Kaye. Harrow had been left to score 55, which was hardly enough to cause a panic. They now opted for the heavy roller before the start of their second innings and later blamed their defeat on this decision. It was not the best of excuses, for the pitch, which had become progressively slower, had surely not been made more difficult by the heavy roller, which may even have quietened it down even more.

With so few runs to bowl at, Eton can hardly have been brimming with confidence when they took the field for the last time, although Fowler himself might have felt something stir inside him. He opened the bowling from the Pavilion End and, finding a certain amount of turn, his quick off-breaks were too much for Harrow. He bowled the hitherto obdurate Wilson with the first ball of the innings. Geoffrey Hopley, who came in third, now hit two fours before he too was bowled by Fowler, and at the same score Thomas Turnbull, a left-hander who had a reputation as a big hitter, had a go and was well caught by Boswell in front of the Pavilion rails.

Harrow were now 8–3 and the Etonian supporters in the crowd of 10,000 were making an awful lot of noise without seriously thinking they were going to win; they could not quite believe what they were seeing, but anyway it was good fun. Earle decided there was no point in hanging around and immediately started to go for his strokes, scoring 13 in a hurry. In the stands the Harrow contingent were giving of their best, for two or three more overs of this and it would be all over. Fowler ran in again, Earle drove and Wigan held on to the catch taken very low down in the slips and for a long time many Harrovians loudly questioned the legality of the catch. They were becoming apprehensive.

It was about now that Lord Manners's butler made his first sortie to the library to give his lordship the encouraging news that Harrow were 21–4. In stentorian tones, his lordship sent him packing. Across London, at White's, Lord Brackley poked his head round the barber's curtain to tell Lieutenant-Colonel C.P. Foley that Harrow were 21–4, without getting too much of a reaction. It soon became 21–5 when Walter Monckton, Winston Churchill's future Minister of Labour, had his stumps spread-eagled by Fowler. Hillyard was then well caught low down at short mid on, which made it 21–6, Fowler having taken all six. It was now that the butler knocked for the second time on Lord Manners's library door to tell him the latest score and again he was told in no uncertain terms to buzz off and not to come back.

Meanwhile, not far away, in White's, Lord Brackley wasted no time in pulling the curtain back again and unleashing on the Lieutenant-Colonel the news that Harrow had now lost their first six wickets for 21 runs. That did it. The Lieutenant-Colonel sprang from his chair with his hair half cut and he and Lord Brackley rushed into the street, hailed a taxi and said, 'Lord's. Double fare if you do it in fifteen minutes.' The Lieutenant-Colonel had a stopwatch and it took 14 minutes 21⅔ seconds and he paid up. On the way into the Pavilion, up the steps which land you in front of the Committee Room, he managed to skewer a large fleeing Old Harrovian in the pit of his tummy. The tip of his umbrella hit him on one of his waistcoat buttons and the umbrella ricocheted out of his hand and over the side rails of the Pavilion.

The Lieutenant-Colonel takes up the story: 'The impact was terrific and the unlucky individual doubling up, sank like a wounded buffalo onto his knees without, as far as I recollect, uttering a sound. I sprang over the body without offering an apology and, shouting out instructions to the attendant to look after my umbrella, dashed into the Pavilion, up the many steps to its summit . . .'

There, he saw Jameson, the opening batsman who was normally a dasher but now still had to get off the mark after 40 minutes at the crease, lying on the ground with a badly cut eye after being hit in the face. When play restarted, the total soon became 29–8 as Fowler yorked Straker.

The Lieutenant-Colonel now resumes his pithy tale: 'The roars from the Harrow stand whenever a run was scored were heard in the Zoological Gardens. [Ogilvie] Graham hit a 3 and then Fowler bowled Jameson. He had scored 2 and was ninth man out, and it was a thousand pities he did not set up a record by carrying his bat through the innings for 0! (32-9-2). [Harold] Alexander, the future Field Marshal Lord Alexander, came in, looking horribly confident. The score crept up slowly. By now the cheering had swollen into such a volume of sound that its overtones included

Paddington Station as well as the Zoological Gardens in its perimeter. Thirteen priceless runs were sneaked or stolen by the indomitable last pair. How I loathed both of them! And just as things began to look really desperate, Alexander edged one to [Walter] Holland in the slips off [Allan] Steel and Eton had won by nine runs.'

History does not tell us how Lord Manners took the news of this famous victory or indeed if his butler dared to go back a third time to give him the result and risk the sack. We would love to know, too, how he explained away to his victorious son his palpable cowardice in deserting what he considered to be a sinking ship. It does not tell us, either, if the Lieutenant-Colonel sported a half-cut head of hair for the weekend at Coombe or whether he had the other half attended to when he returned to White's to pick up his suitcase. It will surely have been his inclination to visit the bar first, where he might have lingered.

We do know, beyond doubt, because Sir Ian Malcolm, in his recollections of Mr A.J. Balfour, Prime Minister from 1902 to 1905, says, 'I can never forget the magnificent finish of the Eton and Harrow match in Fowler's year when, at the close of play, A.J.B., Walter Forbes [a first cousin of A.J.B. who had won the Victoria Cross], Alfred Lyttelton [the first man to play cricket and football for England and, later, Secretary of State for the Colonies in Balfour's government] and two of his brothers all leapt onto the green bench upon which we had been sitting in the Pavilion and waved their hats and cheered Eton in an abandonment of enthusiasm.' The mind boggles.

Fowler's match will surely remain as an unrivalled cricket match. For the record, Robert Fowler made the top score for Eton in both innings (21 and 64) and took 12 wickets in the match. His figures in the second innings were 10–2–23–8. Fowler came from Ireland. In 1924, he played 24 games for Hampshire with reasonable success. In 1925, at the age of 34, he was cruelly cut down by leukaemia, but the story of Fowler's match will remain for ever.

As a postscript, apparently a lady friend of Robert Fowler's mother in Ireland wrote to congratulate her without knowing where she was staying in London. She is said to have written on the envelope, 'Fowler's Mother, London.' And it was delivered to her.

This fixture was always a two-day game until 1982 and is the oldest of all the fixtures still played at Lord's. These two schools first met on 2 August 1805 at the original Lord's Cricket Ground, the first of three, at Dorset Fields, part of which is now Dorset Square, close to Baker Street underground station. Eton, who had been challenged by Harrow, won this first match by an innings and two runs.

ETON COLLEGE v HARROW SCHOOL

At Lord's Cricket Ground, London, on 8–9 July 1910 (two-day match).

Harrow School

T.O. Jameson c Lubbock b Fowler	5	b Fowler	2
T.B. Wilson b Lister-Kaye	53	b Fowler	0
G.W.V. Hopley b Fowler	35	b Fowler	8
T.L.G. Turnbull lbw b Fowler	2	c Boswell b Fowler	0
*G.F. Earle c Wigan b Steel	20	c Wigan b Fowler	13
†W.T. Monckton c Lubbock b Stock	20	b Fowler	0
J.M. Hillyard st Lubbock b Fowler	62	c Lister-Kaye b Fowler	0
C.H.B. Blount c Holland b Steel	4	c and b Steel	5
A.C. Straker c Holland b Steel	2	b Fowler	1
O.B. Graham c and b Steel	6	not out	7
H.R.G.L. Alexander not out	2	c Holland b Steel	8
Extras (18 b, 2 lb, 1 nb)	21	(1 b)	1
Total (all out, 95.3 overs)	**232**	(all out, 19.4 overs)	**45**

1–15 2–84 3–88 4–121 5–133 6–168 7–191
8–201 9–216 10–232

1–0 2–8 3–8 4–21 5–21 6–21 7–26
8–29 9–32 10–45

Bowling, *1st innings*: Fowler 37.3–9–90–4; Steel 31–11–69–4; Lister-Kaye 12–5–23–1;
Stock 7–2–12–1; Boswell 8–4–17–0. *2nd innings*: Fowler 10–2–23–8; Lister-Kaye 3–0–9–0;
Steel 6.4–1–12–2.

Eton College

†R.H. Lubbock lbw b Earle	9		c Straker b Hillyard	9
C.W. Tufnell b Hillyard	5		lbw b Alexander	7
W.T. Birchenough c Hopley b Graham	5		c Turnbull b Jameson	22
W.T.F. Holland c Hopley b Hillyard	2		st Monckton b Alexander	5
*R.S. Fowler c Graham b Jameson	21		c Earle b Hillyard	64
A.I. Steel b Graham	0		c Hopley b Hillyard	6
D.G. Wigan c Turnbull b Jameson	8		b Graham	16
A.B. Stock lbw b Alexander	2	(9)	lbw b Earle	0
J.N. Manners c Graham b Alexander	4	(10)	not out	40
K.A. Lister-Kaye c Straker b Alexander	0	(11)	c Jameson b Earle	13
W.G.K. Boswell not out	0	(8)	b Earle	32
Extras (10 b, 1 w)	11		(2 b, 3 w)	5
Total (all out, 48.1 overs)	**67**		(all out, 73.3 overs)	**219**

1–16 2–16 3–26 4–34 5–36 6–57 7–62
8–64 9–66 10–67

1–12 2–19 3–41 4–47 5–65 6–107
7–164 8–166 9–168 10–219

Bowling, *1st innings*: Earle 12–9–4–1; Hillyard 19–9–38–2; Graham 9–7–3–2; Jameson
4–1–4–2; Alexander 4.1–1–7–3. *2nd innings*: Earle 17.3–3–57–3; Hillyard 23–7–65–3;
Graham 8–2–33–1; Jameson 9–1–26–1; Alexander 14–4–33–2; Wilson 2–2–0–0.

Close of play, *day 1*: Eton College (1) 40–5.

Toss: Harrow School. Last-innings target: 55 runs.
Umpires: J. Moss (Eng), J.P. Whiteside (Eng).

ETON COLLEGE won by nine runs.

7

AUBREY FAULKNER: ONE OF THE TRUE GREATS

An England XI v the Australians
27–30 August 1921; The Saffrons, Eastbourne
An England XI won by 28 runs.

WARWICK Armstrong's Australian side made short work of England in 1921, winning the Ashes series 3–0. As the summer went on, Archie MacLaren, who had captained England in 22 Test matches between 1897 and 1909, continually claimed he could put together a side predominantly of young Englishmen which would beat the Australians. The Saffrons at Eastbourne gave him the chance to prove it when they asked him to bring 'An England XI' to play the Australians. When his side had been bowled out for 43 in about an hour and a quarter on the first day, it looked a pretty feeble boast. The Australians seemed certain to win the considerable bonus they had been promised if they did not lose a match on the tour.

Archie MacLaren was a good batsman and not a bad captain, although Neville Cardus, who worshipped the ground he trod on, did his utmost to persuade his readers that he was the best captain England had ever had. If Cardus was prejudiced about MacLaren, there were times when his hero was equally guilty and MacLaren could be the most inflexible of men. He also had a strong temper, and these are traits which do not always help captaincy at the difficult moments when level-headedness is so important. He was, without doubt, a complex man who survived for much of the time on the edge of bankruptcy, which can make people both cunning and crafty. He fell out with a lot of people, including Lord Hawke, as we have seen, who was chairman of the selectors while MacLaren was the England captain. Their animosity may have cost England the series against Australia in 1902, as chronicled in the description of the fourth Test at Old Trafford.

To try and earn an honest bob or two, MacLaren took on all manner of strange jobs. He was at different times a schoolmaster, an hotel owner, a wine dealer and a slightly bogus assistant secretary of Lancashire County Cricket Club (in order to enable him to continue playing as an amateur). He was secretary for a time to Lionel Robinson, a gung-ho Australian businessman who owned a lovely ground at Old Buckenham near Attleborough in Norfolk. Robinson used his ground to try and buy himself a niche in English society, something he failed to do, although the First World War did not help him in this. With his own uncertain reputation, one can only wonder how much of a help MacLaren will have been to him.

At another time, MacLaren was also to become private secretary to Ranjitsinhji, whose own financial strength was sometimes suspect. There was one hilarious occasion when MacLaren rented a place near Ranji's impressively large house at Shillinglee, close to Chiddingfold in Sussex. When he was taken to court for non-payment of rent, MacLaren claimed that Ranji was the problem because it was he who had rented the house on MacLaren's behalf, but as he was a ruling Indian prince proceedings could not be brought against him. The magistrates disagreed, found MacLaren responsible and forced him to pay. It is thought that Ranji eventually came up with the money. In his splendid biography of Ranji, Simon Wilde says, 'Many of his off-the-field exploits with A.C. MacLaren ... will probably never be known, but it seems clear that sometimes they were not averse to conducting themselves in the fashion of E.W. Hornung's fictional character Raffles, the cricketing burglar.'

MacLaren was saved in the end by his Australian wife, formerly Maud Power, whom he had met when he first toured Australia. She came from a wealthy family and towards the end of their lives inherited a considerable amount of money, which enabled them both to spend their last years living in the style to which he had always felt he should be accustomed. Maud cannot have had the easiest of lives.

MacLaren undoubtedly had a good cricket brain and it was this and his fierce determination which convinced him he could beat Warwick Armstrong's Australians. He complained throughout the summer that the England selectors had not looked at any of the good young players for the Test series. He now chose an excellent blend of youth and experience when the committee at The Saffrons decided to host the match. MacLaren, who was 49, would captain the side, and the others he chose were Aubrey Faulkner, the 39-year-old South African who came out of retirement to play in this match; fast bowler Walter Brearley (45), like MacLaren from Lancashire; Geoffrey Foster (36), from the famous Worcestershire cricketing family; Michael Falcon (33), from Norfolk; and George Wood, the wicketkeeper, who was 28. He had just come down from Cambridge and went on to play three times for England. Then came the youngsters, led by the three Ashton brothers, Gilbert (24), Hubert (23) and Claude (20); a future England captain, Percy Chapman (20); and Clem Gibson (21), a Cambridge Blue who played briefly for Sussex.

Another extremely important figure at the ground – because if he had not been there, the game would have been nothing like so well chronicled – was Neville Cardus, who MacLaren had invited to come down to Eastbourne. In Cardus's eyes, MacLaren could do no wrong. Middlesex and Surrey were fighting for the County Championship over these three days in a crucial game at Lord's which claimed all the other main cricket writers. Cardus, however, had managed to persuade his editor that the train journey from Manchester to Eastbourne was the one to make. He had to withstand much ribbing when MacLaren's side was bowled out for 43 on the first morning and thwart a belated attempt to persuade him to make the journey up to Lord's.

MacLaren's three most important players at The Saffrons were Falcon, Faulkner and Gibson, while Cardus has left us in no doubt that MacLaren's faultless captaincy also had a considerable part to play. At the time, Falcon was the conservative Member of Parliament for East Norfolk, having been elected at what was known as the 'khaki election' in 1918. His parliamentary duties meant that this game at Eastbourne was only his second first-class match of the year, although he had managed to turn out regularly for Norfolk in the Minor Counties Championship. Falcon had bowled at fast-medium with considerable success for Harrow, then for Cambridge for four years and for the Gentlemen pretty regularly, as he was a favourite of Pelham Warner's, but although Warner tried hard to persuade him to play for Middlesex, nothing would budge him from his beloved Norfolk, whom he captained from 1912 to 1946.

At Eastbourne he bowled MacLaren's side back into the game after that disastrous first morning. The Australians had reached 83–1 in their first innings before losing nine wickets for 91, Falcon finishing with 6–67. He moved the ball about in the air and off the seam with great control and cleverly varied his pace. I remember playing for Norfolk myself at the age of 16 and Falcon, grey-haired, smiling, shrewd and helpful, and of course full of fascinating reminiscences, was a wonderful *éminence grise* at the lovely old ground at Lakenham. Even then, he could still be tempted to turn his arm over in light-hearted one-off games. If he had a mentor, it was the great Sydney Barnes, who came down a number of times to Lakenham with the Staffordshire side. They will have discussed their joint art on several occasions. In his description of the 1921 game in the *Manchester Guardian*, Cardus wrote of Falcon that his bowling at Eastbourne was 'far better than any of our Test match bowling'.

Clem Gibson was another Cambridge man who had first captained Eton and then played a season for Sussex before going back to his home in Argentina and leading them to perpetual glory against Brazil. Gibson swung the ball about at fast-medium and had a penetrating off-cutter, as the Australians were now to discover. 'He has a ball which is a good imitation of Barnes's famous ball, the one that pitches on the leg stump and swings away to the off.' Cardus again. Gibson's tall, fair-haired son, another Clem, was my first Eton captain in 1955.

The choice of Walter Brearley was logical because of MacLaren's Lancashire friendship with Brearley who, in spite of being able to play so little cricket for Lancashire because of his business, was a truly formidable fast bowler. He managed to pull a muscle on the first day. He did not bowl a single ball and made one and nought, batting at number eleven. Brearley's injury reduced MacLaren's armoury to three bowlers, which included Aubrey Faulkner's rusty leg-breaks. MacLaren himself never blinked and continued to proclaim that his side would win.

MacLaren had won the toss and decided to bat, only to find that Ted McDonald and Warwick Armstrong were almost unplayable, even though it was a good batting pitch. Armstrong had come on with his leg-breaks in place of Jack Gregory, who, after only two overs, had injured his foot, and both bowlers finished with five wickets. MacLaren's XI was bowled out in an hour and a quarter for 43 and the Australians then made a reasonable start. After Herbie Collins had been bowled by Falcon, Warren Bardsley and Charlie Macartney began to bat well, but soon after they had taken the lead, Faulkner spun leg-breaks past first Macartney and then Tommy Andrews, and with 'Nip' Pellew being quickly picked up in the slips by Hubert Ashton off Falcon, they were in some disarray at 96–4. Bardsley's solid resistance came to an end when he failed to read Faulkner's googly and was lbw. Falcon was capable at times of considerable pace, and now his control, allied to slight movement, proved too much for the remaining batsmen and the Australians were all out for 174, with Falcon taking six wickets and Faulkner the other four. It was a good fightback by MacLaren's side, but the Australians still had a first-innings lead of 131, which in the circumstances seemed likely to be more than enough.

This was confirmed when the England XI now lost their first four second-innings wickets for only 60. MacLaren, who may have felt the time had come for him to make an impact on the game, opened the innings with wicketkeeper George Wood, who was soon beaten by McDonald's pace. They were 8–1 at the end of the first day. The next morning, McDonald soon accounted for MacLaren, in similar fashion to Wood, and Geoffrey Foster then pushed back a return catch to Australia's leading fast bowler. There was a brief flurry of strokes from Gilbert Ashton before he was lbw to one which Armstrong pushed through a little quicker and Faulkner took his place.

Perhaps the most surprising of MacLaren's selections, the South African Aubrey Faulkner had been the game's leading all-rounder before the First World War, but had not played any serious cricket since the Triangular Tournament in England in 1912. Faulkner has to be one of the most important cricketers of that era, known as the Golden Age, and yet he has never received the accolades he deserves. He was almost certainly the best player South Africa has produced and he had a big impact on the game as it developed early in the twentieth century. Although he was blessed with an unusual talent, he always worked hard at his own game and no one has ever had a much better understanding of everything that goes to make cricket the game it is. Faulkner was good-looking, had wide-apart eyes and a friendly, easy-going face and was extremely popular among the ladies. He had fought in both the Boer War and the First World War and had twice been decorated for his bravery. He suffered for much of his life from a particularly nasty form of malaria.

Now at The Saffrons Faulkner played an amazing innings, making 153 in 211 minutes when his side were in a perilous position. He was understandably rusty and, to the irritation of some of the Australians, he audibly coached himself as he went along – and what a good job he made of it. Tall and robust, he was an awkward-looking batsman. He had an unusual grip of the bat and an open, two-eyed stance. His concentration was extraordinary and, being a big man, he hit the ball extremely hard. In spite of his rather homespun appearance at the crease, his footwork and technique were faultless.

His leg-spin bowling was of the highest class, too, and he was one of the first bowlers to perfect the googly. He bowled at medium pace, his disguise was brilliant and batsmen found it unusually difficult to spot his googly. Unlike his fellow leg-spinners in South Africa, Faulkner was able to move seamlessly from the matting pitches at home to turf pitches elsewhere. He also bowled a fast yorker which brought him plenty of wickets and he was able to bowl it without altering his action, which is what made it so dangerous. In spite of the effort that obviously went into everything he did, he always gave the impression that he was enjoying himself. He stayed on to live permanently in England after that triangular series in 1912.

After the war, he established a coaching school in Richmond in Surrey, where he was a great help to many distinguished cricketers. Faulkner himself was a complex character and although the term was not known in those days, he was probably bipolar. He never made the money he might have done from the cricket school or indeed beforehand, and that side of his life was usually in a tangle. This was almost certainly the reason he took his own life at the age of 48.

When Faulkner walked out to join Hubert Ashton, MacLaren's XI still needed 71 runs to make the Australians bat again. He looked really out of sorts to begin with, but his self-coaching paid off and he began to play some wonderful strokes, but, as often happens in this situation, the Australians did not realise what was happening. The last time Faulkner had batted against some of the same bowlers, in Australia in 1910–11, he had made 732 runs in the series. Suddenly this form had returned and while he and Ashton were together, there was a sea-change and it was the Australians who were on the back foot.

At the other end, Ashton went along more quietly, but looked technically the more polished of the two. He and Faulkner had taken the score to 214 when Ashton was suddenly caught in two minds by Armstrong and was lbw. They were 83 ahead at this stage and it was now that Faulkner showed his vast experience. He protected the lower-order batsmen with great skill and he found a particularly doughty partner in Falcon, with whom he added 51 crucial runs for the eighth wicket, of which Falcon made 17. Faulkner was finally out when the two Australian leg-spinners combined and Arthur Mailey caught him off Armstrong. With the last two wickets having added 19 important runs, MacLaren's XI was all out for 326. The Australians will not then have felt there was any chance that they might not be able to score 196 to win.

Before the close of play on this second day, Gibson took his first wicket of the match when he had Collins caught at slip by Hubert Ashton and, at 25–1, they needed 171 more on the last day. The citizens of Eastbourne may have had a sixth sense about it all, because there was a big crowd in position when play began. The second-wicket pair of Bardsley and Australia's 43-year-old wicketkeeper Hanson Carter, who in the first innings had gone in at number eight, his usual position, took the score to 52, when they were both out in quick succession: Bardsley was bowled by Gibson with a beauty which pitched on the off stump, went through Bardsley's defence and hit his leg stump. Before another run had been scored, Falcon bowled a short, fast one to Carter, who cut it late off the middle of the bat. Claude Ashton, who was fielding at third slip, dived forward and somehow got his hands underneath it and held on. It was a magnificent catch.

The score was now 52–3 and although they were making it a little uncomfortable for themselves, Australia still looked to be in control, but the crowd were beginning to sense it was going England's way and there was great and increasing excitement. Falcon now struck perhaps the most crucial blow of all when he bowled Macartney. The ball pitched on a length and moved enough in to the bat to find a way through Macartney's uncharacteristically cross-batted forward-defensive stroke. Australia were now 73–4 and in some trouble. The prospect of them losing their no-defeat bonus ensured their minds were fully on the job. Andrews and Pellew fought on with great determination and managed to reduce the target to double figures, before Gibson found the edge of Pellew's bat and Hubert Ashton held the catch in the slips. The score was 103–5 as the enormously tall figure of Jack Ryder strode to the wicket. He had decided that the best way to go about it was to play his strokes and he made 28 in quick time, with six resounding fours. Each one of his boundaries reduced the spectators to near silence.

At 143–5, with only 53 needed and five wickets in hand, Australia were breathing more easily. Ryder then drove again at Gibson and, in the slips, Gilbert Ashton held on to the edge. This was the final catch taken in a match in which the fielding was exceptional and not one catch was dropped during the three days. Gibson quickly found a way through Jack Gregory's indeterminate defensive push and he seemed to be in front of all three stumps, which the umpire was quick to confirm. This was Gibson's fifth wicket.

Armstrong came massively out to join Andrews. Mailey was later to write that this huge figure was shaking like a jelly, which was hardly characteristic of Armstrong. Maybe this said much for the size of the bonus the Australians were going to receive if they did not lose a match. Anyway, excitement all round the ground was frenzied. Andrews and Armstrong scored ten anxious runs before Faulkner returned because Falcon had suddenly lost his control and was becoming expensive. Almost at once he turned a leg-break more sharply than usual and bowled Andrews, who had batted for more than an hour and a half for his 31. Faulkner now deceived Armstrong with a beauty which came through a bit quicker and he was lbw.

The Australians were 158–9, needing 38 more, as Arthur Mailey, who was lucky to bat as high as number eleven, made his way out to the middle, with the crowd in a frenzy and MacLaren finding it hard to stand still at mid off. Mailey and McDonald scored nine thoroughly unconvincing runs and then, with the crowd on the very edge of its collective seat, Gibson bowled to Mailey, who pushed forward, which is probably rather a kind description of the stroke, and his stumps went over.

MacLaren had done it: his side had won by 28 runs and the Australians had suffered their first defeat of the tour. With his sweater over his shoulder, MacLaren raised his cap to the cheering crowd as he walked off. It was his last game of many against the Australians and what a triumph it was for him. But he had not quite finished. He played his final first-class innings during an MCC tour to New Zealand in 1922–23 and he made 200 not out. What a way to go.

ENGLAND XI v AUSTRALIANS

At The Saffrons, Eastbourne, on 27–30 August 1921 (three-day match).

England XI

G.N. Foster c Gregory b McDonald	5	(3)	c and b McDonald		11
G.A. Faulkner b Armstrong	3	(6)	c Mailey b Armstrong		153
G. Ashton lbw b Armstrong	6	(4)	lbw b Armstrong		36
H. Ashton b McDonald	0	(5)	lbw b Armstrong		75
A.P.F. Chapman b McDonald	16	(7)	b McDonald		11
C.T. Ashton c Ryder b Armstrong	1	(8)	b McDonald		0
M. Falcon b McDonald	8	(9)	c and b McDonald		17
†G.E.C. Wood lbw b Armstrong	1	(2)	b McDonald		2
*A.C. MacLaren b McDonald	0	(1)	b McDonald		5
C.H. Gibson not out	1		not out		0
W. Brearley b Armstrong	1		run out		0
Extras (1 nb)	1		(10 b, 1 lb, 5 nb)		16
Total (all out, 20.1 overs)	**43**		(all out, 91.5 overs)		**326**

1–5 2–9 3–14 4–18 5–26 6–40 7–41 8–41
9–41 10–43

1–5 2–10 3–33 4–60 5–214 6–250
7–256 8–307 9–326 10–326

Bowling, *1st innings*: Gregory 2–0–6–0; McDonald 10–2–21–5; Armstrong 8.1–4–15–5.
2nd innings: McDonald 31–3–98–6; Armstrong 24.5–6–74–3; Gregory 9–0–51–0;
Ryder 5–1–11–0; Mailey 22–3–76–0.

Australians

H.L. Collins b Falcon	19		c H Ashton b Gibson		12
W. Bardsley lbw b Faulkner	70		b Gibson		22
C.G. Macartney b Faulkner	24	(4)	b Falcon		14
T.J.E. Andrews b Faulkner	0	(5)	b Faulkner		31
C.E. Pellew c H Ashton b Falcon	1	(6)	c H Ashton b Gibson		16
J. Ryder b Falcon	10	(7)	c G Ashton b Gibson		28
*W.W. Armstrong b Falcon	13	(9)	lbw b Faulkner		11
†H. Carter c H Ashton b Faulkner	10	(3)	c CT Ashton b Falcon		16
J.M. Gregory not out	16	(8)	lbw b Gibson		0
E.A. McDonald b Falcon	4		not out		9
A.A. Mailey b Falcon	4		b Gibson		0
Extras (1 b, 2 lb)	3		(3 lb, 5 nb)		8
Total (all out, 48.4 overs)	**174**		(all out, 45.4 overs)		**167**

1–32 2–83 3–89 4–96 5–116 6–130 7–142
8–152 9–168 10–174

1–13 2–52 3–52 4–73 5–103 6–143
7–143 8–153 9–158 10–167

Bowling, *1st innings*: Falcon 18.4–2–67–6; Gibson 14–2–54–0; Faulkner 16–1–50–4.
2nd innings: Falcon 18–2–82–2; Gibson 22.4–6–64–6; Faulkner 5–1–13–2.

Close of play, *day 1*: England XI (2) 8–1 (Foster 1*, MacLaren 5*); *day 2*: Australians (2) 25–1
(Bardsley 8*, Carter 4*).

Toss: England. Last-innings target: 196 runs.
Umpires: H.R. Butt (Eng), J.P. Whiteside (Eng).

ENGLAND XI won by 28 runs.

8
COMPTON'S GENIUS

South Africa v England (1st Test)
16–20 December 1948; Kingsmead, Durban
England won by two wickets.

IT was surely compulsory to include in this book at least one match with an extraordinary finish which was orchestrated primarily by the genius of Denis Compton. In the late 1940s, his unique and eternally joyous style of batting helped to keep up the spirits of the country during those first few gloomy post-war years. If his right knee had not been effectively destroyed by his efforts on the football field for Arsenal, he might have held just about every batting record there is, even though there were few things he was less concerned about than breaking records. As it was, his total of 3,816 first-class runs, with 18 hundreds, in 1947 is a record that will never be broken. If any other batsman has been able to turn miraculous improvisation into an art form as he did, it can surely only have been the extraordinary Ranjitsinhji. With a bat in their hands, they were two of a kind.

Before the Second World War, English cricket had taken a fairly lofty view of South Africa when it came to arranging tours to the veldt and, as we saw back in 1905–06, not all the best players were sent. South Africa then toured England in 1947 and had been well beaten. In 1948–49, England went back to South Africa and, with Norman Yardley, the likely captain, being prevented from making the tour by business commitments, Middlesex's

George Mann was chosen to lead the side. Coincidentally, his father, Frank Mann, who had also played for Middlesex, had captained England on the tour to South Africa in 1922–23, before the job passed to Arthur Gilligan. Both Manns were therefore makeshift but winning captains and George had already stamped his mark on this tour by making a hundred in the first match.

The first Test was played in Durban, with South Africa anxious to make amends for that series defeat in England in 1947. Normally the pitch at Kingsmead has few problems for batsmen. It was there that in 1938–39 the fifth Test against England, the last timeless match, was left drawn after ten days so that the England players could reach Cape Town in time to catch their ship home. After that, Tests in South Africa were four-day matches, until the England tour in 1956–57, when a fifth day was added.

Dudley Nourse, the son of the redoubtable A.W. 'Dave' Nourse who we have already caught up with in these pages, will not have thought twice about batting when he won the toss. The pitch was dry, but proved to have its problems. At the Umgeni End the ball lifted off a length while at the other, the Town End, it kept uncomfortably low. England made a splendid and, as it turned out, an appropriate start when, with the score nine, Owen Wynne played Alec Bedser round the corner with the swing and Compton held a brilliant catch at backward short leg. Soon after that Mann gave the ball to Roly Jenkins, who with his third ball in Test cricket had Eric Rowan caught behind the wicket.

In this innings, there were only two stands of note: between Bruce Mitchell and Nourse, who added 51 for the third wicket, and then Denis Begbie and Ossie Dawson put on 49 for the sixth wicket. Both Bedser and Cliff Gladwin found a certain amount of movement in the air, sharing seven wickets between them, and to the audible disappointment of a good crowd, South Africa were bowled out before tea for 161. By then the clouds had been building up at the Umgeni End and only three balls were bowled in the evening session.

By the end of the first day, it looked as if this was destined to be one of those tight, low-scoring matches which often produce more exciting cricket than those high-scoring games which depend on declarations and can often lead to interminable draws. The pitch made life distinctly uncomfortable for batsmen and it was no surprise that Denis Compton and Len Hutton, with their impeccable techniques, played such important roles for England. Their batting was exceptional, especially in the first innings against the two South African spinners, Tufty Mann (orthodox left-arm spin) and Athol Rowan (off-breaks).

When play began the next day it was on a wet pitch which the sun soon turned into an old-fashioned sticky wicket, made for the two South African spinners. Strangely, Nourse did not bring them on until Hutton and Cyril Washbrook, playing with great skill in these awkward conditions, had taken the score past 50, although at times the raw pace of 19-year-old newcomer Cuan McCarthy caused the odd problem. Even then, they had reached 84 before Washbrook made a late decision to try and leave one from Mann and was caught behind. Reg Simpson soon departed to Mann and then there was a brilliant exhibition of batting on this almost impossible pitch by Hutton and Compton, and the score was 144 when the weather brought the second day's play to a premature end.

Two more runs had been scored on the third morning when Hutton tried to drive Rowan, a dangerous stroke on this pitch, and was caught at mid on. The pitch hereabouts was as bad as at any stage and although they added only 26 runs, Compton and the left-handed Allan Watkins, from Glamorgan, batted magnificently. Compton's attempts to improvise against these two spinners were worth the journey out. First he would threaten to come down the pitch, so that the bowler was able to see his intention, and then he would move quickly back, hoping the bowler would drop the ball short, giving him the chance to cut or pull. But Rowan and Mann were not to be fooled and either pitched the ball up or pushed it through quicker. Compton, capless, as splendidly dishevelled as always, black hair gleaming and as well-balanced as ever, danced nimbly around in his crease to try and give himself room to cut. It was all timing and footwork, kept in order by Compton's extraordinary eye. When he succeeded, he found he was frustrated by some brilliant close-to-the-wicket fielding on the off side, but he never let it unsettle him. Watkins meanwhile did his best to give his partner the strike, although he launched one fearsome pull at Mann which brought him four runs. He only made nine, but he can seldom have played better than he did now. They had taken the score to 172 and England's lead to 11 when Watkins pushed forward again to Rowan and was picked up by Nourse falling forward close in on the off side.

Compton found a good partner in George Mann, his captain, also a doughty fighter, who combined an optimistic forward-defensive push with one or two well-timed lusty blows. Compton reached his slowest ever Test fifty, which was as valuable an innings as any he played. They had put on 40 when Eric Rowan caught Mann at short leg off his brother Athol and, at 212–5, England were 51 ahead. The later batsmen did their best and Alec Bedser rather more than that, but it was Compton who kept the innings going, until eventually he got an edge to Tufty Mann, who finished with 6–59 from 37.4 overs. John Arlott wrote, 'I never hope to see a better innings, nor Compton, I believe, to play one.' Thanks to Hutton, earlier, and now Compton, England reached 253, which gave them a hugely important first-innings lead of 92.

Nourse, who played his cricket in Durban and therefore knew the pitch like the back of his hand, did not use a roller between innings. It was now that George Mann badly missed the services of a finger-spinner, whose accuracy would have made best use of this pitch. He turned to Doug Wright, an unusually quick leg-spinner who, when he found his length, was always dangerous.

Soon, Mann brought Jenkins on and so there were two leg-spinners bowling together. England will have been looking longingly at the figure of orthodox left-arm spinner Jack Young, sitting in the pavilion. His recent form had not been good and he had been left out of the side. However, Wright took two wickets that afternoon and Jenkins one, while Bedser removed the most dangerous batsman of all when he caught and bowled Nourse. South Africa ended the third day still two runs behind, at 90–4.

On the fourth and final morning, Billy Wade and Begbie built up the only worthwhile partnership of the innings. They batted through almost until lunch and South Africa seemed to be heading for a comfortable draw. Just before the interval, Bedser took the new ball and immediately suffered the indignity of being swung over midwicket for six by Begbie, but in trying to repeat the stroke, he holed out to Mann. Begbie and Wade had put on 85 for the fifth wicket. Immediately after that, Dawson played Wright to Compton in the gully, where he held another fine catch, and this made the score 179–6 and the lead was 87. The England players will have enjoyed their lunch more than had seemed likely a few minutes earlier, and this fascinating game of cricket had seen the advantage shift once more. The equation between the time left and runs needed was uppermost in everyone's mind.

After lunch, Mann turned to Compton's left-arm spin and he began by bowling nine consecutive maiden overs, and I wonder if he ever did that again in any class of cricket. One does not associate maiden overs with Compton's part-time unorthodox left-arm spin or, indeed, his character. What makes Compton's bowling even more noteworthy was that eight-ball overs were the order of the day in South Africa from 1938–39 to 1957–58. Wade's heroic innings of 63, which had taken three hours, ended when he was bowled round his legs sweeping at Jenkins. After that, the tail fought hard but were undone by the three spinners. Even so, when South Africa were bowled out for 219 the evening rain clouds were gathering at the Umgeni End and they seemed safe.

England's target in the fourth innings on a pitch which was still helping the bowlers was 128 in a maximum of two and a quarter hours, an old-fashioned equation, but one which held good in those days. The rain clouds made it likely that the mathematics would continually be changing.

Hutton and Washbrook now came out in the gloom and the first ball of the innings caused a stir. Cuan McCarthy, the blond-haired 19-year-old fast bowler from Maritzburg University, had only bowled nine overs in the first innings. His first ball now, to Hutton, was short and outside the off stump and Hutton cracked it towards the gully, where Nourse was fielding. It hit him such a painful blow on the knee that five precious minutes were lost while he recovered. Ten runs came in the first over, which was clear evidence that England were going for victory. The score was 18–0 after 15 minutes' play when the rain came back. The break lasted for 15 minutes and seven more runs had then been scored when Lindsay Tuckett, who had opened the bowling with McCarthy, bowled to Hutton. He played a fraction too soon and was well caught close in by Dawson.

This brought in George Mann, who had promoted himself in order to lead by example. The main problem for the batsmen was Tuckett's nagging leg-stump line. Tufty Mann soon replaced McCarthy in the attack and when George Mann tried to swing him away on the leg side, the catch was dropped by McCarthy himself. Washbrook was in great form, but when he had reached 25, Mann slid one back into him which caught him plumb in front of his stumps. England were 49–2 as Denis Compton emerged from the pavilion and, although he did not reach 30, he now played one of the most important innings of his career.

At this point, and to much spluttering in the pavilion, Nourse brought back McCarthy for Mann. Immediately, he had George Mann brilliantly caught in the slips by Mitchell, so Nourse was forgiven. At 52–3, England needed 76 more in 75 minutes, with McCarthy taking almost five minutes to bowl an over. Watkins was just beginning to settle down as Compton's partner when McCarthy beat him for pace and made a dreadful mess of his stumps: 64–4. Reg Simpson hurriedly pushed at the next ball and was caught with great joy by Eric Rowan in the gully: 64–5.

Five of England's six best batsmen had gone, 64 more were still needed, McCarthy suddenly seemed a terrifying prospect, the light was appalling and the South African crowd, sensing victory, was raucously beside itself as Godfrey Evans, at his most ebullient, bounced his way to the middle. He took two most enthusiastic runs off his first ball, grinning broadly at his partner as they crossed in mid-wicket. Evans seemed full of confidence, but McCarthy's answer was to bowl a really quick one with an almost round-arm action, which beat him for pace and comprehensively bowled him: 70–6.

Compton was seven not out as Roly Jenkins, the Worcestershire leg-spinner, came out of the pavilion. The tension round the ground was palpable and there was almost silence as McCarthy accelerated up to the wicket, fair-haired, raw-boned and merciless. Thirteen eight-ball overs had been bowled in the first hour and there were 13 more to come, provided the weather held. Fifty-eight more runs were needed in 63 minutes, and it was Compton and the bowlers who had to get them if England were to win. Compton, restrained because he knew he must not get out, looked assured all the same. Jenkins was anxious, cramped and uncertain, but playing the innings of his life.

Singles and twos kept coming, although Jenkins sometimes looked more as if he was batting out time rather than trying to win the match. Now it was more runs than minutes – 50 runs in 48 minutes – and Athol Rowan came on for Tuckett. They each took three off his first over, five came from McCarthy's next and then it began to rain. A single came from each of the next two overs, with Jenkins pinching the strike, and with 34 needed, England were again behind the clock. Three runs off Rowan, five from McCarthy and five more from Rowan. Three more off

McCarthy and England were again up with the clock. Tuckett came on for Rowan, five off the over and just 13 more runs to get.

The half-changed figures in the England dressing room did not dare move. The light had worsened as McCarthy strode in to Compton. He played the first five balls securely, but the sixth found a way through and bowled him. It was 115–7; 15 minutes remained, 13 runs were wanted and there were three wickets to fall. Compton and Jenkins had put on 45 in 48 minutes. Dudley Nourse later wrote in a book that this was probably the finest innings Compton ever played. Yes, it was that good and, of course, that right knee had not yet been damaged.

Bedser and Jenkins scrambled a single before Jenkins faced McCarthy, as fast and dangerous as ever, and it was now his twelfth over. The second ball lifted on Jenkins, who stabbed at it and Wade behind the stumps held the catch: 116–8, seven minutes to go, 12 runs needed. As Cliff Gladwin left the pavilion, the light and rain made it difficult to identify him. Runs and leg byes produced four runs, then Gladwin was dropped at mid on from McCarthy – an easy catch, but by now the light also made it awkward for the fielders. Gladwin swished at and missed McCarthy's last ball and the debutant had taken 6–43 in 12 overs.

There was now a minute and a half left, time for eight more balls, and England needed eight runs to win, South Africa two wickets. Cricket can never get much better than this. Tuckett was chosen to bowl the last over and looked distinctly uneasy. His first ball was short, hit Bedser on the pad, was half-stopped in the slips and they ran a leg bye. The crowd groaned because they thought it was a catch. The next ball was short on the leg side. Gladwin swung and it steepled away before bouncing over Athol Rowan's head at long leg and going for four. If Rowan had stayed where he was and waited for the ball as he should have done ...

Three runs from six balls and Gladwin mishit the next past short leg and they ran a single. Two from five balls. Bedser played and missed: two from four. He drove the fifth ball to mid on, who fielded cleanly: two from three. Bedser now pushed into the covers for a single and the scores were level. Tuckett in again, Gladwin played and missed and the last ball of the match remained with one wanted.

Tuckett bowled and Bedser, at the non-striker's end, began to run. The ball was short of a length – too short to drive, too full to hook. Gladwin, surrounded by close fielders, swung and missed. The ball hit him high on the leg and rolled out about two yards on the leg side. With Bedser almost in the crease beside him, Gladwin set off for the other end and, being a canny old customer, ran down the line of the fielders so that they couldn't see the stumps to aim at. England had won by two wickets.

SOUTH AFRICA v ENGLAND (1st Test)

At Kingsmead, Durban, on 16–20 December 1948 (four-day match).

South Africa

E.A.B. Rowan c Evans b Jenkins	7		c Compton b Jenkins	16
O.E. Wynne c Compton b Bedser	5		c Watkins b Wright	4
B. Mitchell c Evans b Bedser	27		b Wright	19
*A.D. Nourse c Watkins b Wright	37		c and b Bedser	32
†W.W. Wade run out	8		b Jenkins	63
D.W. Begbie c Compton b Bedser	37		c Mann b Bedser	48
O.C. Dawson b Gladwin	24		c Compton b Wright	3
A.M.B. Rowan not out	5		b Wright	15
L.T.D. Tuckett lbw b Gladwin	1		not out	3
N.B.F. Mann c Evans b Gladwin	4		c Mann b Compton	10
C.N. McCarthy b Bedser	0		b Jenkins	0
Extras (3 b, 2 lb, 1 nb)	6		(1 b, 5 lb)	6
Total (all out, 53.5 overs)	**161**		(all out, 89.3 overs)	**219**

1–9 2–18 3–69 4–80 5–99 6–148 7–150
8–152 9–160 10–161

1–22 2–22 3–67 4–89 5–174 6–179
7–199 8–208 9–219 10–219

England Bowling, *1st innings*: Bedser 13.5–2–39–4; Gladwin 12–3–21–3; Jenkins 14–3–50–1;
Wright 9–3–29–1; Compton 2–0–5–0; Watkins 3–0–11–0. *2nd innings*: Bedser 18–5–51–2;
Gladwin 7–3–15–0; Jenkins 22.3–6–64–3; Wright 26–3–72–4; Compton 16–11–11–1.

England

L. Hutton c McCarthy b A.M.B. Rowan	83		c Dawson b Tuckett	5
C. Washbrook c Wade b Mann	35		lbw b Mann	25
R.T. Simpson c Begbie b Mann	5	(6)	c E.A.B. Rowan b McCarthy	0
D.C.S. Compton c Wade b Mann	72		b McCarthy	28
A.J. Watkins c Nourse b A.M.B. Rowan	9		b McCarthy	4
*F.G. Mann c EAB Rowan b A.M.B. Rowan	19	(3)	c Mitchell b McCarthy	13
†T.G. Evans c Wynne b A.M.B. Rowan	0		b McCarthy	4
R.O. Jenkins c Mitchell b Mann	5		c Wade b McCarthy	22
A.V. Bedser c Tuckett b Mann	11		not out	1
C. Gladwin not out	0		not out	7
D.V.P. Wright c Tuckett b Mann	0		did not bat	
Extras (2 b, 12 lb)	14		(9 b, 10 lb)	19
Total (all out, 99.4 overs)	**253**		(8 wkts, 28 overs)	**128**

1–84 2–104 3–146 4–172 5–212 6–212
7–221 8–247 9–253 10–253

1–25 2–49 3–52 4–64 5–64 6–70
7–115 8–116

Bowling, *1st innings*: McCarthy 9–2–20–0; Dawson 3–0–16–0; Tuckett 6–0–36–0;
A.M.B. Rowan 44–8–108–4; Mann 37.4–14–59–6. *2nd innings*: McCarthy 12–2–43–6;
Tuckett 10–0–38–1; Mann 2–0–13–1; A.M.B. Rowan 4–0–15–0.

Close of play, *day 1*: England (1) 1–0 (Hutton 1*, Washbrook 0*); *day 2*: England (1) 144–2
(Hutton 81*, Compton 17*); *day 3*: South Africa (2) 90–4 (Wade 17*, Begbie 0*).

Toss: South Africa. Balls per over: Eight. Last-innings target: 128 runs.
Umpires: R.G.A. Ashman (SA), G.L. Sickler (SA).

ENGLAND won by two wickets.

9

THE TYPHOON

Australia v England (2nd Test)

17–22 December 1954; Sydney Cricket Ground

England won by 38 runs.

A 38-RUN margin of victory may seem much too comfortable for this match to be included in a book devoted to close and nerve-wracking finishes. Nonetheless, this was a crucially important victory for England and a game of unrelenting excitement, with a huge bearing on the outcome of the 1954–55 Ashes series.

Len Hutton had put Australia in to bat in the first Test in Brisbane and seen them make 601–8 declared and go on to win by an innings and 154 runs. The England selectors had gambled in choosing Frank Tyson and Colin Cowdrey for the tour. Neither had succeeded in this opening match: Tyson took 1–160 in 29 overs and Cowdrey made a total of 50 in the two innings.

Just over two weeks later the second Test began in Sydney. As a captain, Hutton's instincts were defensively inclined and it would not have been surprising if he had preferred to go back to experience rather than unproven talent, although he always stressed the importance of genuine fast bowling. Alec Bedser, whose brilliant fast-medium seam bowling had held England's bowling together since the war, had taken 1–131 at Brisbane, and did not appear to have fully recovered from a bout of shingles on the voyage out. If England had lost this second Test, they would then have been two matches down and in Australia it is not easy to come back after that.

When it comes to selection for Test matches on tour, the captain's wishes are almost sacrosanct and Hutton would have gone into this second Test with the side he wanted. To his great credit, he was prepared to stick with both Tyson and Cowdrey for Sydney, although this was to some extent forced on him by Denis Compton, who had broken his hand crashing into the boundary fence at the Gabba, and perhaps by Bedser's health too. His wish to play Tyson rather than Bedser was understandable. What was not was his unwillingness to tell his vice-captain of his decision before a general announcement was made. Bedser first heard the news when the names of the selected XI were pinned up in the dressing room on the morning of the match, and this after Hutton and Bedser had gone out together to look at the pitch. Bedser himself was, quite understandably, most unhappy at the way he had been treated after such long, faithful and successful service. He deserved better.

Hutton had spent the first part of the tour trying to persuade Tyson to shorten his run, for he saw him as a potential series-winner if his bowling could be properly coordinated. When he had bowled off his long run in the first Test he had been all over the place, although there was more control when at one stage he went onto his shorter run. He worked hard on this in the game against Victoria in between the first two Tests. For the next six or seven weeks, Tyson bowled about as fast as man has ever managed and enabled England to win a series in Australia for the first time since the Bodyline series in 1932–33.

Off 20 paces, Tyson who was strong and extremely fit, came up to the wicket with long, loping strides which seemed to ooze power. Then he went into a fiercely physical action with his right arm just above his shoulder. Just occasionally he would deliber-ately bowl with a lower, round-arm action as a surprise weapon, having copied this trick from Keith Miller. The secret of Tyson's bowling over this short period was the rhythm he was able to find all through his run-up and into his action. This was unusual for someone like Tyson, who was not a natural bowler, and as a result he was later liable to lose this rhythm as suddenly as he had found it. He made bowling look an intensely physical operation, rather as the Australian Jeff Thomson was to do 20 years later.

John Woodcock wrote about this 1954–55 series soon after he had become the Cricket Correspondent of *The Times*. During the tour he asked the Australian opening batsman Arthur Morris just how fast Tyson was. Morris said that the only way he could describe the difference between the pace of Tyson and Brian Statham was to say that it was comparable to the difference in pace between Statham and Trevor Bailey. It is remarkable to think that a bowler could have been that much faster than Statham, who was appreciably quicker than Bailey's fast-medium, and it gives a good idea of how fast Tyson must have been for that short period.

On the next tour of Australia, in 1958–59, Don Bradman gave Woodcock a lift back to his hotel one evening from the Adelaide Oval. The conversation turned to fast bowling and Woodcock asked the Don who was the fastest bowler he had ever seen. Without a moment's pause, the Don said, 'Tyson.' It was the certainty and the speed of the reply which surprised Woodcock and confirmed Tyson's searing pace, although, of course, Bradman never faced him. One wonders if any of the more recent collection of West Indies bowlers were as fast as Tyson, and perhaps Malcolm Marshall was. There cannot have been much in it, and there may have been others.

Although Tyson toured South Africa in 1956–57 and Australia once more in 1958–59, he never again found the same killing pace and rhythm which brought him 25 wickets in the three Tests, at Sydney, Melbourne and Adelaide. The 6–40 he took in the second innings of the fifth Test in Port Elizabeth in 1956–57 owed more to a pitch with a horribly low bounce than to outright pace. And Tyson only played in that match because Statham was unfit.

There was an interesting comparison to be made between Tyson and Australia's supreme fast bowler, Ray Lindwall, who was ten years older than Tyson. Lindwall was a natural bowler with a lovely action and a rhythm which never left him. At his fastest, soon after the war, he cannot have been that much slower. He had an easy, fluent run-up of about 20 paces and moved into his delivery stride without the slightest hesitation and into an almost perfect action. It was all made to seem so effortless. Lindwall purred his way to the crease, while Tyson arrived there looking as if he was going to war.

Arthur Morris, standing in as captain for the injured Ian Johnson, won the toss and put England in to bat. The big crowd settled down to watch Trevor Bailey's relentless forward-defensive stroke for 37 minutes before Ray Lindwall found a way through and removed his middle stump. Soon afterwards, Peter May turned Ron Archer into short leg's hands and when Hutton was brilliantly caught by Alan Davidson at leg slip off Bill Johnston's medium-paced mixture of spin and seam, England were 58–3 and never recovered.

The score had reached 111–9 when Brian Statham joined forces with Johnny Wardle. The left-handed Wardle, using his feet to come down the wicket and leaving himself room when he could to thrash the ball away on the off side, played some remarkable scything strokes, especially against Johnston, whose gentler pace suited his assault. When Wardle skied a catch to mid on, they had put on 43 runs, which would assume great significance by the end of the match, and taken England to 154. As soon as the innings had ended, it began to rain. There was time for a few overs before the end of the day and, shrewdly, Hutton gave the new ball to Statham and Bailey, who were less likely to waste it than Tyson. This paid off when Bailey made the last ball of the day lift nastily from a length and Morris could only fend it to Hutton at leg slip and, at the close, Australia were 18–1.

The next morning, Bailey and Statham did not bowl with their usual control and Les Favell and Jim Burke made steady progress. Bailey then moved to Statham's end and, swinging the ball both ways, recovered himself and bowled extremely well. The score had reached 65 when he found the edge of Favell's bat with an outswinger and Tom Graveney held the catch at second slip. Burke and Neil Harvey now became hopelessly bogged down, much to the irritation of the big crowd. The barrackers enjoyed themselves as they like to on the famous Hill at the SCG. Burke came in for the worst of it and a stentorian voice from under the massive scoreboard on the Hill proclaimed in ringing tones, 'Burke, you're like a statue. I wish I was a pigeon.' Australia were 88–2 at lunch and soon afterwards, after one final jubilant roar, vocal peace returned when Bailey found the edge of Burke's bat. In that afternoon session, Australia lost four wickets for 70 runs.

After lunch Hutton turned to Tyson, who went straight on to the new short run he had been working on since Brisbane. It was the run he had used in the northern leagues before he had joined Northamptonshire, which will have made the change much easier for him. He was all over the place for a couple of overs, but then suddenly found his rhythm. He was bowling to Harvey and produced one with the round-arm action he had picked up from Keith Miller. It lifted sharply to the shoulder of Harvey's bat and was caught by Cowdrey in the gully, and after that there was no holding him. A few runs later a yorker was too fast for Graeme Hole and Australia found themselves at 122–5.

Statham now came back and just when Richie Benaud was beginning to look dangerous, he caught him on the crease and had him lbw. Archer took Australia past the England score with a massive blow onto the Hill for six and he and Davidson had put on 52 when another beauty from Statham removed Davidson's middle stump. The new ball produced a few runs before Archer drove at Tyson and was caught low down by Hutton at third slip. England's fielding was good and they held their catches. By now Lindwall, who had made 64 at Brisbane, was again batting well

A posed but evocative picture of Frederick Spofforth, who may have forgotten to take off his cap and tie.

Good, honest Fred Tate, who found Test
cricket one step too far.

Gilbert Jessop, whose extraordinary
104 at The Oval in 1902 brought him
immortality.

England's chairman of selectors in 1902, Lord Hawke, sits back at Hastings while Jack
Mason and W.G. enjoy themselves.

Aubrey Faulkner, South Africa's leg-spinning all-rounder, one of the great players of the Golden Age.

Kenneth Hutchings, who 'drove' the Australian bowlers to distraction in Melbourne in 1908.

Jack Crawford took eight wickets with his quick off-breaks in the same match

Fowler's Match at Lord's in 1910, with Robert Fowler (Eton) top left.

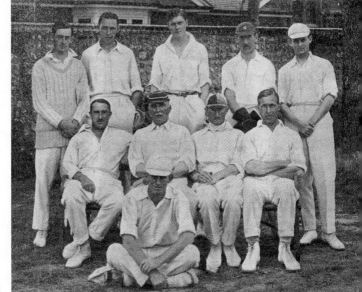

Right: Archie MacLaren's side which beat the Australians at The Saffrons, Eastbourne, in 1921.

Below: Len Hutton, Alec Bedser and Denis Compton start the voyage to South Africa in October 1948.

Denis Compton on his way to 145 not out against Australia at Old Trafford in 1948.

The power of Frank Tyson as he destroyed the Australian batting in 1954–55.

Sonny Ramadhin bowls to Peter May at Edgbaston in 1957. May and Colin Cowdrey put on 411.

The first tied Test match: Joe Solomon throws down Ian Meckiff's stumps at the Gabba in 1960.

The two captains, Richie Benaud and Frank Worrell, in that amazing 1960–61 series in Australia.

England v West Indies, Lord's 1963: the flashing bat of Ted Dexter, left, and the brave determination of Brian Close.

Their most frightening opponent. Wes Hall uncoils his terrific pace from the Pavilion End.

and Tyson, forgetting that there was a code of honour among fast bowlers which ordained that they did not bowl bouncers at each other, let one go at him. It took Lindwall by complete surprise and had him caught behind. He gave Tyson a look which suggested he would not forget his bouncer.

Hutton instructed Tyson to bowl the rest of the over past Johnston's leg stump, so that England would not have to bat that evening. Then, with only ten minutes remaining, Bailey bowled Gil Langley and Australia were all out for 228, which gave them a more-than-useful lead of 74 in what was clearly going to be a low-scoring match. England had only bowled 55.4 eight-ball overs in the day, the equivalent of 74 six-ball overs, but the cricket had been so gripping that not many people will have noticed or have minded if they did. There is usually a garden-party atmosphere at the City or Noble Stand end of the ground during a Test match at the SCG. Picnics are spread out behind the stands on the practice ground and during the lunch interval there is a happy social buzz. In this match, the conversation seldom left the cricket, for there was that extraordinary sustained excitement which an exciting and fluctuating Test match brings with it. Everyone was second-guessing the afternoon session, and beyond, to the accompaniment of popping champagne corks.

There were 32,000 people crammed into the ground each morning of the match. On the third morning, they were again treated to just over half an hour of forward-defensive strokes by Bailey before one of them produced a fatal edge off Archer. Hutton hit two fours off Johnston before being caught off him by Benaud in the gully. Tom Graveney then drove in hope at his third ball and was caught behind off Johnston and, at 55–3, England were still 19 runs behind. Australia looked as if they were sitting pretty when Colin Cowdrey, who had only just come down from Oxford University, joined Peter May, himself not that long out of Cambridge. The two young men were given the toughest of examinations. Lindwall, at his most determined, bowled seven overs straight off before lunch and seven more immediately afterwards. These two saw him off and when, at 118–3, Benaud was brought on, he too was played with a mature confidence. May pulled and drove with textbook perfection and Cowdrey's driving was the product of a lovely natural sense of timing which is seen all too seldom.

Alan Ross, covering the tour for *The Observer*, wrote that 'May split the air with the noise of his strokes, Cowdrey the field with the ease of his timing.' Which nicely summed it up. Just before the end, after a period of watchful defence, Cowdrey lost concentration, came down the wicket and drove a googly from Benaud into the hands of Archer at long off. It was a stupid way to get out late in the day and it was a stroke which lived with Cowdrey for some time. Bill Edrich, who was coming to the end of his Test career, then hooked and drove Johnston for fours and May did likewise. Alan Ross also hit another boundary in the press box: 'This was champagne when one had prepared for indigestion tablets.'

At the close of another absorbing day, England were 204–4, 130 runs ahead, with May 98 and Edrich 16. After Lindwall's opening over on the fourth morning, rain interfered. When play restarted, May pushed his second ball for the two he needed for his hundred. The new ball was now available and in Lindwall's first over, two outswingers were followed by an inswinging yorker which went through May and bowled him. He had batted five hours and his 104 was one of his greatest innings.

England were 222–5 and this brought in Tyson. Lindwall was ready for him: the bouncer was fast and at the batsman. Tyson forgot the first rule for playing bouncers: don't take your eye off the ball. He turned his back to the bowler and ducked into the ball. It crashed into the back of his head and Tyson collapsed in the crease. Edrich, at the non-striker's end, shouted out, 'My God, Lindy, you've killed him.' Tyson, on the edge of unconsciousness, was helped off the field by two ambulancemen. This looked like a double blow for England, in that Tyson's bowling was obviously going to be of great importance in Australia's second innings.

This was underlined when, during the lunch interval, the news leaked out that he was not expected to bat or bowl again in the rest of the match. Then, on the restart, Edrich faced Archer and, in trying to leave a ball alone at the very last moment, played it into his stumps. As Edrich walked off, to everyone's surprise, the batsman emerging from the pavilion was Tyson himself. The crowd quickly caught on, the applause was considerable and just to show all was well, he drove Johnston past cover for four. Lindwall put his arm round him and produced no more bouncers, but he soon bowled him just the same. Godfrey Evans did not last long and when Johnny Wardle was lbw to Lindwall, England were 250–9, 176 runs ahead, which was hardly enough. The Australian crowd was in great voice, while England's supporters were doing their best to keep their spirits up – mostly in the plentiful supply of bars.

It was now that Bob Appleyard was joined by Brian Statham, who had added those 43 much-needed runs with Wardle in the first innings. Statham, a left-handed batsman, showed immediately that his first-innings performance was no fluke when he straight-drove Lindwall for four and cut him wide of gully for another and, to make his point, handed out similar treatment to Davidson. At the other end, Appleyard sheltered behind a well-organised defence and, being the less ambitious of the two, was content to push and steer the ball away for ones and twos. It must have been another infuriating partnership for the Australians. There will have been laughter and joy in the England dressing room, but supreme irritation, not to say dismay, will have held sway just down the corridor. It was forever thus with productive last-wicket stands. When Statham had a wild swing at Johnston and was caught behind, these two had put on 46 crucial runs, which grew dramatically in importance as the match went to its thrilling finish on the last day.

Australia set off midway through the fourth afternoon in search of 223 to win on a pitch which had held up reasonably well. Both Morris and Favell were beaten early on and then Morris was lbw to the second-last ball before the tea interval, trying to swing Statham away to leg. The former Australian leg-spinner Bill O'Reilly, now a vibrant and joyfully argumentative member of the press contingent, described the stroke in his paper the next day as 'a suicidally wild shot borrowed unspoiled from kerosene cricket'.

In the first over after tea, Tyson had Favell caught high up at first slip by Edrich, but Jim Burke and Neil Harvey then took them to 72–2 by the close. They needed another 151 and the next day the batsmen had no trouble in the first few overs on a pitch which was behaving itself, and an Australian win was looking more than probable. For all that, it was a slow start and only five runs had been added when Tyson produced a yorker which removed Burke's off stump. This brought in Graeme Hole and his fourth ball saw an action replay and again the stumps were flying before the batsman had moved his bat. It was 77–4, England were back in charge and Tyson's rhythm and pace were awesome.

Bob Appleyard now came on and after a good off drive, Benaud swept and the ball climbed off the top edge to square leg, where Tyson was having a rest. He circled under the ball, badly misjudging it before getting down on his knees and reaching out despairingly for it with both hands. Miraculously, he got both to the ball and somehow managed to hold on, inches above the grass. Australia were 119–5 at lunch and when four more had been scored, Archer went to square-cut Tyson, only for the ball to jag sharply back at him and hit his off stump. Then Statham pitched one on Davidson's leg stump which moved sharply across him, taking the edge, and Evans threw himself far to his left and hung on to it in his left hand somewhere between first and second slip and it was 127–7.

It was now Lindwall's turn and the fates had decreed he would face Tyson, who was surely still feeling that nasty blow from the retaliatory bumper Lindwall himself had served up. Everyone on the ground, especially Lindwall, was expecting the bouncer Tyson was preparing to deliver, but in the end – with, so he said, a last-second change of mind – he pitched the ball up and Lindwall was bowled trying to cut a half-volley: game, set and match to Tyson, and it was his fifth wicket of the innings.

Gil Langley could do nothing about an inswinger from Statham which hit his leg stump. With the score 145–9, Bill Johnston, the last man, came cheerfully to the crease carrying a bat in one hand and a new stump in the other to replace the one that Statham had just broken when bowling Langley. Harvey launched an attack against all the bowling, trying at the same time to protect his partner as much as he could. Runs came fast, Harvey was batting brilliantly, without any apparent trouble, and Johnston, who knew much more about batting than he let on, defended soundly when he had to.

The score had reached 184, with 39 now needed, and the England players were looking distinctly uneasy. There had been an anxious moment for Australia when Harvey hooked at Tyson and the ball only just cleared Bailey in the deep and bounced inside the boundary before going for four. Was Bailey deliberately standing a few yards in from the boundary, or should he have been right back on the fence? Then, at last, Harvey was kept at the non-striker's end and Tyson had a full over to bowl at Johnston. Johnston kept out the first two balls, which were fast and straight, and scooped the third to short fine leg. At this point, Statham came up and had a word with Tyson, suggesting he should bowl the next one in the same place, but a little shorter and closer to the body. Tyson obliged and Johnston went for that favourite scoop once again, the shot Tyson liked to describe as the 'Victorian palais glide'. He got an edge and Evans took off to his left and held a staggering diving catch in his left glove. Woodcock and one or two others wondered if Johnston had actually made contact with the ball. Four years later, on the next tour to Australia, he asked him if he had touched it. All was well. He admitted that he had.

Tyson had taken 6–85 in the innings and 10–130 in the match. Hutton's faith in him had been more than justified. Tyson went on to take nine wickets in the third Test in Melbourne, which included 7–27 in Australia's second innings, and six more in the fourth in Adelaide, a victory which meant England had retained the Ashes. In the match at Melbourne, Cowdrey made 102 of England's first-innings total of 191. The Australians were sure they would have won the second Test if Lindwall had not bowled that bouncer to Tyson. It made Tyson so angry and he was heard to spout words from William Wordsworth on his way back to his bowling mark in the final innings. He was more than determined to prevent Australia from winning and going two up in the series.

AUSTRALIA v ENGLAND (2nd Test)
At SCG, Sydney, on 17–22 December 1954 (six-day match).

England

*L. Hutton c Davidson b Johnston	30	c Benaud b Johnston	28
T.E. Bailey b Lindwall	0	c Langley b Archer	6
P.B.H. May c Johnston b Archer	5	b Lindwall	104
T.W. Graveney c Favell b Johnston	21	c Langley b Johnston	0
M.C. Cowdrey c Langley b Davidson	23	c Archer b Benaud	54
W.J. Edrich c Benaud b Archer	10	b Archer	29
F.H. Tyson b Lindwall	0	b Lindwall	9
†T.G. Evans c Langley b Archer	3	c Lindwall b Archer	4
J.H. Wardle c Burke b Johnston	35	lbw b Lindwall	8
R. Appleyard c Hole b Davidson	8	not out	19
J.B. Statham not out	14	c Langley b Johnston	25
Extras (5 lb)	5	(6 lb, 4 nb)	10
Total (all out, 54.3 overs)	**154**	(all out, 104.3 overs)	**296**

1-14 2-19 3-58 4-63 5-84 6-85 7-88
8-99 9-111 10-154

1-18 2-55 3-55 4-171 5-222
6-232 7-239 8-249 9-250 10-296

Bowling, *1st innings*: Lindwall 17–3–47–2; Archer 12–7–12–3; Davidson 12–3–34–2; Johnston 13.3–1–56–3. *2nd innings*: Lindwall 31–10–69–3; Archer 22–9–53–3; Johnston 19.3–2–70–3; Davidson 13–2–52–0; Benaud 19–3–42–1.

Australia

L.E. Favell c Graveney b Bailey	26	c Edrich b Tyson	16
*A.R. Morris c Hutton b Bailey	12	lbw b Statham	10
J.W. Burke c Graveney b Bailey	44	b Tyson	14
R.N. Harvey c Cowdrey b Tyson	12	not out	92
G.B. Hole b Tyson	12	b Tyson	0
R. Benaud lbw b Statham	20	c Tyson b Appleyard	12
R.G. Archer c Hutton b Tyson	49	b Tyson	6
A.K. Davidson b Statham	20	c Evans b Statham	5
R.R. Lindwall c Evans b Tyson	19	b Tyson	8
†G.R.A. Langley b Bailey	5	b Statham	0
W.A. Johnston not out	0	c Evans b Tyson	11
Extras (5 b, 2 lb, 2 nb)	9	(7 lb, 3 nb)	10
Total (all out, 55.4 overs)	**228**	(all out, 53.4 overs)	**184**

1-18 2-65 3-100 4-104 5-122 6-141
7-193 8-213 9-224 10-228

1-27 2-34 3-77 4-77 5-102 6-122
7-127 8-136 9-145 10-184

Bowling, *1st innings*: Statham–18–1–83–2; Bailey 17.4–3–59–4; Tyson 13–2–45–4; Appleyard 7–1–32–0. *2nd innings*: Statham 19–6–45–3; Tyson 18.4–1–85–6; Bailey 6–0–21–0; Appleyard 6–1–12–1; Wardle 4–2–11–0.

Close of play, *day 1*: Australia (1) 18–1 (Favell 6*); *day 2*: Australia (1) 228 all out; *day 3*: England (2) 204–4 (May 98*, Edrich 16*); *day 4*: Australia (2) 72–2 (Burke 13*, Harvey 26*).

Toss: Australia. Balls per over: Eight. Last-innings target: 223 runs.
Umpires: M.J. McInnes (Aus), R.J.J. Wright (Aus).

ENGLAND won by 38 runs.

10
RECORDS GALORE

England v West Indies (1st Test)
30 May – 4 June 1957; Edgbaston, Birmingham
Match drawn.

Fᴇᴡ Test matches have produced such remarkable and contrasting cricket as the first between England and the West Indies in 1957. For the first three days of Edgbaston's first Test match for 28 years, England seemed to be heading for a massive defeat, mainly at the hands of Sonny Ramadhin, whose spin bowling, along with that of his left-arm team-mate, Alf Valentine, had destroyed England's batting in 1950, when the West Indies had won their first series in England. Ramadhin now took 7–49 in England's first innings of 186. Strangely, on the morning of the match the West Indian tour selectors had decided not to play Valentine. He was certainly no longer the bowler he had been seven years before, but the psychological advantage of having him at the other end to Ramadhin at the start of the series would surely have been important. He was also the first West Indies bowler to have taken a hundred Test wickets.

Their batsmen then took the West Indies to a first-innings lead of 288, whereupon Ramadhin took two England second-innings wickets. They had reached 113–3 when, after 20 minutes' play on the fourth morning, Colin Cowdrey came out to join his captain, Peter May. The next wicket fell eight hours and 20 minutes later, when Cowdrey holed out to long on, by which time the two of them had put on 411 runs, the third-highest stand in the history of Test cricket at the time, taking England to 524–4. May's declaration half an hour later then left the West Indies with 140 minutes' batting and by the end, at 72–7, they were struggling to hold on for a draw. It was an extraordinary turnaround.

A game like this tends to become submerged in a mass of statistics as endless records are broken. Ramadhin was the joker in the West Indies pack, but now without Valentine, he found he was not able to do it on his own. Ramadhin was a small man with a round, open face which did not give much away. His shirt sleeves were buttoned to his wrists, which helped his inscrutable air, and he twinkled up to the wicket with a quick, short-stepping run-up. His arms came quickly into his action and England's batsmen were mesmerised. They could not read him from the hand and he allowed the batsman little time to see the ball before it left his grip and they found it difficult to tell which way the ball was going to turn. If Ramadhin had played in modern times, his action would surely have raised eyebrows, for there were occasions when it looked as if he threw the ball. The spotlight was not so bright in those days.

After the first innings at Edgbaston, the West Indians will have felt sure that history was about to repeat itself. Their captain, John Goddard, will not have been worried by Valentine's absence. This general feeling of West Indies superiority was forcibly backed up by a brilliant innings of 161 by O.G. 'Collie' Smith. This was mainly responsible for taking them to a total of 474 and a lead of 288. Clyde Walcott, one of the famous three Ws who had done so much for West Indies cricket after the war, made an important contribution of 90, but early on, when going for a quick single, he pulled a muscle in his leg. He was in such pain that he fainted and he needed a runner to enable him to continue batting. Walcott was tall and a big man with it, and for a time he had made an unlikely wicketkeeper for the West Indies. Frank Worrell, another of those Ws, was a right-handed batsman and a left-arm bowler, and was all grace and elegance. He now made 81, but he too hurt himself during his innings and also needed a runner. Everton Weekes, the third W, was amazingly quick on his feet and the best batsman of the three, with a flawless technique, but he had only made nine when he was bowled by Fred Trueman.

The unlucky man who found himself running between the wickets for both Walcott and Worrell was opener Bruce Pairaudeau, who had made just a single before he too had been bowled by Trueman. He had to run for Walcott for three and a quarter hours, but this was no more than a warm-up act because he then had to be on duty for another five hours for Worrell. Talk about having your nose rubbed in it.

There has to be a strong element of sadness in any description of Collie Smith's genius, for he was tragically killed in a car crash just two years later. He was a Jamaican who had burst on the scene in similar fashion to Garry Sobers, with whom he was great friends. Smith had made 104 in his first Test, against Australia in 1954–55 in the West Indies, when he coped brilliantly with the pace of Ray Lindwall and Keith Miller. This 161 at Edgbaston was followed by 168 in the third Test at Trent Bridge. Like Sobers, Smith had a face full of what seemed a slightly naive youthful enthusiasm, although there was nothing in the least naive about their style at the crease. Smith was known affectionately by his team-mates as 'Mickey Mouse', which probably came from his looks, or 'Wayside Preacher', because he enjoyed reading the lesson in church.

He was a wonderfully instinctive and fearless strokemaker and who knows what the future might have brought him. In 1959, he was playing in the Lancashire League for Burnley and in early September, he and two of his West Indian team-mates, Sobers and Tom Dewdney, were driving to London to play in a charity game. At 4.45 in the morning, near Stoke-on-Trent, Sobers, who was driving, was blinded by headlights and they ran into a ten-ton cattle truck. Smith, who was sleeping in the back, died in hospital three days later. John Woodcock, who described both those two big innings Smith played against England in 1957 for *The Times*, later summed him up perfectly when he said, 'He was a true West Indian batsman.' You never knew quite what was coming next, but it was bound to be exciting as he flashed his bat after his quicksilver feet had shimmied into position.

At the time, his 161 at Edgbaston looked as if it would make sure of a West Indies victory when it took them to such a big first-innings lead. If further confirmation of the West Indies dominance was needed, it came when, early in England's second innings, Ramadhin removed Peter Richardson and Doug Insole in successive overs. Brian Close's Yorkshire grit kept him there until soon after the start the next morning, and then a more streamlined Colin Cowdrey than the one who years later stretched out on the benches of the House of Lords joined his captain, who had been successfully sheltering behind his impeccable technique. Although both these two young men – May was 27 and Cowdrey 24 – were outstanding strokemakers, they now had a match to save, and how they buckled down to it.

After Ramadhin had taken seven wickets in the first innings, a good deal of thought and conversation will have gone into trying to work out the best way to cope with him. He did not turn the ball a great deal, but if the batsmen were unable to read him, this did not make it any easier. The middle of the bat is no great distance from the edge and he turned it enough to locate the latter if given the chance by faulty strokeplay. May had already been using his pads more than usual and the general idea was to thrust the pad out at anything Ramadhin pitched wide of the stumps. There was much appealing, but Emrys Davies and Charlie Elliott, like most of their colleagues in those days, were not inclined to give batsmen out if they came onto the front foot. When the ball pitched on the stumps, May and Cowdrey then used their exemplary forward-defensive strokes to smother any spin – 'the prod', as it became known. It did not require high science to work this out, but it required great concentration and judgement to put it into action for long enough to save the situation.

Ramadhin tried to counter this by bowling both quicker and shorter, but both batsmen were up to that. May and Cowdrey were not strangers to this type of innings, for, as we have seen, they had both made heroic hundreds in Australia in 1954–55 which had helped England to win two close Test matches, in Sydney and Melbourne, and then the Ashes. They had all the technical requirements that were needed and they now put them to full use, without ever losing their concentration. It was not a glamorous or exciting partnership in terms of execution, but the situation made it increasingly dramatic, exciting and tense as this fourth day progressed, and their batting was greatly appreciated by a crowd which grew as the day went on.

On the last day, the crowd realised England now had a good chance of salvation and they watched the continuation of this colossal partnership with growing excitement. It was a day when spectators were forever working out the sums of runs needed and minutes left as they willed England on to safety. In the end, the amazing statistical evidence, as one record after another was broken, gave it all an increasing glamour and a tinge of romance too. The prospect of a Ramadhin-inspired West Indies victory became more and more unlikely, before vanishing altogether on that final morning.

Peter May, still arguably the best batsman England has produced since the war, was slim, tall and upstanding and beyond doubt the product of a public school. In his case it was Charterhouse, which has always produced good cricketers, and in May's time they were coached by George Geary, a fast-medium bowler who played 14 times for England and for Leicestershire. May often paid tribute to the importance of the coaching and the advice he received. May was a beautifully fluent strokemaker who hit the ball with an almost clinical precision. It would be difficult to imagine a more perfect stroke than a cover drive by May. Like all great players, he seemed to see the ball earlier than most, his footwork was swift and sure and he was a wonderfully clean striker of the ball. His hallmark was the shot he played off the back foot whipping the ball wide of mid on.

Cowdrey was another batsman who had obviously learned his game at a public school, Tonbridge, and, like May, he made the most of the luck he had to learn the game on true pitches. He was also the most elegant and unruffled of batsmen, although with a mind which sometimes seemed to make the game more complicated for him than it need have been. For such a great player, he allowed himself, especially later in his career, to become becalmed at the crease when he had the skill to break free in ways that mere mortals would have been unable to do. At his best, there was no more felicitous timer of the ball. As they showed at Edgbaston, both their games were based on impeccable defensive techniques. In the second half of the 1950s, England's batting revolved around May and Cowdrey.

Well before the end of the fourth day, captain John Goddard, although a tough, four-square man not often worried by doubts, will have been thinking wistfully of Valentine, who had taken 33 wickets to Ramadhin's 26 in 1950. At the end of every over from Ramadhin which they had safely negotiated with a combination of bat and pad, May and Cowdrey must have been delighted to have an over's respite before starting all over again. If the ball had instead been going straight into Valentine's hands at the other end, the memory of what had happened seven years earlier may have played on their nerves. Even though he did not take a single wicket in the next four Tests, it may have been unwise to leave him out for the first. There must have been a chance too of him producing the occasional unplayable one, and his very presence would surely have been a help to Ramadhin, which would have been important.

Alf Valentine could hardly have been a more different figure from Ramadhin, even though he was just as inscrutable – his sleeves were also buttoned to his wrists. He was a tall, thin Jamaican with a long, narrow, bland and essentially kind face. He had big ears and a wispy moustache above a mouth which occasionally broke into a wide if rather shy smile, revealing a set of front teeth which had the odd gap. He was brisk for a spinner, turning the ball an unusually long way for an orthodox left-arm spinner, and with great accuracy in 1950, in spite of an extraordinary action. He bowled round the wicket without any real delivery stride. It was as if he let the ball go in his run-up, and for the batsman it appeared in a curious and rather puzzling manner from behind his left ear. His delivery looked a little bit like the culmination of a conjuring trick, and there should have been a loud fizz when the ball left his hand.

The essential statistics were that May and Cowdrey's stand of 411 was, at that time, the highest ever in Test cricket for the fourth wicket, as well as being only the third ever of over 400. May's 285 not out was the highest score by an England captain and, with Cowdrey making 154, both batsmen made their highest Test scores. The individual statistics of the two innings show it was unrelenting hard work for both of them. May took 250 minutes to reach his hundred while Cowdrey saw it as his job to drop anchor at the other end. It took him 220 minutes to reach his first fifty and this shows exactly how two wonderful natural stroke-makers had to discipline their games.

The West Indies badly missed Worrell's accurate left-arm seam bowling, and his ability to bowl spinners if wanted may have prompted Valentine's omission. They were further handicapped when Roy Gilchrist had to pull out through injury after bowling 26 overs. England had reached 378-3 by the end of the fourth day, with May 193 and Cowdrey 78. The job was not yet done, for a couple of quick wickets by Ramadhin early on the last morning would have raised all the old fears in the England dressing room. As it was, Ramadhin did not get another wicket and finished the innings with the extraordinary figures of 98–35–179–2. No one had ever bowled so many overs in one innings of a first-class match: not a record Ramadhin will have dwelt on in the circumstances.

As it was, May and Cowdrey continued on their way, with both batsmen beginning to play more like their normal selves. Once again, May was the more expansive of the two and was now playing his strokes with the greater freedom, while Cowdrey went resolutely on to a hundred which took him a little over seven hours. It was then that he suddenly changed gear and his next fifty arrived in only 55 minutes as he began to drive the ball as only he could. The score had reached 524 when, after batting for 500 minutes, which was also the length of the partnership, Cowdrey lifted Collie Smith to long on.

May decided to bat on. This was understandable, for no captain who has managed to save a game as May had done wants to give his opponents the remotest chance of getting back into the match. He and Godfrey Evans added 59 in half an hour before the declaration left a demoralised West Indies to score 296 in 160 minutes. May will soon have been sorry that he had been so cautious with his declaration. After Trueman had dismissed both openers and the West Indies were 9–2, Jim Laker and Tony Lock took over and, turning the ball sharply on a worn pitch, took five wickets between them. Sobers, Walcott and Worrell soon went. Smith followed and Weekes was out 40 minutes before the end, but the later batsmen just managed to hang on, with the captain, John Goddard, batting for 40 minutes without scoring.

The record for the fourth wicket is now held by Adam Voges and Shaun Marsh, who put on 449 for Australia against the West Indies in Hobart in 2015–16. At Edgbaston, May and Cowdrey had not only saved the game for England, they had also transformed the summer. Although they were held to a draw in this first Test, England went on to win the series 3–0 and the ghost of Ramadhin and Valentine had been finally laid to rest. After taking nine wickets in this Test, Ramadhin took only five more in the next four matches, while Valentine remained wicketless throughout.

ENGLAND v WEST INDIES (1st Test)

At Edgbaston, Birmingham, on 30 May – 4 June 1957.

England

P.E. Richardson c Walcott b Ramadhin	47		c sub (Asgarali) b Ramadhin	34
D.B. Close c Kanhai b Gilchrist	15		c Weekes b Gilchrist	42
D.J. Insole b Ramadhin	20		b Ramadhin	0
*P.B.H. May c Weekes b Ramadhin	30		not out	285
M.C. Cowdrey c Gilchrist b Ramadhin	4		c sub (Asgarali) b Smith	154
T.E. Bailey b Ramadhin	1		did not bat	
G.A.R. Lock b Ramadhin	0		did not bat	
†T.G. Evans b Gilchrist	14	(6)	not out	29
J.C. Laker b Ramadhin	7		did not bat	
F.S. Trueman not out	29		did not bat	
J.B. Statham b Atkinson	13		did not bat	
Extras (3 b, 3 lb)	6		(23 b, 16 lb)	39
Total (all out, 79.4 overs)	**186**		(4 wkts, declared, 258 overs)	**583**

1–32 2–61 3–104 4–115 5–116 6–118
7–121 8–130 9–150 10–186

1–63 2–65 3–113 4–524

Bowling, Worrell 9–1–27–0; Gilchrist 27–4–74–2; Ramadhin 31–16–49–7;
Atkinson 12.4–3–30–1. *2nd innings*: Gilchrist 26–2–67–1; Atkinson 72–29–137–0;
Ramadhin 98–35–179–2; Sobers 30–4–77–0; Smith 26–4–72–1; Goddard 6–2–12–0.

West Indies

B.H. Pairaudeau b Trueman	1		b Trueman	7
†R.B. Kanhai lbw b Statham	42		c Close b Trueman	1
C.L. Walcott c Evans b Laker	90	(6)	c Lock b Laker	1
E.D. Weekes b Trueman	9		c Trueman b Lock	33
G.S. Sobers c Bailey b Statham	53	(3)	c Cowdrey b Lock	14
O.G. Smith lbw b Laker	161	(7)	lbw b Laker	5
F.M.M. Worrell b Statham	81	(5)	c May b Lock	0
*J.D.C. Goddard c Lock b Laker	24		not out	0
D.S. Atkinson c Statham b Laker	1		not out	4
S. Ramadhin not out	5		did not bat	
R. Gilchrist run out	0		did not bat	
Extras (1 b, 6 lb)	7		(7 b)	7
Total (all out, 191.4 overs)	**474**		(7 wkts, 60 overs)	**72**

1–4 2–83 3–120 4–183 5–197 6–387 7–466
8–469 9–474 10–474

1–1 2–9 3–25 4–27 5–43 6–66
7–68

Bowling, *1st innings*: Statham 39–4–114–3; Trueman 30–4–99–2; Bailey 34–11–80–0; Laker
54–17–119–4; Lock 34.4–15–55–0. *2nd innings*: Statham 2–0–6–0; Trueman 5–3–7–2; Lock
27–19–31–3; Laker 24–20–13–2; Close 2–1–8–0.

Close of play, *day 1*: West Indies (1) 83–1 (Kanhai 42*, Walcott 40*); *day 2*: West Indies (1)
316–5 (Smith 70*, Worrell 48*); *day 3*: England (2) 102–2 (Close 34*, May 21*);
day 4: England (2) 378–3 (May 193*, Cowdrey 78*).

Toss: England. Last-innings target: 296 runs.
Umpires: D.E. Davies (Eng), C.S. Elliott (Eng).

MATCH DRAWN.

11
THE JUDGEMENT
OF SOLOMON

Australia v West Indies (1st Test)
9–14 December 1960; The Gabba, Brisbane
Match tied.

IT had to happen, but it was a long wait. Not until the 502nd Test match, which was played between Australia and the West Indies in Brisbane, did one end with all the wickets gone and the scores level: match tied. This extraordinary game, which has every right to be regarded as the greatest ever played, was inspired by the attitudes of two outstanding captains, Frank Worrell and Richie Benaud, who were determined to settle for nothing less than victory, at whatever cost. And by 20 other players prepared to give their all in pursuit of victory without ever once considering a draw was a reasonable option. It was, too, a game played in a wonderfully competitive yet friendly atmosphere, for which both captains must take great credit.

After five days of brilliant cricket – as alive, vibrant and exciting as it would be possible to imagine – it all came down to the last over on the last day, and the like of it may never be seen again. Most of the play was of an exceptional standard too. Australia needed six runs from these last eight balls to win the first Test match of the series and the West Indies needed to take three wickets. This, at a time when Test cricket was fast sinking all round the world in a sea of boredom inspired by a generation of players who never appeared willing to try and shake off the ignominy that defeat brings with it. This was a match which flatly refused ever to lie down and die or to bow to contemporary attitudes.

Worrell was the first black West Indian to be asked to captain the side in a full series. George Headley, the only other black man to have captained the West Indies before Worrell, had been appointed for the first Test against England at Bridgetown in 1947–48, but politics and injury meant that this was the only time he led the side. Worrell was the longest-lasting of the famous three Ws. Worrell was supremely calm at all times and was the ideal man to lead this remarkable side, which he was able to forge into a team, holding them together at the tensest and most dramatic moments, the last few overs of this first Test being the tensest of all. His captaincy had a great deal to do with the success of the tour and so did his all-round ability as a player. In Brisbane he made 65 in each innings and, sharing the new ball at just above medium pace with Wes Hall, bowled 46 overs at just under three runs apiece.

In those days the Gabba was a happily ramshackle ground. None of the stands were that tall; the spectators even lay down on the grassy banks of the Hill with its big scoreboard standing in the western corner of the ground. The stands, even at the pavilion end, were delightfully higgledy-piggledy; there were trees on the eastern side of the ground, where the nets stood way behind the boundary. There was a greyhound track running all the way round the boundary and the pavilion was situated underneath the rambling Queensland Cricketers Club, which provided excellent lunches for those lucky enough to find a seat.

The scene was set after Worrell had won the toss and decided to bat. Alan Davidson was a superb all-rounder, and he and Pakistan's Wasim Akram were the two best fast left-arm-over-the-wicket bowlers I ever saw. Bounding in off a strong attacking run, he had, in a terrific opening spell, reduced the West Indies to

65–3 when Frank Worrell came in to join Garry Sobers, who was in brilliant form. Sobers's batting against both Davidson's pace and Benaud's leg-spin was as good as it gets. There was a magisterial elegance about Sobers at the crease. He always had so much time to play his strokes and he never made an awkward move. He played all the strokes, scoring many of his runs square of the wicket on the off side, giving himself room to force off the back foot or to play an elegant square cut. His driving, too, was always fluent and rhythmic. Worrell saw it as his job to make the other end safe and give Sobers as much of the strike as he could, although he also drove and cut in fine style himself.

Sobers's fifty came up in only 57 minutes, a remarkable rate of scoring for the first morning of a Test match against a good Australian side that had just taken three early wickets. These two put on 174 for the fourth wicket and Sobers went to his hundred in just over two hours and batted in all for only 29 overs while making 132. It was as good an innings as he can ever have played. Later, Solomon made an excellent 65 and at the end Wes Hall contributed 50 runs with a variety of invigorating strokes not often seen in a Test match. His frantic running between the wickets was, on its own, worth the price of the ticket. He took the West Indies to 452 before attempting a primeval slog against Lindsay Kline's left-arm spin.

Australia were given a good start by Colin McDonald and Bobby Simpson with an opening stand of 84, and Simpson reached 92 before becoming Sonny Ramadhin's only victim, but the innings really revolved around Norman O'Neill's 181. This stocky, belligerent strokemaker may not have batted as well as he had done at the Gabba against England two years earlier, but since then he had let his previous extrovert intentions be sucked into the cautious, safety-first approach which had come to dominate Australia's cricket at that time. In this innings, the Australians did not score their runs at the same speed as the West Indies, but they still came at a good rate. There was a pleasingly positive and enjoyable approach to their batting, very much in keeping with the spirit of this game. It was enjoyed by the packed crowds on the Saturday and Sunday and it brought a first-innings lead of 52 – which was just not quite enough.

The West Indies set off at the same helter-skelter pace in their second innings, but wickets kept falling and they were soon in a perilous position. Davidson again bowled superbly and took advantage of a certain amount of happy Caribbean strokeplay. Conrad Hunte, always solidly dependable, played some handsome drives at the start and the Australians will have been glad to see him go when he was second out, at 88. He was caught at slip trying to get after the canny medium-paced seam of Ken 'Slasher' Mackay outside the off stump. By then, Rohan Kanhai was playing some good strokes without looking especially safe. The West Indies will have hoped he would be steadied by the calming presence of his captain, Frank Worrell, at the other end.

They had moved the score along to 114 when Davidson bowled Sobers with a beauty which swung in late to the left-hander, and at 127 Kanhai reached outside the off stump at Davidson and was caught behind. This brought in the small figure of Solomon, who was to make such an impact on the match before the end. He and Worrell put on 83 runs for the fifth wicket, with both batsmen going on from where they had left off in the first innings. Worrell, with his sure judgement and unflappable temperament, was always in control, and, just as he had done in the first innings, he brought the best out in the small, chirpy yet determined figure of Solomon, submerged in his large maroon West Indian cap. Even so, neither was able to go on and make the hundred which would have made the game safe for the West Indies.

Davidson remained a constant threat and so too did the skilful captaincy of Benaud, whose thoughtful bowling changes and clever field placings kept the pressure on the batsmen. It was a fascinating battle. In the end, the West Indies were able to set Australia such a tantalising target only because of a most unlikely

and amusing last-wicket stand of 31 between the last two batsmen, Wes Hall and Alf Valentine. Hall batted, as always, like a
runaway windmill, while his partner looked more like a venerable
and mildly lugubrious lamppost. They ran furiously between the
wickets, while Hall's exuberant strokes were a delight until he
tried one drive too many against Davidson.

Australia's target was 233 in 310 minutes, which translated to
69 eight-ball overs at a rate of just under three and a half runs an
over. Australia will have fancied their chances, although not as
much as they would have done today when the influence of the
one-day game has made similar targets much easier to reach than
they used to be. Australia could hardly have made a much worse
start, however, and it was the irrepressible Hall who was their
chief executioner. Working up a great pace from his long and furious run-up, with his arms and legs flying everywhere, he took four
of the first five wickets to fall and reduced Australia to 57–5. The
other wicket, appropriately it seemed, was taken by Worrell.

Hall's innings appears to have fired him up in the most remarkable manner. 'I was fresh, marvellously fresh. I hurtled into the
attack with a vigour which even I found a little amazing. I seemed
to be propelled by a jet during the early onslaught,' was how he
put it in his autobiography. He found the edge of Simpson's bat in
the first over and Neil Harvey's soon afterwards, to leave Australia
wobbling at 7–2. McDonald and O'Neill then clawed their way to
49, when O'Neill reached out to drive at Hall and was caught
behind. Before another run had been added Worrell, who had
been ambling up to the wicket in his economical way and always
doing just a little with the ball, threaded one through McDonald's
defensive stroke and bowled him. Australia were 49–4 and the
crowd, which never quite reached 5,000 on this unbelievable last
day, were stunned into as near silence as an Australian crowd ever
gets.

Australia's hero of the match, Alan Davidson, now strode out
to join Les Favell. In the two West Indies innings, Davidson had

taken 11 wickets for 222 and he had made 44 invaluable runs in the first innings. There has never been a much more wholehearted competitor in the history of the game than the thickset, strong and determined Alan Davidson. But almost before he could get under way, Favell turned Hall round the corner into Solomon's hands at backward short leg. Ken Mackay, chewing gum as never before, took his place and Davidson began to hook and drive with a single-minded authority which even at this stage must have made the West Indians wince. The left-handed Mackay was as obdurate as ever and the score went quietly along to 92 before he came forward to Ramadhin and left room for the ball to turn through him into the stumps.

With six wickets down, Australia needed 141 more to win as an unruffled Benaud walked confidently out to join Davidson. Almost from the first ball of their partnership, these two changed the complexion of the game. Both batsmen seemed full of confidence and their strokes were firm and convincing. You would never have guessed that they were, at that point, fighting to save the match. Benaud's approach was splendid and was made apparent by a short conversation he had with Sir Donald Bradman, the chairman of the Australian selectors, during the tea interval. Australia then needed 124 in 120 minutes with four wickets left.

'What is it going to be?' Bradman asked him.

'Well, we're going for a win,' came the reply.

'I am very pleased to hear it,' Bradman said.

In that situation, I cannot think of many Test captains who would not only have answered as Benaud did but then gone on to bat as he did a few minutes later. The thought of a draw did not go through his mind. Both he and Davidson played their strokes and cleverly pushed and ran for singles, which not only kept the score moving, but upset their opponents' equilibrium. There were misfields, wayward throws and overthrows and it was then that Worrell did a splendid job keeping his side together, although by the middle of that last session of the game, the Australians were firmly in control of the match.

With only 12 minutes left, it looked as if they would win without much difficulty. They were 226–6, needing another seven runs, when Benaud pushed Sobers away just in front of square leg, as he had done so many times before, and called his partner for a run. For once, Davidson was a little slow in starting and Solomon, about 25 yards from the stumps, pounced on the ball and hit the one stump that he could see from square on. Davidson was comfortably out and said many years later that if he had been Usain Bolt, it would not have made any difference. An extremely nervous-looking Wally Grout took his place and managed one run before Wes Hall began the last over of the match, from the pavilion end. They were eight-ball overs in Australia in those days, and needing six runs with three wickets in hand, the Australians were still the favourites.

Has there ever been a more extraordinary over in Test cricket? Wally Grout was on strike and the first ball was short of a length and lifted sharply on him, hitting him a painful blow on the body. Benaud was off like a greyhound from the non-striker's end and Grout, doubled up with pain and clutching his midriff, somehow made it to the other end as about six West Indians tried to prevent the run. Five were wanted from seven balls. Worrell had told Hall not to bowl too many bouncers, but now he let one go. Benaud instinctively hooked, got a touch and Gerry Alexander took the catch behind the stumps. The West Indians could not believe their luck and, great sportsman that he was, Benaud walked off without showing any rancour or disappointment. The tall left-handed Ian Meckiff took his place and the atmosphere was febrile in the extreme, but if Australia held their nerve . . .

Hall came bounding in again, like a one-man cavalry charge, and Meckiff, in goodness knows how many minds, succeeded in pushing the ball back to the bowler almost as if by mistake. Now it was five from five. Hall could not get back to his mark quickly enough and Worrell came across for a calming word. Meckiff was ready and the cavalry charge began again. As Hall's arm came over, Grout from the non-striker's end began to sprint. Meckiff swung and missed. The ball went down the leg side and as it sank into Alexander's gloves, Meckiff was off, going hell for leather towards the bowler's end. Alexander threw the ball to Hall, who was not all that far down the pitch and just to the leg side. He caught the ball, turned and with all three stumps to aim at, had Meckiff at his mercy. His throw was a foot wide. Hall's head was in his hands. Four from four.

Hall bowled another bouncer and Grout, who had never been scared of fast bowling, went, like Benaud, for the hook. The ball hit the top edge of the bat and ballooned high into the air and seemed to hover over short midwicket, where Kanhai was stationed. Hall's adrenaline now took over. Somehow, he managed to change direction in his follow-through and went charging after the ball, almost hitting Kanhai out of the way, reached up for the ball and dropped it. 'The Good Lord's gone and left us,' was Hall's immediate exclamation, which almost unnerved Col Hoy, the umpire, who was expecting something much more electrifyingly down to earth.

It was now three from three. Meckiff got ready to receive the next ball from Hall after Worrell had done his best to calm him down. His run in now was plain terrifying, but Meckiff held his nerve and, with what was really a slog, hit him hard and high away on the leg side and, at first, it looked as if it had to be a boundary and four runs. The batsmen ran furiously for two, but by the time they touched their bats down for the second run, the ball had been picked up by Hunte a few inches from the boundary. Meckiff and Grout decided to take on the throw and they came charging back for what would have been the winning run. Hunte let go the throw of his life. It was flat and unerringly accurate into the gloves of Alexander, who turned and lunged at the stumps. Grout was at least a foot short of his crease and trudged off.

This was a moment of indirect controversy. Benaud later said that when he had arrived at the Gabba that morning, 'I could see white flowers dotting the turf [in the outfield]. They were clover flowers. It was obvious the ground hadn't been mown this morning. I ask for a mowing, but the curator tells me there was a heavy shower just after seven o'clock and he hasn't been able to get the mower on the ground. Now he hasn't the time to do it. I don't suppose it matters a great deal really, we'll only have a bit over 200 to make.' Which was another instance of famous last words. If the outfield had been mown that morning, maybe that blow of Meckiff's would have gone for four and it would have been all over.

Lindsay Kline took Grout's place and his frame of mind was perfectly illustrated when he took time to leave the pavilion because he could not find his batting gloves. It transpired that he had been sitting on them. With the scores level, one was needed from the last two balls and Kline had to face Hall. Worrell was as calmly in control as he had been at any time in the match. He walked over from short midwicket and warned Hall not to bowl a no-ball. 'They'll never let you back into Barbados if you do.' It's not easy to be quietly humorous at a moment like this.

The stage was set for the final scene. After five days of thrilling, pulsating cricket, with the advantage all the time going backwards and forwards, it came down to the last two balls. The world stood still. Hall raced in, kept his right foot behind the bowling crease and Kline played the ball comfortably away to square leg and set off. Meckiff was already on his way. Just in front of square leg, Solomon and Peter Lashley were both converging on the ball. Lashley started from square leg and as he approached the ball he heard Solomon shout, 'Move, move, move!', and Lashley left it to the little Guyanese, although it was going to his left and wrong hand. But Solomon not only managed to pick it up, but he also threw with deadly accuracy in almost the same movement and, for the second time in two overs, hit the one stump he could see and Meckiff was just short of his ground. Some years later I asked Col Hoy, the square-leg umpire who gave Meckiff out, how far out he had been. He shook his head and smiled. 'I don't know, but he wasn't there,' was all he said.

If all Test cricket had been played in the spirit of this game, there may never have been a need to invent the one-day game.

AUSTRALIA v WEST INDIES (1st Test)

At Woolloongabba, Brisbane, on 9–14 December 1960.

West Indies

C.C. Hunte c Benaud b Davidson	24	c Simpson b Mackay	39
C.W. Smith c Grout b Davidson	7	c O'Neill b Davidson	6
R.B. Kanhai c Grout b Davidson	15	c Grout b Davidson	54
G.S. Sobers c Kline b Meckiff	132	b Davidson	14
*F.M.M. Worrell c Grout b Davidson	65	c Grout b Davidson	65
J.S. Solomon hit wkt b Simpson	65	lbw b Simpson	47
P.D. Lashley c Grout b Kline	19	b Davidson	0
†F.C.M. Alexander c Davidson b Kline	60	b Benaud	5
S. Ramadhin c Harvey b Davidson	12	c Harvey b Simpson	6
W.W. Hall st Grout b Kline	50	b Davidson	18
A.L. Valentine not out	0	not out	7
Extras (3 lb, 1 w)	4	(14 b, 7 lb, 2 w)	23
Total (all out, 100.6 overs)	**453**	(all out, 92.6 overs)	**284**

1–23 2–42 3–65 4–239 5–243 6–283 7–347
8–366 9–452 10–453

1–13 2–88 3–114 4–127 5–210
6–210 7–241 8–250 9–253 10–284

Bowling, *1st innings*: Davidson 30–2–135–5; Meckiff 18–0–129–1; Mackay 3–0–15–0; Benaud 24–3–93–0; Simpson 8–0–25–1; Kline 17.6–6–52–3. *2nd innings*: Davidson 24.6–4–87–6; Meckiff 4–1–19–0; Benaud 31–6–69–1; Mackay 21–7–52–1; Kline 4–0–14–0; Simpson 7–2–18–2; O'Neill 1–0–2–0.

Australia

C.C. McDonald c Hunte b Sobers	57	b Worrell	16
R.B. Simpson b Ramadhin	92	c sub (Gibbs) b Hall	0
R.N. Harvey b Valentine	15	c Sobers b Hall	5
N.C.L. O'Neill c Valentine b Hall	181	c Alexander b Hall	26
L.E. Favell run out	45	c Solomon b Hall	7
K.D. Mackay b Sobers	35	b Ramadhin	28
A.K. Davidson c Alexander b Hall	44	run out	80
*R. Benaud lbw b Hall	10	c Alexander b Hall	52
†A.T.W. Grout lbw b Hall	4	run out	2
I. Meckiff run out	4	run out	2
L.F. Kline not out	3	not out	0
Extras (2 b, 8 lb, 4 nb, 1 w)	15	(2 b, 9 lb, 3 nb)	14
Total (all out, 130.3 overs)	**505**	(all out, 68.7 overs)	**232**

1–84 2–138 3–194 4–278 5–381 6–469
7–484 8–489 9–496 10–505

1–1 2–7 3–49 4–49 5–57 6–92
7–226 8–228 9–232 10–232

Bowling, *1st innings*: Hall 29.3–1–140–4; Worrell 30–0–93–0; Sobers 32–0–115–2; Valentine 24–6–82–1; Ramadhin 15–1–60–1. *2nd innings*: Hall 17.7–3–63–5; Worrell 16–3–41–1; Sobers 8–0–30–0; Valentine 10–4–27–0; Ramadhin 17–3–57–1.

Close of play, *day 1*: West Indies (1) 359–7 (Alexander 21*, Ramadhin 9*); *day 2*: Australia (1) 196–3 (O'Neill 28*, Favell 1*); *day 3*: West Indies (2) 0–0 (Hunte 0*, Smith 0*); *day 4*: West Indies (2) 259–9 (Hall 0*, Valentine 0*).

Toss: West Indies. Balls per over: Eight. Last-innings target: 233 runs.
Umpires: C.J. Egar (Aus), C. Hoy (Aus).

MATCH TIED.

12
A BROKEN ARM
DOES ITS DUTY

England v West Indies (2nd Test)
20–25 June 1963; Lord's Cricket Ground, London
Match drawn.

For the second time in just over two years, Wes Hall found himself bowling the last over of a Test match with all four results possible. England needed eight runs to beat the West Indies at Lord's with two wickets in hand, although one of the remaining batsmen, Colin Cowdrey, had a broken arm. In December 1960 in Brisbane, as we have just seen, Australia had needed six runs to win with three wickets in hand and after Hall had bowled seven balls of an eight-ball over, the match was tied. Now, at the end of a six-ball over, England were six runs short with one wicket left and Cowdrey standing at the non-striker's end with his arm in a plaster cast.

England were grateful for the draw, having fought their way valiantly through a damp afternoon in appalling light. From the moment that Frank Worrell, who had also been in charge of the West Indies in Brisbane, had won the toss and decided to bat first, the match was always poised on a knife edge, with the advantage changing almost by the hour. It was a match which had the cricketing world firmly in its grip for the five days and it was full of remarkable and heroic individual performances.

One big surprise before the match began was the selection of Derek Shackleton, the 38-year-old medium-paced seamer from Hampshire, to open the bowling with Fred Trueman. He had been preferred to Trueman's long-standing partner, Brian Statham, who had not taken a wicket in the first Test at Old Trafford, which the West Indies had won by ten wickets. It is not known what Trueman said when he first heard the news.

Most of the main West Indies batsmen contributed in their own individual styles to their first innings on a pitch which always gave the quicker bowlers something to hope for. At this point, Trueman was at the pinnacle of his career and he took four of the first five wickets to fall, finishing with 6–100 in 44 overs. His venerable partner, who had never taken fewer than a hundred wickets a year for his county for more than a decade, finished with 3–93 in 50 overs and the West Indies were all out for 301.

England soon lost both their Surrey openers, Micky Stewart and John Edrich, before Ted Dexter came in and began to bat like a Boy's Own hero. In the gloaming, he hooked and drove the fierce pace of Hall and Charlie Griffith, who was considered by many people to have a doubtful action, like a man possessed. I was lucky enough to watch almost every ball of this match, purely as a spectator, in the back row of the top deck of the Warner Stand, immediately below the press box. I shall never forget Dexter, under whose captaincy I had played a few games for Cambridge University in 1958, smiting Hall and Griffith through the covers off the front foot. They were just about the most thrilling strokes I have ever seen played. His fifty came from 51 balls, but when he had made 20 more, Worrell called up Garry Sobers to bowl fast left-arm-over-the-wicket at the Pavilion End and very soon Dexter tried to play him away on the leg side with the ball angled across him and was lbw.

It was now that Ken Barrington, who had first played for England in 1955 and was still looking for his first Test hundred in England, shored up the innings, although in the end it was a splendid 52 by off-spinner Fred Titmus that took England to within four runs of the West Indies total. The match was watched by big crowds and on the third day, with England 244–7 overnight, the gates were shut on a full-house crowd ten minutes before the start. And what a day it was. After Titmus's splendid batting first thing, Trueman and Shackleton, sharing the early West Indies wickets, reduced them to 84–4, which became 104–5 when off-spinner David Allen had Joe Solomon well caught low down at forward short leg by Stewart.

While this had been going on, Basil Butcher, the small right-hander from Guyana who had been promoted to number four, was batting wonderfully well and making light of both the conditions and some excellent bowling. While the West Indies were still very much under siege, he came down the wicket to Allen and drove him magnificently over mid on for six. It requires both technique and bravery to play a shot like this when batting is such a struggle. If Butcher had not played his cricket for the West Indies in the shadow of Sobers and Kanhai and the others, we would, I am sure, have heard a lot more about him. Only a batsman of the highest class could have played as he did in this innings. It almost goes without saying that he found the partner he badly needed in his captain, Worrell, who, as always, produced the calming, measured influence that West Indies cricket has often lacked in highly charged situations. They put on 110 for the sixth wicket, taking the score to 214–5 by the close, when the West Indies had their noses in front.

All that changed in a matter of moments on the fourth morning. Worrell was caught close to the wicket off Trueman before a run had been scored and in 25 minutes Shackleton and Trueman had taken the last five wickets for only 15 runs, Trueman finishing with 5–52 and Shackleton 4–72. England had to make 234 to win and made a bad start. The openers again went quickly. Hall, faster and more demon-like than ever, soon found the edge of Edrich's bat and his pace was too much for Stewart. Dexter, whose knee had been badly bruised by Griffith in the first innings, was seriously handicapped and was soon bowled by Lance Gibbs, reducing England to 31–3.

Barrington, at his most unflappable, was joined by Cowdrey and somehow they managed to withstand a fierce battering from Hall and Griffith, in spite of being frequently hit on the body and the fingers. Hall was bowling in highly questionable light from the Pavilion End, where there was no sightscreen in those days and the ball therefore came out of the Long Room windows and the faces of the members sitting in the front of the Pavilion. Cowdrey had got to 19 when Hall bowled one which was only a fraction short of a length and lifted sharply. It hit him a fearful crack just above his left wrist and broke his arm. Ironically, Cowdrey was batting near his best and had been coping well.

This brought together England's two staunchest fighters, Ken Barrington and Brian Close. Their intentions were similar. Both were single-minded in their pursuit of victory, selling their own wickets as dearly as they could, and both were indomitable fighters. One, Barrington, was from the south, Surrey, while Close was a northerner, from Yorkshire, and as redolent of Yorkshire as it would be possible to be. When, in later life, he came to captain Somerset, it was an unholy but, all the same, satisfactory mixing of metaphors. Barrington, who was of about medium height under his crimped dark hair, was a man of great good humour and when, after he had retired, he became an England coach, no one was more loved and respected by the players. He was, too, a wonderful middle-order batsman, best known for his adhesiveness at the crease and, even so, for his delightful party trick of reaching a hundred with a six, which I saw him do on two or three occasions. He also bowled cheerful leg-breaks which were good enough to break a number of potentially important partnerships.

Close purveyed off-breaks and would never in a million years have stooped to the frivolity of leg-spin. As a race, Yorkshiremen are disdainful of leg-spin, at least they seldom produce one of their own. Leg-spinners can be profligate. Close, a left-handed batsman who led with his belligerent bald head, was more than prepared to take on any bowling, however fast – with his bare chest if need be, as he did now at Lord's and, in 1976, against the West Indies and Andy Roberts and Michael Holding at Old Trafford at the age of 45. He had first played for England in 1949 at the age of 18 and is still the youngest ever to do so, but his cussed north-country nature never allowed him to make the most of his talents. Barrington, on the other hand, made 6,806 runs in Test matches with an average of 58.67. There is no gainsaying those figures.

Now it was a combination of temperament, guts and bloody-mindedness, and some splendid strokes too, that kept the pair together until the close on the fourth day. Worrell and the West Indies threw at them everything they could, but they held fast and it was an heroic partnership, made more so by the gloomy light. It was a remarkably tense battle to watch and the crowd was as nervous and involved as any I can remember. While they preserved their wickets until the end of the day, Close clenched his teeth and hung on; Barrington did so with some composure. There was an audible sigh of relief that evening when the last ball had been safely negotiated and the players turned to the Pavilion as the spectators rose from their seats.

The next day was darker still and it rained for most of the morning. A big crowd huddled together to protect themselves, but no one thought of leaving. When a start could eventually be made, at 2.20, time had become another important factor in the equation. England needed 118 more runs in 200 minutes which, considering the appalling over rate of the West Indies, was barely long enough. This was underlined when Hall and Griffith started the bowling and at once both batsmen were being hit painful blows on the upper body. Much rubbing ensued and more time was lost.

It was typical of Close that he should suddenly change tactics and try to upset the rhythm of the bowlers by coming down the pitch to them and moving around in the crease. It worked too, and you could feel Close relishing these duels, while Barrington was now not at all at ease. It was 45 minutes before he scored his first run and the two fast bowlers had him jumping all over the place. His form of the evening before had completely disappeared. He still did his best to score runs, but kept either missing the ball or finding the fielders. The first hour produced 18 anxious runs and you could feel Barrington's frustration. In the end he tried to cut Griffith, a shot he probably would not have attempted if runs had been coming normally, and was caught behind, for 60.

Jim Parks took his place and immediately began to go for his strokes. He had made 17 good runs before he was lbw to a full-length ball from Griffith which he did not seem to pick up. Parks's decision to take on the bowling must have been right, for siege warfare had never been his game. When he came in, 104 were needed and if he had stayed for a little longer it would have made an important dent in the target.

England had reached 171–5 at tea when 63 more were needed in 85 minutes, but that figure was worse than it seemed because of the abysmal over rate of only 14 an hour, which made a difficult task even harder. Close and Fred Titmus, with great skill and shrewdness, added 45, at which point England had the advantage, but then Hall intervened. Another ball rose sharply from near a length to Titmus, who could only fend it to short leg. Trueman was caught behind pushing at the next ball and the West Indies were back on top. David Allen helped Close take the score to 219, with each run being wildly cheered by the crowd, particularly by the big gathering in front of the famous Tavern.

After three hours and 50 minutes of both considerable bravery and stirring defence, Close himself suddenly became an unlikely victim of the unbelievable pressure. He had decided earlier to change his tactics to try and unsettle these ferocious fast bowlers. He began to come down the pitch to both Hall and Griffith in an attempt to upset their length. For a time it worked. Then he attempted a huge and wild swing at Griffith and was caught behind. Of course, he was blamed in some quarters, but if it had come off, he would have been a hero for playing the same stroke. Hindsight can be as unkind as it can be unnecessary, and in this case the margin between success and failure is about a centimetre and a bit. Close's approach was applauded by Dexter, his captain, who stressed that it had so nearly worked, while Close himself said, 'It wasn't unthinking bravado. Far from it. I made Hall lose his cool. His line and length suffered.'

As Shackleton came out to join Allen, England's official target was 15 in 19 minutes, with Colin Cowdrey padded up in the dressing room ready to go to war if needed. He had been practising batting left-handed so that his left arm was protected by his body. England were still going for a victory and a curious assortment of seven agonising runs were scrambled from some strange strokes, and some extraordinary running between the wickets.

Eight runs were needed from Hall's last over. Shackleton was facing, and what an ask this was for a 38-year-old who had not been near a Test match for 11 years and was accustomed only to the crowds at county matches, which were both modest and quiet. He somehow negotiated the first ball. He stopped the second, which fell at his feet, and set off on a middle-aged attempt at a sprint, with Allen coming at full speed in the other direction. Hall himself charged all the way down the pitch, but Allen just beat him to it. Seven were wanted from four balls and Hall bowled a yorker. Allen was ready for it, digging it out towards square leg, and they ran a single. Six were needed. Shackleton swung in hope at the next, but it was too fast and went through him to Deryck Murray. They started to run and Murray threw the ball quickly to Worrell at short mid on. Worrell had a quick look at where Shackleton was and rather than throw to Hall or anyone else – for in the general frenzy, with fielders running all over the place, anything might have happened – he ran calmly to the bowler's end and took the bails off himself. Job done.

Six were still needed and now it was the turn of Cowdrey, with a plaster cast round his left arm. He emerged rather gingerly from the Pavilion to great cheers, which he greeted with a wide grin, and started on his stately way to the middle. In his book *West Indies at Lord's* Alan Ross wrote of Cowdrey's arrival, 'There was something of Wodehouse about it, something of Sapper. Allen had the strike, there were two balls to go. The batsmen conferred, but the obligation was indisputable.' Allen greeted Cowdrey, who was still smiling: 'I have not yet given up hope of winning. If I have the luck to get a four off the first ball, we'll scamper the last run.' By my arithmetic, this would have left them one short, but it was a frenzied moment.

Hall pitched the next ball up to Allen and he calmly kept it out of his wicket. An English win was now unthinkable. Hall went back to his mark, preparing to bowl the last ball at Allen, when Worrell stopped things, walked over from short mid on and spoke to Hall. Dexter reported later that he believed he had said, 'Make sure you don't bowl a no-ball,' which was precisely what he had said to Hall at Brisbane two and a half years before when the Australian and West Indies scores were level with two balls to be bowled.

Hall waited impatiently until Worrell had gone back to his position. He had shown incredible stamina and had bowled unchanged since play began at twenty past two; his hostility and enthusiasm had never dimmed. He ran in now with even greater zest, intending to bowl what must have been the fastest ball of his life. It was aimed at Allen's middle stump. Allen, remarkably relaxed, played calmly forward and that was that. From where I was sitting in the Warner Stand, I could hear behind me through the window, 'It's a draw!' from a bellowing Brian Johnston as he passed on the news to his BBC television viewers. It was a close-run thing, not least because heavy rain came down five minutes later, but who minded getting wet after all that?

ENGLAND v WEST INDIES (2nd Test)

At Lord's Cricket Ground, London, on 20–25 June 1963.

West Indies

C.C. Hunte c Close b Trueman	44		c Cowdrey b Shackleton	7
E.D.A.S. McMorris lbw b Trueman	16		c Cowdrey b Trueman	8
G.S. Sobers c Cowdrey b Allen	42	(5)	c Parks b Trueman	8
R.B. Kanhai c Edrich b Trueman	73	(3)	c Cowdrey b Shackleton	21
B.F. Butcher c Barrington b Trueman	14	(4)	lbw b Shackleton	133
J.S. Solomon lbw b Shackleton	56		c Stewart b Allen	5
*F.M.M. Worrell b Trueman	0		c Stewart b Trueman	33
†D.L. Murray c Cowdrey b Trueman	20		c Parks b Trueman	2
W.W. Hall not out	25		c Parks b Trueman	2
C.C. Griffith c Cowdrey b Shackleton	0		b Shackleton	1
L.R. Gibbs c Stewart b Shackleton	0		not out	1
Extras (10 b, 1 lb)	11		(5 b, 2 lb, 1 nb)	8
Total (all out, 133.2 overs)	**301**		(all out, 98 overs)	**229**

1–51 2–64 3–127 4–145 5–219 6–219
7–263 8–297 9–297 10–301

1–15 2–15 3–64 4–84 5–104 6–214
7–224 8–226 9–228 10–229

Bowling, *1st innings*: Trueman 44–16–100–6; Shackleton 50.2–22–93–3;
Dexter 20–6–41–0; Close 9–3–21–0; Allen 10–3–35–1. *2nd innings*: Trueman 26–9–52–5;
Shackleton 34–14–72–4; Titmus 17–3–47–0; Allen 21–7–50–1.

England

M.J. Stewart c Kanhai b Griffith	2	c Solomon b Hall	17
J.H. Edrich c Murray b Griffith	0	c Murray b Hall	8
*E.R. Dexter lbw b Sobers	70	b Gibbs	2
K.F. Barrington c Sobers b Worrell	80	c Murray b Griffith	60
M.C. Cowdrey b Gibbs	4	not out	19
D.B. Close c Murray b Griffith	9	c Murray b Griffith	70
†J.M. Parks b Worrell	35	lbw b Griffith	17
F.J. Titmus not out	52	c McMorris b Hall	11
F.S. Trueman b Hall	10	c Murray b Hall	0
D.A. Allen lbw b Griffith	2	not out	4
D. Shackleton b Griffith	8	run out	4
Extras (8 b, 8 lb, 9 nb)	25	(5 b, 8 lb, 3 nb)	16
Total (all out, 102 overs)	**297**	(9 wkts, 91 overs)	**228**

1–2 2–20 3–102 4–115 5–151 6–206 7–235
8–271 9–274 10–297

1–15 2–27 3–31 4–130 5–158
6–203 7–203 8–219 9–228

Bowling, *1st innings*: Hall 18–2–65–1; Griffith 26–6–91–5; Sobers 18–4–45–1;
Gibbs 27–9–59–1; Worrell 13–6–12–2. *2nd innings*: Hall 40–9–93–4; Griffith 30–7–59–3;
Gibbs 17–7–56–1; Sobers 4–1–4–0.

Close of play, *day 1*: West Indies (1) 245–6 (Solomon 34*, Murray 12*); *day 2*: England (1)
244–7 (Titmus 23*, Trueman 5*); *day 3*: West Indies (2) 214–5 (Butcher 129*, Worrell 33*);
day 4: England (2) 116–3 (Barrington 55*, Close 7*).

Toss: West Indies. Last-innings target: 234 runs.
Umpires: J.S. Buller (Eng), W.E. Phillipson (Eng).

MATCH DRAWN.

13
A KNOTT REFUSES TO BE UNTIED

West Indies v England (5th Test)
28 March – 3 April 1968; Bourda Oval, Georgetown
Match drawn.

Some of the best games of cricket ever played have ended in draws, and this last Test match on England's tour of the West Indies in 1967–68 was, for me, probably the most exciting of any in this book. I was sitting in the press box, perched between Jim Swanton (*Daily Telegraph*) and Keith Miller (*Daily Express*), on my first major England tour as a journalist. Colin Cowdrey's side came to Georgetown in Guyana just one match up in the series and, in accordance with the rules at the time, because the series was still undecided with one game left, this last game was given a sixth day. Bourda was a small, exciting and charmingly dated cockpit for cricket perched on the South American mainland. It was a lovely little ground which held only 13,000 people, which was clearly too few for a game which contained just about all the drama you could possibly cram into one cricket match. At the end of those six extraordinary days, it all came down to the last over of the match, bowled by off-spinner Lance Gibbs, who had already taken six wickets in the innings, to England's last man, Jeff Jones.

England had won the previous match, in Trinidad, after Garry Sobers had suddenly clapped his hands and waved the players in, leaving England to score 215 in 165 minutes. When Sobers arrived in Georgetown the next morning he was given a police guard, for it was felt by some that by leaving England such an easy target he had been playing with West Indian nationalism, when he had simply thought, mistakenly, that he had a chance of winning the match. This feeling had considerably increased the tension which gripped proceedings over the next ten days when we were in Guyana for the fifth and final Test.

One nice little twist to the last two Test matches of this series was that England had summoned left-arm spinner Tony Lock from Perth, where he had just led Western Australia to the Sheffield Shield title. Off-spinner Fred Titmus, Cowdrey's vice-captain, had unfortunately had four toes cut off in a boating accident in Barbados before the third Test and it was decided that England needed another spinner in addition to the other off-spinner, Pat Pocock, for the last two Tests, in Port-of-Spain and Georgetown. Lock bowled without a great deal of success in either match, but in Georgetown his batting became one of the principal reasons that England managed to hold on for a draw and win the series. Coming in at number nine in the first innings, he and Pocock put on 109 for the ninth wicket, with Lock making 89, his highest score in 654 first-class matches in which he made over 10,000 runs, the most anyone has ever made without scoring a hundred.

Guyana embraces both the West Indies and South America. In Georgetown, with its architecture and its canals, the Dutch influence is strong. The Stabroek Market would have found a home in Amsterdam, while the cathedral was then the tallest wooden building in the world. The three huge rivers, the Demerara, the Essequibo and the Bernice, which carve their way far into Guyana, are closely related to the nearby Amazon, and are pure South America. The surrounding country, which includes the Kaieteur Falls, one of the tallest although not the most magnificent, waterfall in the world, is also South America rather than the West Indies. The swaying fields of sugar cane and the rum distilleries were distinctly West Indies, while the night-time revels at the Belvedere in Georgetown itself added an interesting cosmopolitan touch, even if with a strong rum-based bias. The Georgetown Club is irrevocably empire and colonial, as were the two superbly turned-out police horses standing throughout the six days' cricket on either side of the sightscreens at Bourda, ridden by impeccably turned-out policemen.

The elegant, wooden pavilion built at the end of Queen Victoria's reign and standing in one corner of the ground was brim-full and positively humming when we all arrived an hour and a half before the start. The rest of the ground, with one-storey stands ringing the playing area, was also full, with the 13,000 spectators augmented by a few who had found their way in without tickets and others perched in the surrounding palm trees. The noise was already terrific. When Sobers and Cowdrey came out to toss, the excitement, like the noise, increased and when Sobers indicated that he had won, it boiled over. The West Indies lost three wickets for 72, but then Sobers and Rohan Kanhai, a local boy, joined forces before lunch and, not without a certain amount of early luck, batted on until just after lunch the following day, by which time both, playing magnificently for a long time, had reached 150.

On the second morning, England took the new ball. The first two hours produced 72 runs, but no wicket. There were no better batsmen in the world and a succession of wonderful strokes flowed from both their bats. Sobers, tallish and slim, played everything with time to spare. His strokes were unhurried, his judgement impeccable on a pitch that already had an uneven bounce, which was to grow worse. There was always a supreme classical elegance about Sobers, whether defending or playing his strokes, and he made batting look so easy. At the other end, the much smaller, vibrant Kanhai, of Indian descent, was a busier, more bustling figure, with twinkling wrists and lightning-fast footwork as he got himself into position to play a wonderful range of strokes. He seemed more impetuous than his partner, in the way of smaller batsmen who do not have the height to help them. Their greater reach allows taller batsmen to use their front feet to attack and unsettle a bowler's length more than their smaller brethren, who tend to compensate off the back foot, driving, cutting, pulling and improvising generally. It is rare to see two great batsmen playing at their best in tandem, and this was one such occasion for me.

They had reached 322 when Kanhai played rather a rough-hewn pull at Pat Pocock and was caught by John Edrich at square leg. Clive Lloyd, who should have been caught by Cowdrey at slip when he was nine, helped Sobers take the score to 385. Sobers then suddenly lost concentration, drove carelessly at Ken Barrington and was picked up by Cowdrey at slip. John Snow, who had bowled beautifully throughout, and Tony Lock took the last five wickets between them for only 29 runs. The West Indies were therefore all out for 414 and, considering that Sobers and Kanhai had each made 150, England had every reason to feel reasonably happy. To win the series, all they had to do was save the match, but more than four days remained. It was going to be a long, hard struggle and it was important that the batsmen should not concentrate only on defence and, in so doing, surrender the initiative.

The West Indies first innings had exposed a recurring problem in the days before neutral umpires were used for international cricket matches. The two standing at Bourda were, quite rightly, highly respected, even though this was only the sixth Test for Cecil Kippins, who came from Guyana. His partner, Cortez Jordan from Barbados, a smaller man, was standing in his 17th. With the West Indies and their supporters badly wanting victory to draw level in the series, the umpires were under considerable pressure. Every decision they gave was endlessly scrutinised by a passionate crowd, especially those that went against the local team. The umpires were under almost more pressure than the players. On a pitch which turned increasingly, the pads often came into play and there was always going to be much appealing. This was not helped by the way in which batsmen of that time used their pads as much as their bats to play spin bowling. Almost every time the ball hit the pad the fielders went up and, to make it worse for the umpires, it was an each-way bet for the fielding side. If it was not lbw, the umpire might decide it was a catch off bat and pad to one of the close fielders.

In all the many games of cricket I have watched, I have always felt that if ever the umpires were likely to give a home-town decision, this was it. The fact that the game was drawn speaks volumes for the honesty of Messrs Kippins and Jordan. Kippins did have one nasty moment during the first innings, however. When England took the second new ball at the start of the second day, Jones was bowling to Sobers. The last ball of the first over kept horribly low and hit Sobers on the ankle as he went onto the back foot. The appeal could have been heard in Barbados. Kippins, the taller of the two, was at the bowler's end. He looked long and hard but refused to raise his finger. Two days later, on the fourth evening of the match, Kippins announced he would be retiring as a Test match umpire because of the personal threats he had received, and there had been an attempt to burn down his house. The reason for this is unlikely to have been his decision to keep Sobers at the crease.

An hour and a half of the second day remained when Edrich and Geoffrey Boycott began the England first innings. Belying his reputation, Boycott hit three spanking fours in Wes Hall's first two overs, before Edrich followed Sobers outside the off stump without much of the necessary footwork and was joyously caught behind by Deryck Murray. It was not long before Cowdrey leant into one of those lovely cover drives against Sobers, the product of pure timing, when the ball seemed almost to purr as it made its way to the cover boundary. England were 40–1 at the end of the day, with the last few overs appearing to be more anxious than they probably were.

On the third day, rain prevented more than two and three-quarter hours' cricket. Boycott and Cowdrey went uneventfully along, taking the score to 146–1, at which point England looked in a good position to draw the match. The next morning, Boycott's 18th four, a straight drive off Lester King, took him to a superb hundred. At 176–1, Sobers took the new ball and after a last lovely off drive against Hall, Boycott felt for a short one outside the off stump and was caught behind, which brought the crowd leaping to its feet. When Cowdrey pushed half forward to the first ball of the next over from Sobers and was lbw, the noise reached crescendo level. Just before lunch, a diving catch by Kanhai off Sobers at backward short leg got rid of Barrington. Early in the afternoon, Tom Graveney tried to drive Hall off the back foot and was caught behind and England had slumped to 240–5. Then, in quick succession, Basil D'Oliveira, Alan Knott and John Snow were out and, at 259–8, the West Indies seemed certain to take a sizeable first-innings lead, while the crowd were making us think they had already won the match. It was now that the ever-genial Pat Pocock strode out to join the redoubtable Tony Lock.

Lock had always been the most formidable of opponents. He had thickened out in cricketing old age – he was 38 – but his enthusiasm was as great as ever. For many years, there had been a mounting suspicion about his action, especially when he bowled his quicker ball, which came through at a frightening pace. He had not been worried by this until he saw a film of himself bowling during the 1958–59 tour of Australia and New Zealand. He was appalled by what he saw and decided, then and there, to change his action, even though he was by then into his thirties. He did so with great success, reverting to the high action he had used at the start of his career. He had first changed to a lower action in order to try and spin the ball more. When he reverted more or less to his original action, his left arm wheeled over higher and more slowly and no one could have doubted its legality.

There was something belligerent about Lock's baldness, although it was now covered by a cap with the peak at a warlike angle. Tony Lock had never taken prisoners and his instincts will have been as sharp as a hawk's. The knotted handkerchief round his neck seemed also to make a pugnacious statement of intent. With Lock against you, you knew you were in a battle, and I do not think there can have been many innings which reflected a batsman's character as accurately as this one did now. He was like a dreadnought reporting for duty at Scapa Flow.

In between his resolute 'thou shalt not pass' defensive strokes he went for his attacking strokes whenever he had the chance. He began by driving David Holford over extra cover, before he swept and cut Lance Gibbs to the fence. When he had another go at Holford, he skied the ball to deep extra cover, where local boy Stephen Camacho dropped the catch, to the groaning dismay of the crowd. At the time, it seemed unimportant, but this dropped catch cost the West Indies the match. After tea, Lock went from strength to strength, playing an array of resounding strokes, each one of which was accompanied by a good deal of vibrant chatter. When Lock reached 50, Pocock was still not yet off the mark. By now, both the West Indies and the crowd were becoming distinctly uneasy. The new ball came at 347–8 and the batsmen then had the satisfaction of seeing the last ball of the day slide down the leg side for four byes, encouraged verbally, no doubt, by Lock.

At the close, with two days left, England were 352–8, 62 runs behind, with Lock and Pocock's stand worth 93. The next morning they took it to 109 in 127 minutes, before Pocock pushed an easy catch back to King and then Lock had a final heave and was bowled. He had batted for 140 minutes and hit 13 fours. The West Indies lead was now 43. Lock was still talking when he climbed the pavilion steps on his way back. He had not been summoned all the way from Perth to score runs, but with a bat in his hand the old trouper, treading the boards for the last time, had done England proud.

The West Indies second innings began with a top edge for six by Seymour Nurse off Snow which really set the crowd going. The West Indies were trying to score as quickly as they could, for they must have been hoping to bowl a few overs at England with the new ball that evening. They were 72–0 from 17 overs at lunch, but afterwards John Snow was at his best as he removed both openers and Lloyd, reducing them to 86–3. The rest of the innings belonged to Sobers who, in his feline way, again produced a succession of wonderful strokes and passed 6,000 runs in Test cricket. Wickets fell regularly at the other end and there was no question of a declaration that evening, for, more than anything, Sobers will not have wanted to get it wrong two matches running. When Snow bowled Gibbs, Sobers was left on 95 at the non-striker's end and it was cruel that he was not able to reach his second hundred of the match. As it was, he had left West Indian supporters in no doubt that the declaration in Port-of-Spain had been nothing more than a miscalculation. He walked off the field with his usual good-natured loping stride, modestly acknowledging the applause as he went.

John Snow, who had just taken his tenth wicket of the match, grasped his sleeveless sweater from the umpire, threw it over his shoulder and stalked off. Snow was not one for showing his emotions and you would not have known from looking at him whether he had taken 6–60 or 0–110. Fielding at long leg after bowling a brilliant over and taking an important wicket, he would stand expressionless and look bored. When the ball was turned to long leg he would set off in that long-striding predatory way of his. He would field it perfectly and then uncurl that fierce low throw which would zip into Alan Knott's gloves at the top of the bails. Then Snow would mooch back to his original position. He would have made a good poker player.

It was a tense evening as we swallowed more Mateus Rosé than perhaps we should have done in the Palm Court restaurant, next door to the Tower Hotel on Main Street where most of us were billeted. Four of the five Test matches had gone down to the wire as we had cavorted round the Caribbean for just over three months and it had all come down to the final day of the series. The next morning, Edrich pushed defensively at the third ball of the day and it rolled agonisingly back about half an inch wide of the leg stump. Already, we knew it was going to be that sort of a day. In the press box I can remember Jim Swanton's booming voice trying to sound matter-of-fact about it all, but not succeeding. Keith Miller, when he turned up, kept us smiling and Les Ames, the England manager, visited briefly and did his best to make a joke. The noise of the crowd was now almost ear-shattering and the two police horses, just to our left by the sightscreen, were more restless than usual.

As in the first innings, Boycott played some fine strokes early on against both Hall and Sobers. This made us remember that England had been left a target of 308 to win, not that that was anything more than a mathematical possibility. Then Boycott pushed forward to Sobers and edged the ball. Kanhai, at first slip, dived to his right, got his hand under it, but could not hold on. Seventeen overs were bowled in the first hour, which just shows what bowlers can do if the need is there, and England were 33–0. In the next over, Edrich played forward to Sobers and Gibbs held a quick catch at short leg. Cowdrey played Gibbs with his front pad and both players and crowd appealed for all they were worth, but the umpire did not agree with them. Boycott tried to cut one which pitched well wide of the off stump but turned such a long way that it bowled him. It was 37–2 and it was as if the crowd were already celebrating a West Indies victory.

Gibbs now bowled to Graveney with four men round the bat. He turned the second ball off the front foot out of the meat of the bat. It hit Sobers, at backward short leg, on the metal toecap of his left boot and rebounded into the gloves of Murray. In the second innings of the second Test in Kingston, Graveney had played

Gibbs away off the front foot, the ball had bounced off Camacho's thigh at forward short leg and had flown to Charlie Griffith at mid on. That time, Graveney had thrown away his bat in disgust; now, he merely shook it. Soon after this, Barrington reached forward to Gibbs and the hugely tall Lloyd threw himself forward from silly mid off and scooped up a splendid catch. Two runs later, Gibbs flighted one enticingly to D'Oliveira, who obligingly pushed it straight back to the bowler. Gibbs, unemotional like Snow, had taken 4–4 in nine wonderful overs in which he had barely allowed himself a smile, and England were 41–5. Their hopes of winning the series had surely gone.

But then 21-year-old Alan Knott, looking even more impish than usual, came so jauntily out of the pavilion, it almost made us feel that things were not quite as bad as the score suggested. This feeling was confirmed when Gibbs bowled him a faster ball and, quick as a flash, he went onto his back foot and late-cut it for four. When he tried the stroke again, he got an edge and Murray dropped the catch behind the stumps. Lloyd, at silly mid off, was so unhappy it was almost as if he had had a premonition.

The all-Kent partnership of Cowdrey and Knott had taken the score to 68–5 at lunch, with three and a half hours remaining. In every country the crowds have their own special characteristics and no crowd is so passionately involved in a game of cricket as they are in the West Indies. For more than five days the crowds at Bourda had lived every ball, and now that the West Indies had the match in their grasp, they went over the top – and who can blame them. After lunch the noise and the general jubilation had reached such a level that soon after the afternoon session had begun, Cowdrey walked away from his crease and refused to continue until they quietened down. Of course, the crowd's immediate reaction was to redouble their efforts and it became considerably worse. It was only after an announcement over the loudspeakers that they realised they were preventing play and it grew quieter.

When play restarted, Knott went forward to a leg-break from Holford and Kanhai, diving to his right at slip, dropped a low catch. When Cowdrey had dispatched Holford for two more fours, he again moved away from the crease as the noise of rhythmical clapping took over. The process was repeated, although there was quite a pause before the game was able to continue.

Sobers was now becoming agitated. There was not all that much time left and he still needed five more wickets. A square cut by Knott off Holford brought up the hundred stand. Three fours came in the next over from Gibbs, which produced 13 runs. Sobers made seven bowling changes in the hour after lunch and suddenly there was a different feel to the game. The crowd were growing both anxious and quieter, and the tension among the players was now easy to see. When Cowdrey pulled Sobers for four to reach 50, there was scarcely a ripple of applause.

The new ball was taken one run later and although Knott all but played Sobers into his stumps, both batsmen were still there at tea, when England were 153–5. There was now only an hour and a half left and England were inching their way to safety. When Gibbs came back, Knott cut him for four and I remember Cowdrey shaking his head at the other end, for the ball had turned back a long way and would have hit the stumps. Knott then pushed at the next ball and it rolled back towards the stumps before Knott, in the nick of time, knocked it away with his bat.

All through his innings, Cowdrey had been coming forward and playing Gibbs with his front pad, just as he had done to Sonny Ramadhin at Edgbaston in 1957. The appealing then had been constant, but as was happening now at Bourda, the umpires had kept shaking their heads. Now, once more he came half forward to Gibbs, letting the ball hit his front pad, and umpire Jordan, after some thought, gave him out. One wondered what he had seen that had not been there on the countless other occasions when he had shaken his head – or why his finger had not gone up before this.

Cowdrey had made 82 and the pavilion stood to him as he came back. The scoreboard showed 168–6 and England's last four wickets had to hold on for 73 minutes. It could hardly have been more nerve-wracking, and the encouragement of the crowd for the West Indies was now turned up to full volume as Snow, in his seemingly uninterested way, strode out to join Knott.

Sobers at fast-medium now took over from Gibbs and Snow survived two anxious and noisy maiden overs. At the other end, the nimble and puckish Knott – there was always humour in his batting, just as there was with his keeping – pulled Holford to midwicket for a four which took him to his fifty. He celebrated by twice square-cutting him to the boundary. It was so important for Knott to score runs where he could, because it prevented the West Indies from putting a stranglehold grip round the England batsmen with platoons of close fielders. Knott, with his shirt sleeves buttoned to his wrists, was so obviously enjoying himself, despite the dire circumstances. Snow, too, was splendid in defence and he stuck it out for 45 minutes. Then he came forward to Sobers, played no stroke and umpire Kippins's right index finger sent him on his way. It was five past five; 25 minutes remained and there were three wickets left.

There were 19 minutes left when Tony Lock pulled a long hop from Sobers into Lester King's tummy at mid off. Lock strode off as if looking for someone to beat up and England were 200–8. A single off Gibbs's last ball enabled Knott to keep the strike but, aiming to do the same off the last ball of Sobers's next over, he made the mistake of hitting a four and Gibbs was able to bowl to Pocock with six men round the bat. Pocock played a pretty confident maiden over, with the crowd – and all of us – living each ball as we fidgeted away in the press box. The palm trees all round the outside of the ground were filled with spectators and suddenly there was a rough tearing noise behind us as a branch broke under the weight of at least six occupants, who were deposited into the narrow canal between the stand and the road.

Knott played out a maiden against Basil Butcher's leg-spin before appealing against the light. There was as much chance of that being answered in his favour as there was of a cloudburst. I have never known an appeal against the light turned down so quickly; the umpires did not even meet. Gibbs bowled again to Pocock and now there were seven round the bat. There were six minutes to go as Pocock thrust forward to the fifth ball and it flew to Lloyd at square short leg. Pocock thought he had hit the ball into the ground and stayed where he was. The whole of Georgetown seemed to appeal and umpire Jordan's finger went up.

It was down to Jeff Jones, the last man, and what must he have felt like as he walked out? What was going on in his mind? He was hemmed in by so many close fielders, it was almost impossible to see him. Somehow he kept out the last ball of the over. Knott played out the next, from Sobers, but was unable to get the single which would have given him the strike. The last over was to be bowled by Gibbs to Jones, who one can only describe as a worthy number eleven, with the outcome of the series depending upon these six balls.

Knott and Jones met mid-wicket for a chat which went on long enough to make sure there would only be time for one more over. There was no one sitting still in the entire ground and the noise was so great that even Jim Swanton was unable to make himself heard in the press box, although it was not for want of trying. In my whole life, I have never experienced anything quite like those few minutes. The next day in the aeroplane on the way back to London, I asked Knott what he and Jones had talked about when they met before that last over. 'What did we talk about?' With a mischievous twinkle in his eye, he fired back at me, 'We sang the first verse of "Land of My Fathers".'

Somehow – and I daresay he never quite knew how – Jones played out perhaps the most gut-wrenching over I have ever watched. Jones played each tortuous ball; three with the front pad, each of which produced a blood-curdling appeal. It was greatly to the credit of umpire Kippins, after all he had been through, that he was brave enough to shake his head on all three occasions – the second time, only after a long pause – regardless of the consequences. When Jones somehow kept the last ball out, the crowd leapt over the fencing and invaded the field. One huge West Indian swooped on Alan Knott at the non-striker's end, picked him up and carried him triumphantly into the pavilion. That, somehow, said it all. It had been just about the perfect Test match.

WEST INDIES v ENGLAND (5th Test)

At Bourda, Georgetown, Guyana, on 28 March – 3 April 1968 (six-day match).

West Indies

S.M. Nurse c Knott b Snow	17		lbw b Snow		49
G.S. Camacho c and b Jones	14		c Graveney b Snow		26
R.B. Kanhai c Edrich b Pocock	150		c Edrich b Jones		22
B.F. Butcher run out	18	(6)	c Lock b Pocock		18
*G.S. Sobers c Cowdrey b Barrington	152		not out		95
C.H. Lloyd b Lock	31	(4)	c Knott b Snow		1
D.A.J. Holford lbw b Snow	1	(8)	b Lock		3
†D.L. Murray c Knott b Lock	8	(7)	c Boycott b Pocock		16
L.A. King b Snow	8		b Snow		20
W.W. Hall not out	5		b Snow		7
L.R. Gibbs b Snow	1		b Snow		0
Extras (3 lb, 4 nb, 2 w)	9		(1 b, 2 lb, 3 nb, 1 w)		7
Total (all out, 150.4 overs)	**414**		(all out, 66.2 overs)		**264**

1–29 2–35 3–72 4–322 5–385 6–387 7–399
8–400 9–412 10–414

1–78 2–84 3–86 4–133 5–171
6–201 7–216 8–252 9–264 10–264

Bowling, *1st innings*: Snow 27.4–2–82–4; Jones 31–5–114–1; D'Oliveira 8–1–27–0; Pocock 38–11–78–1; Lock 28–7–61–2; Barrington 18–4–43–1. *2nd innings*: Snow 15.2–0–60–6; Jones 17–1–81–1; D'Oliveira 8–0–28–0; Pocock 17–1–66–2; Lock 9–1–22–1.

England

J.H. Edrich c Murray b Sobers	0	c Gibbs b Sobers	6
G. Boycott c Murray b Hall	116	b Gibbs	30
*M.C. Cowdrey lbw b Sobers	59	lbw b Gibbs	82
T.W. Graveney c Murray b Hall	27	c Murray b Gibbs	0
K.F. Barrington c Kanhai b Sobers	4	c Lloyd b Gibbs	0
B.L. D'Oliveira c Nurse b Holford	27	c and b Gibbs	2
†A.P.E. Knott lbw b Holford	7	not out	73
J.A. Snow b Gibbs	0	lbw b Sobers	1
G.A.R. Lock b King	89	c King b Sobers	2
P.I. Pocock c and b King	13	c Lloyd b Gibbs	0
I.J. Jones not out	0	not out	0
Extras (12 b, 14 lb, 3 nb)	29	(9 b, 1 w)	10
Total (all out, 163.2 overs)	**371**	(9 wkts, 120 overs)	**206**

1–13 2–185 3–185 4–194 5–240 6–252
7–257 8–259 9–368 10–371

1–33 2–37 3–37 4–39 5–41 6–168
7–198 8–200 9–206

Bowling, *1st innings*: Sobers 37–15–72–3; Hall 19–3–71–2; King 38.2–11–79–2; Holford 31–10–54–2; Gibbs 33–9–59–1; Butcher 5–3–7–0. *2nd innings*: Sobers 31–16–53–3; Hall 13–6–26–0; King 9–1–11–0; Gibbs 40–20–60–6; Holford 17–9–37–0; Butcher 10–7–9–0.

Close of play, *day 1*: West Indies (1) 243–3 (Kanhai 113*, Sobers 75*); *day 2*: England (1) 40–1 (Boycott 21*, Cowdrey 13*); *day 3*: England (1) 146–1 (Boycott 93*, Cowdrey 43*); *day 4*: England (1) 352–8 (Lock 76*, Pocock 7*); *day 5*: West Indies (2) 264 all out.

Toss: West Indies. Last-innings target: 308 runs.
Umpires: H.B.D. Jordan (WI), F.C.P. Kippins (WI).

MATCH DRAWN.

14
ITB IN EXCELSIS

England v Australia (3rd Test)
16–21 July 1981; Headingley, Leeds
England won by 18 runs.

Few games of cricket have stayed in the memory like this one and few players have stayed in the memory like Ian Terence Botham. The build-up to this extraordinary game began in February 1980, when Mike Brearley retired from the England captaincy after the Golden Jubilee Test match against India in Mumbai. It was said to be his recommendation that the job should pass on to Botham, who in that celebratory match had made 114 and taken 13 wickets. Two series followed, at home and away, against the West Indies, both of which were lost, and Botham's captaincy had been at best questionable.

Australia came to England in 1981. They won the first Test at Trent Bridge, then the second at Lord's was drawn and, at the end of the match, Botham resigned the captaincy, moments before he was going to be relieved of the job. With the next Test, at Headingley, only nine days away, Mike Brearley, still captaining Middlesex, was brought back to lead the side for the rest of the series.

This was drama enough before a ball had been bowled. Brearley proceeded to win his ninth Test match against Australia as captain, beating W.G. Grace's record of eight wins. More than that, a psychoanalyst in the making, he was able to transform Botham in those nine days and somehow turn him back into the most compelling and destructive cricketer of his generation. Who knows what went on between the two of them? The main magic may not have come so much from words of wisdom, as from the simple fact of Brearley's vastly reassuring presence once more being there for him, and this more than anything was what Botham needed if his genius was to be restored to full working order.

At this point I must admit that I was a member of the BBC's *Test Match Special* commentary team for this Test, which meant I could hardly have been more closely involved with the extraordinary events of those five days in Leeds. At the end, I also had the luck to be on the air when Bob Willis bowled Ray Bright with the last ball of the match.

For the first three and a half days there was no hint of the drama that was to follow. After Australia had won the toss and decided to bat, the cricket was as drab as the grey, damp weather. It was a comfort for English eyes to see the familiar, modest yet purposeful figure of Brearley leading the side out. Behind him came the slim 25-year-old Ian Botham, playing his 38th Test match and looking, on that first morning, as sprightly as ever. There was a lot of public sympathy for him, a certain amount of the optimism he always inspires and also the fear that this was perhaps a little too soon. For all that, you could sense the colt-like enthusiasm in his stride which, with every step, left one in no doubt he was once again loving the challenge. He came out at Headingley with a relish and a bounce which may not have been so evident when he was the captain.

Brearley did not give him the new ball, however, and he found he was the fourth bowler to be used that first morning. By the time the ball was thrown to him, the openers, John Dyson and Graeme Wood, had given Australia a solid start. The score had reached 55 when, to the huge delight of the players and the crowd, Botham trapped Wood plumb in front. The rehabilitation process had begun. Dyson, known for his lengthy occupation of the crease rather than his strokeplay, went on to reach his first Test century and was principally responsible for taking Australia to 203–3 by the end of the first day, which had lost nearly an hour to rain. Australia's progress continued to be slow the next day, as half-centuries from captain Kim Hughes and Graham Yallop took Australia to 401–9 declared. By then, England had won an important psychological trick, even if they did not know it at the time. After tea on this second day, Botham had come on and taken 5–35, giving him 6–95 in all. He was back among the wickets and this could only have made his sense of well-being even more jaunty, which was important for England.

The next day, in typically English conditions, the three Australian quicker bowlers – Dennis Lillee, as menacing as ever; Terry Alderman, as precise as ever; and Geoff Lawson, as raw-boned as ever – shared the wickets. But there was another shaft of bright light for England. They were 87–5, with the ball moving all over the place off the pitch, when Botham strode out to bat. He decided to take the bowlers on and made 50 in quick time before being caught behind by Rod Marsh off Lillee. This was the catch which gave Marsh his record 264th catch in Test cricket and it was appropriate it should have been one of the 95 he held off the bowling of Lillee. Even though England, 227 runs behind on first innings, had been forced to follow on before the end of the third day, Botham was once again able to locate the middle of his bat.

It was a day which had a most unhappy ending too. After tea, there was a long stoppage for bad light. At five minutes to six o'clock, the close of play, the umpires, Barrie Meyer and David Evans, came out, consulted their light meters and called off play for the day. As soon as they had gone back into the pavilion, the light improved and the sun even made an appearance. The crowd were loud in their condemnation of the umpires and demanded to be told why they were not allowed the extra hour the regulations provided for, to make up for some of the time that had been lost. The scenes invoked memories of a similar situation at Lord's the previous year when spectators, including members of the MCC in the Pavilion, hurled both abuse and cushions at Dickie Bird and David Constant during the Centenary Test between England and Australia.

It was late on this third day, when England followed on, that Ladbrokes, whose main cricket adviser then was the former England wicketkeeper Godfrey Evans, with his magnificent mutton-chop whiskers, made an interesting and entertaining contribution. Evans was one of post-war cricket's great players and characters and he now persuaded Ladbrokes to offer odds of 500–1 against England winning the match. This was during the period when the players were off the field because of bad light, so when the operator of the electronic scoreboard heard these odds were being offered, he flashed the details up on the board. Dennis Lillee saw them and, being a betting man, realised that odds of 500–1 in a two-horse race were too good to miss. His first thought was to put 50 pounds on England, but he was talked out of that by his colleagues, particularly Rod Marsh, who at first refused to bet even a fiver against Australia. In the end, Lillee settled on ten pounds and the next morning, just before play began, he enlisted the services of their coach driver, Peter 'Geezer' Tribe, to put the money on for him in the Ladbrokes tent. Seeing 'Geezer' walking round to the tent, Marsh, on his way out to the middle, had second thoughts. He shouted to the coach driver, to attract his attention, and then held up five fingers to indicate he wanted to put five pounds on England. 'Geezer' shook his head, as if to tell Marsh not to waste his money. Marsh shouted back, holding up five fingers a second time, and then clenched his fist to show what might happen if he ignored him. The money went on and Lillee and Marsh won £7,500 between them.

If this had happened in today's politically correct world, goodness knows what would have happened. As it was, it was considered to be a good bit of fun by two devout Aussies who would never in a million years have 'sold' a match to England. In the end, Ladbrokes paid out about £40,000 in all, for what was surely a wonderfully cheap piece of publicity. One or two others in the dressing rooms and the commentary boxes wanted to have a bit of it too. The unlucky Bob Taylor had set off for the betting tent ten minutes before play began and was prevented from getting there by a crowd of autograph hunters. Ted Dexter and Richie Benaud in the television box had left a note for Godfrey Evans, who usually visited the box each day before the start of play, but unfortunately for them, that morning, thinking the game was virtually all over, he had decided to go home.

England's batting in the first part of the fourth day was no better than it had been in the first innings. The score was 105–5 when Botham came out to join Geoffrey Boycott, whose impeccable defensive technique had served him as well as ever for more than three and a half hours. Botham began with two thumping off drives which made it clear how he was going to bat. This pair had taken the score to 133 when Boycott was caught in two minds by a ball which Alderman may have held back a fraction, played too soon and across the line and was lbw. Boycott made it abundantly clear that it was a decision he was not happy with. When Taylor went almost at once, offering a dolly catch to short leg, England were 135–7, still 92 runs behind, and he will have been glad he had hung on to his money. In the dressing room, as the tall, fair-haired Graham Dilley walked out to bat, the England players must have been pleased they had booked out of their hotel that morning. But by the end of the day, after three hours' cricket which was as unbelievable as it was unexpected, the city's principal hoteliers had been assured of another night's takings.

In the old commentary box at the top of the football stand, arguably as uncomfortable a box as any I ever commentated from, the atmosphere among the English contingent was of resigned and, I hope, good-humoured inevitability. We did our best to be cheerful, but Trevor Bailey and Fred Trueman found it hard going in the summariser's chair. Brian Johnston was as cheerful and amusing as ever, but when Don Mosey discussed the failings of the England batsmen, his tone suggested he might have been presiding over a more than unusually gloomy convention of pessimists. Then there was Australia's Alan McGilvray, a fine commentator and never slow to embrace Australia's cause. Up to this point, he had done nobly to keep his Australian sympathies in check. If only he had known what lay just around the corner, I am sure he would have been tempted to let his hair down a bit more during those first three and a half days. In the scorer's corner, Bill Frindall was, statistically speaking, having the time of his life and never wasted a chance to get a word in when he could. Peter Baxter, our producer, was a blur of perpetual motion, trying to cater for the needs of all the many BBC programmes that wanted their money's worth as this match built to its unforgettable climax. If John Arlott was listening in his new home in the island of Alderney, he can only have regretted that he did not delay his retirement for one more year.

Those first two off drives by Botham against Terry Alderman had been described as pleasant but irrelevant splashes on a canvas where the main picture had already been indelibly drawn. Even though it was no less a man than Botham, surely the only target that might still be reached was the minor satisfaction of making Australia bat a second time. The 92 more runs needed to achieve even that seemed a huge mountain to climb.

Botham's powerful strokes continued to come. He now turned his attention to Lillee, driving him twice to the square-cover boundary with shots which sounded like the crack of a gun as the ball sped from his bat. To our amazement in the commentary box, and surely to everyone else's, Dilley, a left-handed batsman, stood up tall and crashed the ball through the covers with power and elegance, as if he was nothing more or less than a left-handed

Botham. We knew about Botham, but Dilley, whose batting was normally of the just-occasional car-boot-sale variety, began to play strokes which would have hung in the National Gallery. While Botham, always restless, wearing a long-sleeved sweater throughout his innings, prowled around in his crease, Dilley stood quietly at the other end, tall, blond, reserved and modest. His drive off the back foot for four past cover's left hand off Alderman was as good as it gets. It made one wonder what on earth he was doing batting as low as number nine. In between balls, Dilley would sometimes stand with his bat raised across his chest and, with masses of curling hair fluffing out from under his helmet, he looked almost schoolboyish. There was one nasty moment when he might have been run out. Botham had pushed Alderman to Trevor Chappell at cover and set off for a run which was never there. Botham changed his mind and went back into his crease, with Dilley more than halfway down the pitch. Marsh could not get up to the stumps in time to take Chappell's throw, which went for four overthrows. If Marsh had been able to get there and had thrown the ball back to Alderman, Dilley would have been stranded.

England went cheerfully into the tea interval at 176–7, with Botham 39 and Dilley 25. It was the first time in the match that England's batting had offered worthwhile resistance to the Australian bowlers. It was entertaining and the crowd loved every stroke, but 51 more runs were still needed to make Australia bat again. In the commentary box, even amongst ourselves, we were doing no more than hoping that England might just save the follow-on. The ball was still doing plenty off the pitch and even Fred Trueman had not yet started to shake his head and say, 'You know, funny things can happen in this game of ours,' in that inimitable Yorkshire voice.

A crashing cover drive off the back foot from Botham against Alderman gave the evening session a good start. Then, later in the over, when he pitched short, Botham came forward, waited and, with a delightful flick of the wrists, late-cut him most elegantly for four more. When he attempted another massive drive off Alderman, the ball went off a thick inside edge to the midwicket boundary, which took him to 50 off 57 balls with eight fours. Botham now seemed to be throwing his bat at almost everything. There was one extraordinary, almost primeval, stroke off Alderman which he played off the back foot. He threw everything at the ball which soared over mid on to the boundary – and yet it had come off the splice of the bat. It was the sheer power of the man that made it possible. It was a stroke which any good, honest caveman would have envied.

Eight were needed to save the follow-on when he went for another huge drive off Alderman. The ball streaked away off the edge over the slips, which reduced it to four. Then he stood up on his toes and drove a short one off the back foot past cover and Australia had to bat again. Just to make the point, the next ball also disappeared for four, and I think this was the moment when it suddenly began to occur to people that maybe something truly remarkable might be just beginning to happen. Another heaved pull drive for four brought up the hundred stand in 70 minutes. Then a lovely cover drive took Dilley to his first Test fifty. He stood still and waved his bat with what seemed an endearing air of mild embarrassment, as if he was not quite sure what to do. He had scored six more when Alderman went round the wicket. Dilley tried to play another stroke square of the wicket on the off side and was undone by the angle of delivery, which brought the ball into him, and he was bowled.

These two had put on an extraordinary 117 for the eighth wicket and yet England were still only 25 runs ahead. At this point, none of the Australians would have had even the slightest doubt that they were going to win the match with ease. Chris Old, tall and upright, made his way out to bat. Old's batting had never produced as many runs as it should have done, but now he too rose to the occasion. He defended solidly and produced a few lovely left-handed strokes, which brought him 29 runs. He helped Botham, who continued unabated, add another 67 for the ninth wicket.

Botham was now batting like a tidal wave. His power was extraordinary. The strokes he only half hit were finding the boundary, and one such to midwicket brought him to his hundred off only 87 balls, with 19 fours and one six. When Old departed, being bowled pushing defensively at Lawson, England were 319–9, only 92 runs ahead. The Australians were not worried and although English voices were talking of miracles, they were not sure they really meant it.

The sight of the huge Bob Willis coming to the wicket with a bat in his hand normally brought the groundsman out of his hut knowing that it wouldn't be long before he had to roll the pitch. But on this occasion Willis offered a straight defensive bat when he had to and helped his partner add 37 runs, which turned out to be the deciding runs of the match. Botham's bat continued to cut all sorts of curves as he improvised between the impressively orthodox and the outrageously unorthodox. These two took England's score to 351–9 that evening, when they were 124 runs ahead of Australia. In all honesty, was that enough for this England side to become only the second to win a Test match after following on? It had last been done by A.E. Stoddart's England team at the Sydney Cricket Ground in 1894, when they won the first Test by ten runs.

The sheer magnificence of Botham's strokeplay and the galvanising effect this astonishing innings will have had made some people feel that a miracle had to happen. Of course, the pitch, which had been a great help to the seam bowlers throughout the match, was badly worn and would make batting difficult on the fifth day. In a commentary box where the BBC demands impartiality from its employees, it was becoming harder and harder to be fair and even-handed. Every run brought another feverish calculation of England's lead. There was much talk of how in the past good batting sides have lost their way chasing small totals in the fourth innings. There was also great joy and relief that there would now, after all, be a fifth day's play, but was it not really expecting too much to think there was even an outside chance of England pulling off an unthinkable victory?

Botham's innings took us through the full range of emotions. When he arrived at 105–5 it was doom and despond from the England point of view. By the close of play three hours later, the English were gleefully beginning to count their chickens well before they had hatched. The Australians were applauding Botham's magnificent innings while remaining convinced that it had done nothing more than delay their victory. It was a strange evening of make-believe and conjecture which may have been made possible by one man, but, as he will have been the first to realise, he could not have done it without the help of Graham Dilley, Chris Old and Bob Willis. In fact, England's four fast bowlers had comprehensively won the batting honours. There was plenty to talk about that night when we sat down to dinner in our rebooked hotels.

The next morning, Botham hit his 27th four before Willis was caught close to the bat. The final scene was set. Australia needed 130 to win. A good crowd gathered and the ground was bristling with a vibrant sense of expectancy, or were the spectators simply hanging on to a healthy imagination? As so often happens when expectations are huge, nothing much occurred for the first hour. It seemed appropriate that the first wicket should fall to Botham, when with the score 13, Graeme Wood, after hitting two good leg-side fours off Botham in the first over, was caught behind. Wood did not like it and may have felt he hit the ball on the full toss and into the ground before it went through to Taylor. In those days, there was no review system (DRS) to sort these things out. The roller had temporarily quietened the pitch and Dyson and Trevor Chappell now put on 43 without seeming to be in any great danger. At 56–1, the target of 130 will have seemed a doddle.

Willis had come on as first change at the Football Stand End, which meant he was bowling up the hill and into the wind. He was clearly most unhappy. Willis was a bowler who, when he felt the odds had been stacked unfairly against him, made his feelings clear. He had a word with Brearley, who soon agreed to let him bowl downhill from the Kirkstall Lane End with the wind behind him. Willis said later he told Brearley he was too old to bowl up the hill. The transformation was astonishing.

With lunch approaching, Australia needed 74 more; it was difficult to get too excited. Chappell was facing and suddenly Willis made one rear unpleasantly from just short of a length. The effects of the heavy roller were wearing off. Chappell could only fend it away as it lifted towards his face and the ball lobbed gently into the gloves of Bob Taylor. Two runs later, Willis began what was to be the last over of the morning. He bowled fast and short to Kim Hughes, who tried to get in behind it. The ball took the outside edge of his bat and Botham, swooping low to his left at third slip, came up with a marvellous catch. This brought in the left-handed Graham Yallop; two balls later he played Willis away on the leg side out of the middle of the bat. Just in front of square at short leg, Mike Gatting held a terrific reflex-action catch low down in front of him. This was exactly the pre-lunch aperitif England needed. At the interval, Australia were 58–4, still needing 72 to win. The fifth-day crowd was in full cry. Suddenly, it was not quite such a doddle.

Seven more anxious runs came after lunch before Allan Border faced Chris Old, who so far had not taken a wicket in the match. Border was now caught on the crease by a ball he might have gone forward to. As it was, it flicked the inside edge of the bat and went into the stumps. Australia were 65–5. Still the faithful Dyson was soldiering on at the other end, but, at 68, he tried to hook Willis, was hit on the glove and the jubilant Taylor held another catch behind the wicket. It became 74–7 when Rod Marsh was unable to resist another short one from Willis. He hooked and the ball steepled into the air towards fine leg. While the world held its breath, Dilley, who had started to come in, judged the ball perfectly, back-pedalling a few paces before clutching it into his chest not much more than a yard from the boundary. In these tense circumstances it was an outstanding catch. The ball seemed to hang in the air for ever, yet Dilley's concentration never wavered. I was on the air at that moment. I shall never forget the silence that came over the ground as the crowd waited for that ball to come down. Dilley, as calmly as you could wish, made the catch look simple. The roars of delight and relief told the story. Dilley immediately threw the ball back to the middle and seemed almost to hesitate before running in and taking part in the celebrations.

We were now much nearer the edge of our seats and I don't think any of us could really believe it. We had hardly had time to get our breath back before Lawson felt for Willis outside the off stump and Taylor was celebrating his fourth catch of the innings: 75–8, with 55 runs still needed by Australia. In the commentary box we did our best to add caution to our English excitement, while Alan McGilvray was being graciously philosophical about it all. Which was the last thing Dennis Lillee was being. A great competitor, he now strode out in his sleeveless sweater, his moustache bristling with a jaunty militancy, to join Ray Bright. Lillee was certainly not a man who was thinking about collecting his winnings. On the other hand, the crowd were as good as celebrating an England victory, which will only have increased his determination.

Willis bowled short to him and, as cool as anything, Lillee waited in the crease and, with skill and versatility, deliberately uppercut the ball over the slips for four. Within seconds the game was transformed and suddenly we had two batsmen who were in control. You could almost sense them meeting in mid-pitch and saying, 'What's all the fuss about?' The England bowlers, so near to their goal, were now guilty of trying too hard. They had got where they were by bowling short and what was good enough for

Hughes and Yallop must surely have seemed good enough for Bright and Lillee. When Old pitched short to Bright, he swivelled and pulled him handsomely to the midwicket boundary. Moments later, he lifted him away from near the off stump to midwicket for another four. Runs were coming easily and 75–8 became 100–8.

Willis was short again to Lillee, who once more waited for him. This time he cut him with power and precision, neatly bisecting third man and deep backward point. Four more classy runs. When he had played another good-looking cut for four off Willis, Brearley decided to step in. He ran from first slip to have a word with the hyped-up Willis, who was striving frantically for every inch of extra pace. He was probably not in the best mood to take advice which, in simple terms, must have been to 'pitch it up'. Brearley trotted back to first slip, Willis steamed in again, the crowd held its breath. The ball was up to the bat on about middle and leg. Lillee, slightly off balance, tried to chip it away on the leg side. The ball spooned into the air towards Gatting at mid on. For an agonising moment, he obviously did not pick up the flight of the ball. After a split second's hesitation, he came tearing in and then lurched forward in a despairing tumble and came up with the catch with the backs of his hands almost on the ground. Lillee, furious with himself, walked off and I will guarantee the betting tent never entered his mind. He and Bright had put on 35 runs and had looked to be winning the match for Australia.

It was not quite all over, for the almost demure-looking Alderman, in his gleaming white helmet, was now twice dropped by Old at third slip, both difficult low chances. Willis began his next over with Australia needing 19 more runs. I remember thinking, as I described it all in the commentary box, that when he ran in now to bowl to Bright, it was even more ferociously than before. Bright started to push half forward, but the ball was through him and the middle stump was cartwheeling back towards Taylor.

England had won an incredible victory by 18 runs and Bob Willis had taken 8–43 in the defining spell of his career. The celebrations began, and what celebrations they were too. The match has gone down in history as Botham's Match; Willis and Brearley should both get a mention too.

ENGLAND v AUSTRALIA (3rd Test)

At Headingley, Leeds, on 16–21 July 1981.

Australia

J. Dyson b Dilley	102	(2) c Taylor b Willis	34
G.M. Wood lbw b Botham	34	(1) c Taylor b Botham	10
T.M. Chappell c Taylor b Willey	27	c Taylor b Willis	8
*K.J. Hughes c and b Botham	89	c Botham b Willis	0
R.J. Bright b Dilley	7	(8) b Willis	19
G.N. Yallop c Taylor b Botham	58	(5) c Gatting b Willis	0
A.R. Border lbw b Botham	8	(6) b Old	0
†R.W. Marsh b Botham	28	(7) c Dilley b Willis	4
G.F. Lawson c Taylor b Botham	13	c Taylor b Willis	1
D.K. Lillee not out	3	c Gatting b Willis	17
T.M. Alderman not out	0	not out	0
Extras (4 b, 13 lb, 12 nb, 3 w)	32	(3 lb, 14 nb, 1 w)	18
Total (9 wkts, declared, 155.2 overs)	**401**	(all out, 36.1 overs)	**111**

1–55 2–149 3–196 4–220 5–332 6–354
7–357 8–396 9–401

1–13 2–56 3–58 4–58 5–65 6–68
7–74 8–75 9–110 10–111

Bowling, *1st innings*: Willis 30–8–72–0; Old 43–14–91–0; Dilley 27–4–78–2;
Botham 39.2–11–95–6; Willey 13–2–31–1; Boycott 3–2–2–0. *2nd innings*: Botham 7–3–14–1;
Dilley 2–0–11–0; Willis 15.1–3–43–8; Old 9–1–21–1; Willey 3–1–4–0.

England

G.A. Gooch lbw b Alderman	2	c Alderman b Lillee	0
G. Boycott b Lawson	12	lbw b Alderman	46
*J.M. Brearley c Marsh b Alderman	10	c Alderman b Lillee	14
D.I. Gower c Marsh b Lawson	24	c Border b Alderman	9
M.W. Gatting lbw b Lillee	15	lbw b Alderman	1
P. Willey b Lawson	8	c Dyson b Lillee	33
I.T. Botham c Marsh b Lillee	50	not out	149
†R.W. Taylor c Marsh b Lillee	5	c Bright b Alderman	1
G.R. Dilley c and b Lillee	13	b Alderman	56
C.M. Old c Border b Alderman	0	b Lawson	29
R.G.D. Willis not out	1	c Border b Alderman	2
Extras (6 b, 11 lb, 11 nb, 6 w)	34	(5 b, 3 lb, 5 nb, 3 w)	16
Total (all out, 50.5 overs)	**174**	(all out, 87.3 overs)	**356**

1–12 2–40 3–42 4–84 5–87 6–112 7–148
8–166 9–167 10–174

1–0 2–18 3–37 4–41 5–105 6–133
7–135 8–252 9–319 10–356

Bowling, *1st innings*: Lillee 18.5–7–49–4; Alderman 19–4–59–3; Lawson 13–3–32–3. *2nd innings*: Lillee 25–6–94–3; Alderman 35.3–6–135–6; Lawson 23–4–96–1; Bright 4–0–15–0.

Close of play, *day 1*: Australia (1) 203–3 (Hughes 24*, Bright 1*); *day 2*: England (1) 7–0 (Gooch 2*, Boycott 0*); *day 3*: England (2) 6–1 (Boycott 0*, Brearley 4*); *day 4*: England (2) 351–9 (Botham 145*, Willis 1*).

Toss: Australia. Last-innings target: 130 runs.
Umpires: D.G.L. Evans (Eng), B.J. Meyer (Eng).
Man of the Match: I.T. Botham.

ENGLAND won by 18 runs.

15

SECOND BITE OF THE CHERRY

Australia v England (4th Test)
26–30 December 1982; Melbourne Cricket Ground
England won by three runs.

THERE are few cricketing locations as dramatic or exciting as the Melbourne Cricket Ground (MCG) on Boxing Day morning, especially when the Ashes are the prize. On their tour of Australia in 1982–83, Bob Willis's England side arrived for this fourth Test two matches down, having lost in Brisbane and Adelaide. Their narrow and incredibly exciting victory, by just three runs, sent them on to Sydney with the chance of drawing the series, but a draw at the SCG meant that Australia regained the Ashes.

This match in Melbourne was the first Test in which all four innings were completed within ten runs of each other. England, who were put in to bat, were bowled out for 284. Australia replied with 287 and then dismissed England the second time for 294, before being themselves bowled out for 288 in the final innings. England's three-run margin of victory was, at the time, the equal lowest in an Ashes Test match. Australia had won by three runs at Old Trafford in 1902.

This was another dramatically exciting Test match which I watched from the commentary box and, just as I had been the year before at Headingley, I was lucky enough to be on the air when the last ball was bowled. So often, exciting finishes turn up as a surprise at the end of three or four days of fairly uneventful cricket. This game at the MCG, a huge stadium designed in its present form for the Olympic Games in 1956, was exciting from the first ball to the last. The only great individual performance came from a mildly unexpected source when fast bowler Norman Cowans, in the high moment of a Test career which brought him 51 wickets from 19 matches, took six wickets in Australia's second innings. No batsman made more than Chris Tavaré's 89 in England's first innings and, as was usual, he took his time. There was a neat and unusual symmetry to the proceedings too, in that the first three days each saw one complete innings. The only point in the five days when the batsmen took control came in the first two sessions on the first day and the last two sessions of the match, when Allan Border and Jeff Thomson almost took Australia to victory.

Greg Chappell won the toss for Australia and gave the England batsmen first use of a questionable surface. The pitch had been recently relaid and the bounce, which was uneven at the start, became progressively lower. Edges accounted for the first three batsmen, Graeme Fowler, Geoff Cook and David Gower, and England were struggling at 56–3 immediately after lunch. The usual large Boxing Day crowd – there were just over 83,000 in the ground – were in typically boisterous form when Chris Tavaré was joined by Allan Lamb and they put on 161 for the fourth wicket. Strokeplay was always hazardous, but on this first after-noon, these two, in their sharply contrasting styles, put together the biggest partnership of the match.

Even so, the bowlers will always have known there was some-thing in it for them and both batsmen needed a certain amount of luck. They had taken England's score to 217 before Jeff Thomson found the edge of Tavaré's bat and ten runs later Bruce Yardley turned an off-break to Lamb much further than he should have been able to on the first day of a Test match. After that, the innings subsided and England were all out for 284, moments before the close of play. That evening, no one was quite sure where the advantage lay, but there seemed little doubt we were in for a gripping few days. Batting had been harder work than usual on the first day at the MCG and pitches like this which prevent massive totals being compiled often produce the most exciting matches.

The second day saw a smaller crowd, probably as a result of the chaos at the turnstiles on the first morning when surprisingly few were open and many spectators were forced to queue for up to an hour and a half before getting into the ground. Opener Kepler Wessels, the first South African Test cricketer to play for Australia, gave them something to cheer about early on as he cut and carved away outside the off stump in his angular and rather awkward-looking left-handed way. Wessels, always an invaluable competitor, was not a batsman you would go along especially to watch.

The Australians were going along smoothly, however, at 55 for no wicket, when suddenly the 21-year-old Norman Cowans, playing in his first series, sent back John Dyson and Greg Chappell with successive balls. Dyson was lbw shuffling across his stumps and Chappell hooked his first ball, a bouncer, and it steepled away to the backward-square-leg boundary, where Lamb had been placed with some precision. From then on, the innings became a splendid dogfight in which Kim Hughes's careful defence was lightened by some customary flashing left-handed strokes from David Hookes. Australia had inched their way to a slender lead of three when, moments before the end of the day, Geoff Miller bowled Thomson through a wild slog.

Midway through the next day, which produced much tense cricket, England's second innings was not well placed at 85–3. The left-handed Graeme Fowler, also on his first tour, now played his best innings of the series. He had passed 50 when he received a nasty yorker from Thomson. He attempted to dig it out and the ball flicked the bottom of his bat before landing on the big toe of his right foot, which it broke into three pieces. Fowler told Bernard

Thomas, the England physiotherapist who had rushed onto the ground, that he could not stand on his right leg and should go off. Thomas cheerfully suggested he should try standing on the other one and prepare for a one-legged battle with Thomson – which Fowler was unlikely to win. David Gower, who probably needed some persuasion to do this particular job, came out as his runner. Predictably, the next ball was a bouncer. By his own admission, Fowler, unable to move, flapped rather than hooked at it and it flew straight to Bruce Yardley, who was almost standing on the fine-leg boundary. Fowler was in considerable pain and was probably quite relieved, but a moment later he heard the umpire shout 'no-ball' and had to resume the contest. He was soon put out of his agony when he was bowled by Rodney Hogg.

The ball was now coming through appreciably lower, but England's later batsmen fought hard in the difficult conditions. Ian Botham hung around for an hour and a half, playing a few extravagant strokes and hitting eight fours. Then Derek Pringle and Bob Taylor added 61 invaluable runs and England finished with 294, which turned out to be the highest total of the match and, in the end, was a really good effort. Australia had been left to score 292 to win, with two full days in which to get them, and it was not going to be an easy task.

England's second innings had finished just before the end of the day, and Australia set off in pursuit of their target at the start of a cloudy fourth day which promised rain. The one thing in their favour was the lightning speed of the outfield caused by the recent severe drought. Kepler Wessels and John Dyson made a reasonable start, with each run being loudly cheered by another good crowd. I think everyone was expecting something dramatic to happen in this last innings, for it had been that sort of game. The crowd were on the edge of their seats from the first ball.

Australia had progressed anxiously to 37 when Norman Cowans struck the first blow for England. Wessels pushed out in defence round his front foot, as was his habit, and was bowled off the pad. This brought in Greg Chappell, who in the first innings had been out first ball to Cowans. His first ball now was fast and short on his body. He turned it at catchable height through Cook at short leg who, if he had been standing a yard and a half deeper, would have been able to see the ball and take the catch. Instead, Chappell was off the mark and Cowans looked like a man who had been robbed. In his next over but one, Cowans bowled again to Chappell. This time it was a short ball just outside the off stump and he played a firm stroke off the back foot which was a mixture of cut and drive. Ian Gould, England's reserve wicketkeeper, fielding as a substitute for Fowler, was at cover point and, diving low to his left, held on to a brilliant catch. Chappell's dismissal knocked a bit of the stuffing out of Australia.

Kim Hughes and Dyson then took the score along to 71, when Dyson drove at an outswinger from Botham and was beautifully caught in the slips by Tavaré. At 71–3, just before lunch on this fourth day, Hookes came out to join Hughes. During the hours of the afternoon they put on exactly a hundred and shifted the balance back towards Australia, just as they had done in the first innings. Hughes, a somewhat enigmatic character, always longing to be loved, was now circumspect and determined and so obviously exerting massive self-control over his natural inclination to play his strokes. This was in sharp contrast to Hookes who, left-handed, fair-haired, angular and elegant, and a great favourite with the crowds, was always looking for every chance to play his strokes. He knew no other way.

Their stand ended, to the huge disappointment of a crowd which was having a great time riding the crest of this particular wave, when Kim Hughes got into a muddle with a sweep against Geoff Miller. Behind the stumps, Bob Taylor quickly changed direction and held a tumbling right-handed catch which had come off the batsman's body. Two runs later, at 173, England will have felt they were back in charge when Hookes's innings came to an end. Although tea was fast approaching, he decided to pull

Cowans and the ball steepled up on the leg side. Willis went after it, running away from the wicket and watching the ball as it came down over his left shoulder, and held on to an extremely awkward catch. It was not in Hookes's character to go carefully with the tea interval imminent.

Cowans kept going after tea and in a couple of overs it seemed that he had just about won the game for England. Off the first ball of his second over he won an lbw decision against Marsh which looked as though it could have gone either way. The sixth ball was short and kept low and made a mess of Bruce Yardley's stumps as he tried to slash what he expected to be a lifting ball. Australia were 190–7 and Cowans had taken 3–5 in 20 balls in the best spell of his career. After two firm blows, Geoff Lawson hooked Pringle to fine leg, where Cowans judged the catch well, and at 218 Cowans had Rodney Hogg leg before, although most of Australia felt the ball was too high.

Cowans, England's unlikely hero that day, seemed at times to lack the sheer hostility of some of his fellow West Indians – Cowans was born in Jamaica. He bowled steadfastly for Middlesex and then Hampshire for 15 years, and also for England in 19 Test matches. He swung the ball but did not have the searing pace or bite of some West Indian bowlers, generally speaking. In this Test match he was decidedly sharp and was helped by the uneven bounce. Cowans was not an extrovert but a seemingly shy and sensitive man who probably never had the confidence in his own ability to enable him to make the most of what he had. On this tour of Australia one felt that Willis did not have all that much confidence in him either, for he was seriously underbowled until this fourth Test. The ironical reason for this may have been that Willis himself had a badly upset tummy and was hardly fit to bowl. It was an occasion when everything came together for Cowans. He was a bowler who struggled to find and then keep his rhythm, but now suddenly it all worked for him. As a result, he bowled with greater self-belief than maybe ever before, which helped him to find another half a yard in pace; his control was unusually good too. Sadly, he was never able to do it again.

Australia were 218–9 and Jeff Thomson was the only remaining Australian batsman. Willis decided that the way to proceed was to get Allan Border off the strike at every possible opportunity and to attack Thomson, but it was a tactic which badly misfired. To the increasing delight of the crowd, Thomson began to play an innings that was as well conceived as it was put together and therefore completely unexpected. In order to keep Border on strike, these two refused no fewer than 29 singles, and while Border still managed now and then to find the way to the boundary, Thomson produced some inimitable off drives of his own, with his feet so far apart that he was almost doing the splits.

As captain, Willis lost control and England acquired at least three additional captains as Taylor, Gower and Botham all frantically waved their arms as they tried to rearrange the field. Meanwhile, the two batsmen were looking as secure as any in the match. It then seemed as if a heavy shower would end the day, but when the rain stopped, the players had to come back at twenty past six, twenty minutes after the normal finishing time, so that the last two overs of the day's ration could be bowled. It was a great moment for England to put both batsmen under as much pressure as they could, but, to Border's amazement and relief, Willis kept the same field and nine more comfortable runs were added.

When Jeff Thomson had first come out to join Allan Border, England must have thought it was all over, but Border, ever the gritty Australian, at times of crisis such as this looked to be made more of reinforced concrete than flesh and blood. He had not been in good form for some while and knowing this, Thomson, wanting to gee him up, said to him when he came in, 'Let's beat these fruits.' Border had been going through one of those spells which unaccountably seem to happen to just about every good batsman, with the exception of Don Bradman, in the history of the game. Border's last 15 innings for Australia had produced only 245 runs, and Ian Botham had done his bit to try and help him by giving him one of his spare bats, a decision he will now have been regretting as Border put it to such excellent use in this second innings.

One can only say that he was greatly helped in his task by Willis's captaincy. Knowing from experience that prolonged occupation of the crease by Thomson was unlikely, he had decided to place his fielders deep for Border in order to give him a single whenever he wanted, so that his bowlers would be able to spend more time attacking Thomson. It was a ploy which did not work, partly because of the quality of the bowling and partly because of the size of the ground. Border was still able to find the fence, because the MCG is so large that the fielders on the boundary were necessarily a long way apart, and to steer the ball into the gaps for comfortable twos.

Gradually, as the partnership built up, the crowd began to see what was happening and were greeting every run with wild cheering, while England's supporters watched in an almost morbid silence. At the end of the fourth day, Australia were 255–9, Border and Thomson having added 37, leaving them to score 37 more to win the match on the last day. England's mood of profound gloom will have been lifted a little by the thought that after six overs the next morning the new ball would be available.

Bob Willis may not have been the best captain England ever had, but no more determined cricketer will ever have played for his country. The England manager, Doug Insole, was not such a successful player as Willis, having played only nine Test matches, but when it came to determination and patriotism he was up there with the captain. It would be interesting to know if the two of them had a conversation that evening and, if so, how it went. Surely, they must have spoken and equally surely Insole must have tried to persuade Willis that there were other ways of trying to break this infuriating partnership. One of them might have been to put Border himself under a little bit more pressure, whether he was wielding Botham's bat or not. This will have been discussed extensively around the dinner tables that evening not only in Melbourne, but just about everywhere cricket was played. For four days, the excitement of this extraordinary Test match had gripped a world that stretched far beyond the boundaries of cricket itself.

With only one wicket to fall, the ground authorities at the MCG agreed to let the crowd come in for free the next morning. After all, it might be over in one ball. When the first over was bowled, more than 18,000 people were sitting in the stands. We saw at once that if Insole had tried to get into Willis's ear, he had not made much of a job of it. Intriguingly, Insole himself was a man who found it uncommonly difficult to change his mind. He will have met his match in Willis. Cowans bowled the first over, from the pavilion end, and, without the slightest difficulty, Thomson, surrounded by close fielders, played out a maiden. Border was then on strike and, apart from the wicketkeeper, there was not a fielder within earshot of the batsman.

The atmosphere was febrile. In the Outer, where most of the 18,000 were gathered, fervent and mainly good-natured patriotism reigned supreme. In the confines of the pavilion and in all the various cubby-holes occupied by the media, generous attempts were made to disguise passionate prejudice with open-handed generosity. 'No matter who wins, what a triumph for the game of cricket' was much bandied about, without anyone really believing a syllable of it. *Test Match Special* was perched in the open air on the top terrace of the pavilion. The perfectly reasonable line we adopted to try and hide any eagerness for England to win was that, with Australia two matches up in the series, victory for England would keep the series alive for the last match, in Sydney.

Border and Thomson needed to score 37 more runs, while England wanted just one more wicket. The new ball was imminent, and this surely would be the key to it. Or so England supporters hoped. Predictably, Willis bowled the first over from the southern end and he and Cowans kept going for the six overs before the new ball was due. Thomson was exemplary; he dug out yorkers and, apart from one flash outside the off stump at Cowans, did not take the semblance of a risk. Border even took a single off the first ball of Willis's second over and Thomson played out the remaining five as if he had been doing it all his life. Four runs had come before the new ball, which was taken by Cowans. He bowled to Thomson, who at once pushed for a single. Border hit a few quickly run twos and the crowd greeted each of them as if they were the stroke that had won the Ashes. There was one chance of running out Thomson, but Lamb and Gould knocked each other over and the crowd roared its approval.

The partnership had reached 50 in just over an hour and a half and Border's own fifty came after he had been in for three and a quarter hours, which shows one exactly the sort of innings it was. Five overs had been bowled with the new ball when Botham took over from Willis at the southern end. Drinks came next and by then 23 runs had been added and 14 more were needed. There was a fiendishly difficult chance to Tavaré in the slips off Botham, followed by a misfield, and nine was now the target. Thomson hit a three and the roof nearly came off, and then an edge for two brought the target down to four. The batting was convincing and the Ashes were as good as back in Australia's hands.

The MCG was bubbling over with excitement as Botham moved in to begin his fourth over with the new ball. His first ball, the 103rd of the morning, swung away from the right-hander and was short of a good length. Thomson could have safely left it alone, but he was drawn to it as if he wanted to run it to third man and he seemed to hesitate in mid-stroke as if he suddenly realised he should not be tempted. He got a thick-ish edge and the ball flew fast to Tavaré at second slip.

During the match on this slow pitch the ball had often dropped short of the slips. Before the start of the day, Willis had told the slips to come up closer to the bat, saying, 'We may drop the catch, but at least if we're a bit closer it will give us a chance.' Of course, the hardness of the new ball makes it travel that much faster. While Tavaré had moved forward, Miller, at first slip, had stayed where he was for the new ball, a yard behind Tavaré. The ball now flew from Thomson's bat at an eminently catchable height up by his left shoulder, burst through Tavaré's hands, having arrived rather more quickly than he expected, hit him on the left shoulder and bounced away. Miller saw the ball balloon behind Tavaré and, moving quickly across to his right, caught it with both hands at about knee height. He thought for a moment about throwing it aloft, but decided to hang on to a valuable trophy and ran flat-out into the pavilion. If he had also come up a yard and a half, he would never have been able to get round Tavaré.

Thomson just stood there in the crease, rather as Brett Lee did at Edgbaston all those years later, although he was at the non-striker's end. Thomson said a long time afterwards, 'I could not talk about it for years. It was one of the all-time low moments of my life.'

At the microphone, I almost burst a gasket I was so excited. From the very first ball it had been an incredible game of cricket. I am still not quite sure who deserved to win.

AUSTRALIA v ENGLAND (4th Test)

At MCG, Melbourne, on 26–30 December 1982.

England

G. Cook c Chappell b Thomson	10	c Yardley b Thomson	26
G. Fowler c Chappell b Hogg	4	b Hogg	65
C.J. Tavaré c Yardley b Thomson	89	b Hogg	0
D.I. Gower c Marsh b Hogg	18	c Marsh b Lawson	3
A.J. Lamb c Dyson b Yardley	83	c Marsh b Hogg	26
I.T. Botham c Wessels b Yardley	27	c Chappell b Thomson	46
G. Miller c Border b Yardley	10	lbw b Lawson	14
D.R. Pringle c Wessels b Hogg	9	c Marsh b Lawson	42
†R.W. Taylor c Marsh b Yardley	1	lbw b Thomson	37
*R.G.D. Willis not out	6	not out	8
N.G. Cowans c Lawson b Hogg	3	b Lawson	10
Extras (3 b, 6 lb, 12 nb, 3 w)	24	(2 b, 9 lb, 6 nb)	17
Total (all out, 81.3 overs)	**284**	(all out, 80.4 overs)	**294**

1–11 2–25 3–56 4–217 5–227 6–259 7–262
8–268 9–278 10–284

1–40 2–41 3–45 4–128 5–129
6–160 7–201 8–262 9–280 10–294

Bowling, *1st innings*: Lawson 17–6–48–0; Hogg 23.3–6–69–4; Yardley 27–9–89–4; Thomson 13–2–49–2; Chappell 1–0–5–0. *2nd innings*: Lawson 21.4–6–66–4; Hogg 22–5–64–3; Thomson 21–3–74–3; Yardley 15–2–67–0; Chappell 1–0–6–0.

Australia

K.C. Wessels b Willis	47	(2)	b Cowans	14
J. Dyson lbw b Cowans	21	(1)	c Tavaré b Botham	31
*G.S. Chappell c Lamb b Cowans	0		c sub (I.J. Gould) b Cowans	2
K.J. Hughes b Willis	66		c Taylor b Miller	48
A.R. Border b Botham	2	(6)	not out	62
D.W. Hookes c Taylor b Pringle	53	(5)	c Willis b Cowans	68
†R.W. Marsh b Willis	53		lbw b Cowans	13
B. Yardley b Miller	9		b Cowans	0
G.F. Lawson c Fowler b Miller	0		c Cowans b Pringle	7
R.M. Hogg not out	8		lbw b Cowans	4
J.R. Thomson b Miller	1		c Miller b Botham	21
Extras (8 lb, 19 nb)	27		(5 b, 9 lb, 3 nb, 1 w)	18
Total (all out, 79 overs)	**287**		(all out, 96.1 overs)	**288**

1–55 2–55 3–83 4–89 5–180 6–261 7–276
8–276 9–278 10–287

1–37 2–39 3–71 4–171 5–173
6–190 7–190 8–202 9–218 10–288

Bowling, *1st innings*: Willis 15–2–38–3; Botham 18–3–69–1; Cowans 16–0–69–2; Pringle 15–2–40–1; Miller 15–5–44–3. *2nd innings*: Willis 17–0–57–0; Cowans 26–6–77–6; Botham 25.1–4–80–2; Pringle 12–4–26–1; Miller 16–6–30–1.

Close of play, *day 1*: England (1) 284 all out; *day 2*: Australia (1) 287 all out; *day 3*: England (2) 294 all out; *day 4*: Australia (2) 255–9 (Border 44*, Thomson 8*).

Toss: Australia. Last-innings target: 292 runs.
Umpires: A.R. Crafter (Aus), R.V. Whitehead (Aus).
Man of the Match: N.G. Cowans.

ENGLAND won by three runs.

16
FEELING THE HEAT

India v Australia (1st Test)

18–22 September 1986; Chepauk Stadium, Chennai

Match tied.

THE second tied Test match was set up by an interesting, adventurous and old-fashioned declaration by Australia's captain, Allan Border, who might have been pushed into making it by the team coach, Bobby Simpson. Simpson himself had played for Australia in the only other tied Test match, against the West Indies in Brisbane in 1960–61. This game in Chennai, which had been little more than an inevitable runfest on the flattest of pitches, was brought to life on the fifth day when Border declared Australia's second innings at their overnight score of 170–5. This left India the whole day, which in the end amounted to 87 overs, to score 348 to win.

It was a Test match which contained much good cricket from the best players on both sides. There were also important contributions from one or two of the less well-known players. Dean Jones, fighting serious dehydration in the latter part of his innings of 210, Kapil Dev, Sunny Gavaskar and Border himself batted as only they can, but no one played a more important part in this game than Greg Matthews. He took 10–249 in the match with his tirelessly enthusiastic off-breaks, bowling 40 overs in succession on the last day in great heat. Not content with this, he was only out once in the match and made 71 invaluable runs. Matthews was a much underrated cricketer, even though he played in as many as 33 Test matches. This match in Chennai was probably the high moment of his career.

He was a fine all-round cricketer, as well as being an incorrigible and irrepressible character, which probably came to count against him, for he undoubtedly got on some people's nerves. While he may not have been the easiest of men to control, he was always anxious to be in the thick of it, but on his own terms. There cannot have been many more wholehearted players, for he gave everything to the cause all the time, but his way of going about it will not have suited everyone. Matthews lived in an alternative world and was uninhibited in everything he did. He was easy to spot in the field, for he always looked the odd man out and was never ready to conform if it did not suit him. In appearance, he was not so much scruffy as different. His shirt sleeves were rolled up in their own way and also had minds of their own; his shirt was tucked reluctantly into the waistband of his trousers. In the field there was an eager enthusiasm in everything he did, and with the bat in his hand he was always up for the fight and anxious to get on with it. He never took a prisoner at any time in his career – or in the commentary box, when it was over.

This was where I met him after he had retired and where he was as wonderfully alternative as he had been as a player. He was invariably lively and outspoken, with, at times, a highly unusual and irreverent way of looking at both the game and life. He took a delight in being different and knocking attitudes he considered to be old hat and absurd. He liked to shock. I do not remember him arriving anywhere except in a bit of a fluster and with a story to tell. You never knew what you were going to get from a face which portrayed a deceptive wide-eyed innocence. The game has always needed a few of these one-off characters; they keep everyone on their toes.

There was something about him that was both irritating and admirable, for he never shirked a challenge with either bat or ball.

In the end, his lively and obtrusive manner did not sit comfortably with the Australian side of the 1990s and he played his last Test in 1993, when he was 33 and still had plenty more in him. By then, he was not producing the figures to justify his disturbingly irrepressible nature and the game was the poorer without him. It was all well and good when his team-mates were happy with his *modus operandi*, but when it became too irritating, there was no place for him.

Ray Bright, the orthodox left-arm spinner, was his partner at Chennai, also taking five wickets in India's second innings, to add to the two he picked up in the first. In all, Bright played in 25 Tests and ironically is probably best remembered for his batting, at Headingley in 1981. He was the last man out when Australia, needing 130 to win, were bowled out for 111. When Bob Willis removed his middle stump England had won by 18 runs and the photograph of this dismissal achieved wallpaper status. Bright, a cheerful, avuncular-looking figure, was in and out of the Australian side between 1977 and this tour of India in 1986. Subcontinental pitches usually suit spin bowlers and Bright now took 7–182 to add to the 10–111 he had taken six years before against Pakistan in Karachi.

Australia won the toss in Chennai and after the pugnacious-looking David Boon, with his black moustache bristling, had got them off to a good start, the innings centred round Jones, whose 210 was the highest score made by an Australian in a Test match in India. This was only Jones's third Test match and he played an innings which showed off his class as a tall, upright, classical strokemaker. It also demonstrated a remarkable ability to concentrate in the high heat and, in the second half of his innings, extraordinary bravery which enabled him to continue when he became badly dehydrated. Jones the man was Jones the batsman. There was the same open, fair-haired cheerfulness in his batting as there was in the way he lived his life. He was always looking to get onto the front foot and now it was a joy to see him use his feet to the Indian spinners and also his willingness to hit the ball over the heads of the in-fielders. It was a dreadful irony that he should have died at the age of 59 while in India commentating for television on an Indian Premier League game in Mumbai in 2020.

Boon's 122 was his third Test hundred since being moved up the order to open the innings a year earlier. He was out just before the end of the first day, when he nibbled outside the off stump at Chetan Sharma and was caught in the slips and Australia were 211–2 at the close. Jones batted with Border for much of the second day while they put on 178 for the fourth wicket. Australia's main problem became Jones's health. He suffered progressively from leg cramps, repeated vomiting and pins and needles. Jones wanted to retire, but Border, himself made of near-granite, was reluctant to let him go. He psyched him into staying in the middle by telling him he was glad to have a tough Queenslander, in Greg Ritchie, coming in next. He ribbed Jones about being a weak Victorian, and Jones later admitted that it was only his captain's words which had kept him batting. When Jones was rushed to hospital immediately after he was out, having spent 502 minutes at the crease, Border thought, 'Oh my God, what have I done?' During his innings, Jones lost eight kilograms and it took him nine months to get his weight back.

Australia declared on the third morning at 574–7 and were soon among the Indian wickets after Kris Srikkanth had made a typically hectic fifty. Greg Matthews, bowling as usual in his cap, removed both openers: Sunil Gavaskar, who in this match became the first man to play in a hundred successive Test matches, and Srikkanth. Flighting the ball cleverly, he took four of the first six wickets. Most of the main batsmen made a good start, but only Kapil Dev went on to reach a hundred, in one of the most impressive innings he ever played for India.

Kapil Dev was one of the game's most magisterial figures and should surely have been the Maharajah of Something or Other. Whether bowling, batting, fielding or simply going for a walk, his was a commanding presence. Now, he stood at the crease for 214 minutes, in which he dismissed each of the Australian bowlers from his presence with strokes which had that inescapable ring of authority. Kapil was tall for an Indian and his black moustache – India's answer to Boon – seemed to add to this general stamp of authority. He played this unmistakable role in three Test matches in this series, even if his best efforts now were to save the follow-on, rather than to take his side to victory as in a fairer world they surely would have done. If one stroke could sum up this innings, it was the hook for four off Craig McDermott which took him to his hundred. You do not often see such an overwhelmingly decisive shot. But the nineties were never especially nervous for Kapil.

By the end of the fourth day, Australia had reached 170–5 in their second innings after almost three and three-quarter hours' batting. It came as a surprise when Border declared first thing the next morning, leaving India all day to score 348. Many captains would have given in to the temptation to bat on for a few more minutes to make sure India had no chance of victory. Border sometimes erred on the side of caution and the coach, Simpson, may, as I have already suggested, have had a hand in this. By giving India an outside chance of victory, it undoubtedly lured them to self-destruction. This has always been one of the main reasons for making a declaration, but the tendency nowadays in what has increasingly become a safety-first cricketing world is to make a game completely safe before declaring.

Whoever it was who inspired this decision to declare in Chennai should be congratulated, for it produced an extraordinary last day's play and a wonderful finish. The only downside to it was that the relations between the two sides had deteriorated as the match went on, and the high temperatures will not have helped, but it is interesting to compare this tied Test match with the one in 1960–61. The behaviour and the standard of sportsmanship in that match was exemplary. Different times, different customs. And two strong and independent captains, Richie

Benaud and Frank Worrell, who were not one-of-the-boys in the way captains were later to become.

Border's decision to declare caught the public in Chennai on the wrong foot. There was hardly anyone in the ground when play began on the last day. Not surprisingly, the prospect of watching the Australians having batting practice did not appeal. News of the declaration soon got round and almost immediately all the switches to television and radio sets, like all roads in Chennai, led to the Chepauk Stadium (as the M.A. Chidambaram Stadium is known).

India made a good start too. Gavaskar was in appropriate form for his hundredth consecutive Test. He was short in stature, being only five foot five inches tall, and it is no exaggeration to say that the Indian batting stood on his broad shoulders for the sixteen years of his Test career. Like a number of other small batsmen – Don Bradman, Neil Harvey and the two West Indians, Rohan Kanhai and Basil Butcher, are four others that come immediately to mind – he was a wonderful player of fast bowling. He was an outstanding strokemaker with an impeccable technique, limitless powers of concentration and a passionate dislike of being dismissed. To get rid of Gavaskar gave any of India's opponents a big psychological boost.

India went into lunch on the third day at 94 for the loss of Srikkanth who, as always, had got the innings off to a dramatic start. Gavaskar then put on 103 with Mohinder Amarnath, who was being barracked because the crowd felt he was going too slowly. Amarnath was second out at 158, caught close in on the leg side off Matthews. In contrast to Amarnath's rather laboured progress, Mohammad Azharuddin's mercurial and elegant wrists were soon pushing the score along. His partnership of 46 with Gavaskar produced some of the best batting of the day, to the delight of a crowd who were living every ball as they waved flags and yelled in encouragement and appreciation.

India had reached 193–2 at tea and needed 155 more from the last 30 overs. It was excitingly poised, with both sides still interested in victory, although with Gavaskar still there, India will at that point have felt they were in the better position. The situation then was later put into its true perspective by Ravi Shastri who said, 'Big chases are not really planned, they tend to happen as things progress.' Things progressed rapidly after the interval. Eleven more had been scored when Gavaskar came forward to drive Bright through the covers. He was beaten in the air, found himself reaching for the ball and Jones, who had recovered from the side effects of his long innings, held the catch in the covers. Just for a moment that formidable concentration had slipped and Gavaskar was furious with himself as he walked off. He was certain that if he had stayed in until the tea interval, India would have won, which was fair enough.

Bright was now bowling in tandem with Matthews, who had come on after eight overs and kept going with remarkable determination and control until the end of the innings. In spite of the heat and humidity, he wore his sleeveless sweater for much of the day. The spectators loved him, for when he was fielding on the boundary he engaged with them after almost every ball and they enjoyed the humour of his antics. He was full of little idiosyncrasies. When fielding, for example, he wore a white floppy sun hat, but when bowling he put on his Australian cap. It was never clear whether this was from superstition, a need to keep his hair out of his eyes, his love of wanting to be different, or for some other unfathomable reason. It was his way of doing it. The crowd, which in the afternoon had grown to capacity, was loving every moment and living it at the top of their voices.

It was now, at 204–3, that Azharuddin was joined by Chandra Pandit, the Bombay wicketkeeper. He was playing as a batsman because Dilip Vengsarkar had pulled a back muscle in the one-day international just before this match. In the end, Pandit had to keep wicket, for Kiran More went down with food poisoning on the first day of the match. While Pandit now played a lovely cameo of an innings, Azharuddin continued in his inimitable wristy way at the other end. Runs came fast and, with seven wickets in hand, India must have won if they had not let the situation get to them.

Whenever they seemed to be in complete control, a wicket would fall. Pandit's innings now was full of exciting improvisations, but at 251 Azharuddin departed. He came rushing down the wicket to Bright and was caught by Greg Ritchie at long on. A mental aberration perhaps, but if it had cleared Ritchie and gone for six, it would have been hailed as a wonderful stroke. All eyes were now on Kapil Dev as he strode confidently to the middle. He tucked his first ball away for a single and then faced Matthews. Perhaps he was too aware of what all India was expecting from him and felt he had to deliver at once, before he was ready. His second ball was not that short, he went to pull it and the ball looped off the top edge to Bright saving one behind square on the leg side.

Shastri, India's vice-captain, was next in and he waited until he knew which side of the sightscreen his captain would walk on his way back to the pavilion. He went out the other side because he was sure India could still win and did not want to be told by Kapil Dev that he should no longer go for the runs. Shastri took guard, shimmied two paces down the pitch to his first ball and drove Bright to the extra-cover boundary. Point made. Shastri played some wonderful strokes, driving Matthews for two huge sixes, and between balls he egged the crowd on to even greater and more noisy levels of excitement, using his bat as a conductor's baton, which will hardly have helped the Australian state of mind.

After putting on 38 with Shastri, whose 48 not out was perhaps the best, if not the largest, innings he ever played for India, Pandit stepped far away to leg against Matthews to give himself room to cut him into the unguarded off side, but succeeded only in playing the ball into his leg stump. Matthews had plenty to say to Pandit as he left the crease. In the closing stages the umpire, Dara Dotiwalla, had words with Border about the way Australia were trying to slow the game down as they wasted time after almost every ball, anxious to keep the number of overs to a minimum. Then, Chetan Sharma threatened Australian wicketkeeper Tim Zoehrer with his bat handle after what had presumably been a lively conversation. Tempers were becoming increasingly frayed.

While Shastri and Sharma were engaged in a stand of 40 in 40 minutes, Bright succumbed to the heat and almost collapsed leaving the field. After a few minutes in the dressing room, Bright asked Dave Gilbert, who was not playing in the match, to go out and ask Border if he needed him back on the field. Border said he wanted him at once and so back he came and in double-quick time proceeded to take three wickets, just when it seemed India must win.

With 30 balls left, 18 were needed with four wickets in hand. When umpire Vikramraju, standing in his second Test match, turned down an lbw appeal against Sharma, Matthews's body language had to be seen to be believed. In the 17th over of the last 20, Sharma charged down the pitch at Bright and was easily caught by Craig McDermott at long on. Shastri, who was now on strike, as the batsmen had crossed while the ball was in the air, played the next two balls into gaps for a two and a single. Kiran More then shuffled across his crease to his first ball and was lbw to Bright and India were 334–8 with 14 needed from three overs. Matthews bowled to Shivlal Yadav, floated one up and Yadav flailed wildly at it and, after hanging in the air for a long time, it finally went over long on for six. Four were wanted off nine balls when Yadav played a sweep at Bright and was bowled off his pad. Maninder Singh, a number eleven who more than justified his position, somehow defended Bright's last two balls.

Matthews bowled the last over, his 40th in succession. The fielders were spread far and wide in the hope that Shastri would take a single. He blocked the first ball. The second was pitched up and he aimed to play it to midwicket. It hit a thick inside edge and went out to deep square leg, where Steve Waugh did not pick it up cleanly and they were able to scamper back for a second, leaving Waugh to think he had cost Australia the match. Shastri played the third ball calmly to deep midwicket and they ran the single which levelled the scores. Shastri's thinking was that if he took the single, it was the last thing Border wanted him to do, for it meant that India could not lose. But Border was not in the least upset: 'I was very surprised and relieved that he gave us the opportunity to bowl at Maninder for those last few deliveries.'

Three balls were left. Shastri told his partner to take great care with the next two balls and, if necessary, to have a go at the last. Maninder dutifully blocked the fourth ball of the over, but was hit on the pad while trying to defend the next. There was a huge appeal and umpire Vikramraju's finger was up above his head almost before the appeal had begun. It was a tie. But Maninder had no doubt that he had got an inside edge on the ball and nor did Shastri. More significantly, Border, who was fielding at silly point, was also sure the ball had hit the inside edge of the bat. The umpire himself had no doubt it was out: 'The bat was not near the pad. And he was plumb in front of the wicket.' The Board of Control for Cricket in India (the BCCI) had the last word: Vikramraju never umpired another Test match.

INDIA v AUSTRALIA (1st Test)

At Chepauk Stadium, Chennai, on 18–22 September 1986.

Australia

D.C. Boon c Kapil Dev b Sharma	122	(2)	lbw b Maninder Singh		49
G.R. Marsh c Kapil Dev b Yadav	22	(1)	b Shastri		11
D.M. Jones b Yadav	210		c Azharuddin b Maninder Singh		24
R.J. Bright c Shastri b Yadav	30		did not bat		
*A.R. Border c Gavaskar b Shastri	106	(4)	b Maninder Singh		27
G.M. Ritchie run out	13	(5)	c Pandit b Shastri		28
G.R.J. Matthews c Pandit b Yadav	44	(6)	not out		27
S.R. Waugh not out	12	(7)	not out		2
†T.J. Zoehrer did not bat			did not bat		
C.J. McDermott did not bat			did not bat		
B.A. Reid did not bat			did not bat		
Extras (1 b, 7 lb, 6 nb, 1 w)	15		(1 lb, 1 nb)		2
Total (7 wkts, declared, 170.5 overs)	**574**		(5 wkts, declared, 49 overs)		**170**

1–48 2–206 3–282 4–460 5–481 6–544
7–574

1–31 2–81 3–94 4–125 5–165

Bowling, *1st innings*: Kapil Dev 18–5–52–0; Sharma 16–1–70–1;
Maninder Singh 39–8–135–0; Yadav 49.5–9–142–4; Shastri 47–8–161–1; Srikkanth 1–0–6–0.
2nd innings: Sharma 6–0–19–0; Kapil Dev 1–0–5–0; Shastri 14–2–50–2;
Maninder Singh 19–2–60–3; Yadav 9–0–35–0.

India

S.M. Gavaskar c and b Matthews	8	c Jones b Bright	90
K. Srikkanth c Ritchie b Matthews	53	c Waugh b Matthews	39
M. Amarnath run out	1	c Boon b Matthews	51
M. Azharuddin c and b Bright	50	c Ritchie b Bright	42
R.J. Shastri c Zoehrer b Matthews	62	b Matthews	39
C.S. Pandit c Waugh b Matthews	35	c Bright b Matthews	1
*Kapil Dev c Border b Matthews	119	not out	48
†K.S. More c Zoehrer b Waugh	4	c McDermott b Bright	23
C. Sharma c Zoehrer b Reid	30	lbw b Bright	0
N.S. Yadav c Border b Bright	19	b Bright	8
Maninder Singh not out	0	lbw b Matthews	0
Extras (1 b, 9 lb, 6 nb)	16	(1 b, 3 lb, 2 nb)	6
Total (all out, 94.2 overs)	**397**	(all out, 86.5 overs)	**347**

1–62 2–65 3–65 4–142 5–206 6–220 7–245
8–330 9–387 10–397

1–55 2–158 3–204 4–251 5–253
6–291 7–331 8–334 9–344 10–347

Bowling, *1st innings*: McDermott 14–2–59–0; Reid 18–4–93–1; Matthews 28.2–3–103–5;
Bright 23–3–88–2; Waugh 11–2–44–1. *2nd innings*: McDermott 5–0–27–0; Reid 10–2–48–0;
Matthews 39.5–7–146–5; Bright 25–3–94–5; Border 3–0–12–0; Waugh 4–1–16–0.

Close of play, *day 1*: Australia (1) 211–2 (Jones 56*, Bright 1*); *day 2*: Australia (1) 556–6
(Matthews 34*, Waugh 5*); *day 3*: India (1) 270–7 (Kapil Dev 33*, Sharma 14*);
day 4: Australia (2) 170–5 (Matthews 27*, Waugh 2*).

Toss: Australia. Last-innings target: 348 runs.
Umpires: D.N. Dotiwalla (Ind), V. Vikramraju (Ind).
Man of the Match: Kapil Dev, D.M. Jones.

MATCH TIED.

17
WELCOME TO
THE CARIBBEAN

West Indies v South Africa (One-off Test)
18–23 April 1992; Kensington Oval, Bridgetown
West Indies won by 52 runs.

SOUTH Africa was readmitted to the world of international cricket in 1991 when the country's hideous policy of apartheid was abolished. Their reintroduction came with an ODI series in India; their first Test match since 1970 was played a few months later, against the West Indies in Bridgetown, Barbados, which was both a condemnation of this dreadful system and a celebration that at last it had been consigned to history. Appropriately enough, it was a wonderful game of cricket which, against all odds, South Africa came close to winning, having outplayed their illustrious opponents for most of the match. Only at the very end were the West Indian fast bowlers able to exert their devastating influence when they took the last eight South African wickets for 25 runs before lunch on the fifth morning of the match.

It was sad that this game should have fallen victim to a parochial protest by the cricket-lovers of Barbados at the whims of the West Indies selectors. They allowed themselves to feel insulted by the omission of their own fast bowler, Anderson Cummins, from the West Indies side. As a result, they boycotted a wonderfully exciting game of cricket which said so much about a newer and fairer world. A total of only just over 6,000 spectators watched the five days' cricket and, of course, the atmosphere suffered. It was grossly unfair on the South Africans and an insult, too, to the West Indies side under their new captain, Richie Richardson. Maybe the empty seats had something to do with their disappointing performance for so much of the match.

It took place during the period I was lured away from *Test Match Special* for three years, which was the time it took for me to show those in charge of Sky Sports that I would never make a television commentator. I watched the match from the Sky commentary box and, in spite of the empty stands all round Kensington Oval, it was one of the most memorable games of cricket I have seen. It was made so by the cricket itself, inevitably intertwined with the political significance which formed such an important background to the match.

South Africa's first act caused no surprise. When they won the toss they asked the West Indies to bat, something visiting sides made a habit of doing at Kensington Oval, for fear of what the West Indies fast bowlers might get up to themselves. After Desmond Haynes and Phil Simmons had put on a seemingly effortless 99 as an opening stand, wickets began to fall to the South African seam attack. There were no spinners in the side; they had none good enough at this point, and also they will have felt that an extra batsman was another guard against the fast-bowling threat. Haynes, Richie Richardson and Keith Arthurton all made useful if largely unexciting contributions and South Africa's four bowlers did well to restrict them to 262. Richard Snell, with 4–83, was the best of them, while the reputation of Allan Donald, who took two wickets, had preceded him. He did not seem to be quite the eye-blinking fast bowler reports had promised, but maybe even he was going to take time to acclimatise himself to Test cricket. Nonetheless, they will have been happy that the West Indies score had been kept within bounds as it had.

Before this one-off Test match, they had already played three one-day internationals, one in Kingston and two in Port-of-Spain, and the West Indies had won all three. The crowds had been good and there had been no animosity towards the South African party who, in Omar Henry, included just one coloured player. It was only three weeks before the tour began that the South Africans had voted to end apartheid. The cricket everywhere had been hard-fought and played in a good atmosphere. While we were in Jamaica I had interviewed Michael Manley, their former Prime Minister, who was, of course, a fiercely outspoken critic of apartheid. He was cautiously optimistic about the new way of things. It was the first interview of this calibre that I had done and I do not think I got too many out of ten for it.

It felt strange, and nowhere more than in the commentary box, to be talking about such a significant game with no one in the ground. The players themselves will have understood the importance of the occasion more than anyone, but this complete lack of atmosphere must have made them feel it was all more than a little surreal. The few who came to the match and those watching on television will have been expecting the West Indies to win. But when South Africa's batsmen began to gain the upper hand, it was a situation which produced pressure, and the atmosphere which came with it helped all of us pick ourselves up and start giving the game all that it deserved.

The first day had been interesting and gripping in its way, although not especially glamorous, but thereafter it turned into a thrilling, red-blooded Test match. The unlikely central character as South Africa took control was the 27-year-old Andrew Hudson, who, like all except for Wessels, was playing in his first Test match. He was not a big man, but sturdy, with a deceptively boyish face, for he was brim-full of guts and determination as he fought on for more than eight and a half hours. At first sight, he did not look like someone who would be able to tame the considerable fast-bowling strength of the West Indies, who were not at their best until the last day of the match. Surprisingly, for South Africa have been playing Test cricket since 1889, until they were ostracised in 1970, Hudson became the first South African to score a hundred in his first Test match. Being the symbolic match that this was, played between two sides who, until apartheid was abolished, were a great deal more than the Atlantic Ocean apart, it somehow made it even more impressive.

For 519 minutes he not only withstood Curtly Ambrose, Courtney Walsh, Patrick Patterson and Kenny Benjamin, also playing in his first Test match, but he hit 20 fours, mostly with delightful off drives, on his way to 163. It was an innings which will be remembered more for its concentration and its cumulative effect than for its elegance or the power and versatility of the strokeplay. Having said all that, this was still a truly heroic innings, and if it had not been for Hudson, South Africa would have been easily beaten, surely within four days. He defended meticulously and played some good strokes on both sides of the pitch in addition to that off drive.

In the final analysis, the West Indies had only themselves to blame, because they dropped him at long leg when he was 22 and behind the wicket when he was 66, but his determination never faltered and he did not allow the clatter of wickets at the other end to upset his equilibrium. He found a good partner in his captain, the peripatetic Kepler Wessels, whom we have seen earlier in these pages, carving away outside the off stump ten years before this in Melbourne for Australia against Bob Willis's England side. He was never an object of great beauty when batting, but he was effective and difficult to dismiss. He now helped Hudson put on 125 in almost two and a half hours before getting an edge to Ambrose. South Africa were 139–2 and were then steered almost single-handedly by Hudson to a first-innings lead of 83, which did not prove to be quite enough.

The only other batsman to give him worthwhile support for any length of time was Adrian Kuiper, playing his only Test match. He came in at 187–4 and, making 34 in three and a quarter hours, which gives some idea of what a hard-fought battle it was, helped Hudson add 92 for the fifth wicket. The most surprising thing about the South African innings now was that it was brought to an end by the left-arm spin of Jimmy Adams. Adams, another newcomer to Test cricket, tended to push the ball through and he caused problems with his variations of flight and pace and was a better bowler than he may have looked. He took 4–43 in 21.5 tight overs, including the last three for only five runs. Hudson's innings ended when he was bowled through an understandably tired-looking defensive push. In the end, the West Indies will have been happy their deficit was only 83, but they soon lost their way again in their second innings.

It must have been strange to play in such an exciting Test match in front of empty stands, just as it was to describe it in the commentary box. Richard Snell, again the fourth South African bowler to be used, caused difficulty early on. He was not quite top pace, in spite of a long, straight run, but his control was excellent and he found just a little movement off the pitch. He sent back Desmond Haynes, caught behind, and Richie Richardson, leg before, both of whom were dismissed by Snell for the second time in the match, and the West Indies found themselves at 68–3. Brian Lara went on to reach his first fifty in a Test match, although he should have been out when he trod on his off stump against Tertius Bosch. Amazingly, neither umpire saw it happen and he was allowed to stay. This was the only moment in the match when the two sides had words, and of course DRS was not even a figment of anyone's imagination.

Lara and Keith Arthurton put on 52 before they both fell to Allan Donald. The rest of the innings revolved round some fine batting by the impressive Adams, whose 79 not out took 221 minutes with 11 good fours. He sheltered behind a compact left-hander's defence while never wasting the chance to score runs. Even so, wickets kept falling at the other end and when Walsh was ninth out at 221, the West Indies lead was only 138. Adams was now joined by fellow Jamaican Patrick Patterson, who was repeatedly beaten by all the bowlers but somehow managed to preserve his wicket while they put on the 62 runs for the last wicket which ultimately took the West Indies to victory and saved their 57-year unbeaten record at Kensington Oval. This was their eleventh victory there in succession. The reluctance of the South African captain, Wessels, a somewhat inflexible thinker, to put a man out on the backward-point boundary to block Adams's square cut cost South Africa many runs and possibly the match. When Patterson was eventually bowled by Bosch, the West Indies had reached 283 and South Africa needed 201 to win.

It was an important psychological moment when the West Indies lead reached 200. This was soon underlined when Hudson, the hero of the first innings, was caught by Lara close to the wicket off Ambrose from the second ball of the innings. The score became 27–2 when Ambrose also bowled the other opener, Mark Rushmere, and Wessels was joined by Peter Kirsten, at 36, the second oldest South African to play his first Test match – the 40-year-old fast-medium bowler Geoff Chubb being the oldest, against England in 1951 at Trent Bridge. Wessels and Kirsten, both batting in their usual rather idiosyncratic ways, had put on 95 in 40 overs by the end of the fourth day, leaving South Africa well placed at 122–2, needing only 79 more.

Who knows what went on that evening in terms of team talks and general West Indian motivation, but the next morning it was a different West Indies side which took the field. It was as if they had suddenly realised they were in great danger of losing a Test match on a ground which was redolent of West Indian cricket, perhaps more than any other. It had been the scene of so many of their famous victories, and also it was a ground which had produced a considerable number of the great West Indies players. The present team were playing for the past as well as the present.

Now, on a dramatic last morning, it was another Jamaican, Courtney Walsh, who set the scene. It was somehow difficult to communicate the full excitement of a game which was so intriguingly poised, even if the match seemed to be leaning towards the visitors when play began. Only about 6,000 spectators attended for the full five days and on this final day there were five hundred in the ground at the most. Whenever a South African wicket fell, the expected roar of the crowd turned out to be little more than a few happy rattles from one or two remote vantage points where there was a small knot of spectators.

It was most noticeable that the island's favourite cricketing character, King Dyal, who normally came religiously to his seat in the front row of the Kensington Stand, had stood by the protesters and had not watched the match. His brightly coloured shark-skin suits, his pith helmet, white gloves and white clay pipe were much missed. At the end, he graced the occasion by parading up and down the road behind the pavilion in a gleaming yellow suit with his pipe at the ready in his hand as he spoke to his friends, happy that his men had maintained their unbeaten record at Kensington Oval, if still saddened by the omission of Anderson Cummins.

Only one more run had been scored when Brian Lara caught Wessels, and this was the wicket the West Indies needed the most. If they had failed to get Wessels, they would almost certainly have lost the match. After his dismissal, it all happened at great speed. Hansie Cronje, a bag of nerves, had made two when he got a thin edge to Ambrose and one run later Kuiper was also caught behind, off Walsh. A wicket seemed likely to fall almost every ball. South Africa edged their way to 142, when Kirsten, who had just reached fifty, was bowled by Walsh after batting for 223 minutes and South Africa were 142–6. Although they only needed 59 more, it was clear they would now need a miracle to get them.

The West Indies had recently seen some of their greatest players come to the end of their careers. Viv Richards, Gordon Greenidge and Malcolm Marshall were three pretty decent ones to be going on with. The present side may not have been quite as distinguished, but when the force was willing, there was no stopping them. After Snell had been caught in the gully off Walsh,

Ambrose went like a hurricane through the last three: Meyrick Pringle's stumps went all over the place, David Richardson was caught behind, the next ball bowled Donald and South Africa were all out for 148.

The West Indies had saved their unbeaten record at Kensington Oval and in the end it had not been that close either. Ambrose, tall, determined, unsmiling and frightening, strode triumphantly off with 6–34 under his belt and a gleam in his eye, while Walsh, almost as tall, ferocious with a ball in his hand, genial and smiling without it, with an eventual tally of 519 Test wickets, came more easily behind him. On this last day it was Walsh who had shown the way, taking 4–31 and destroying South Africa's all-important middle order.

South Africa had done wonderfully well in their first Test match since 1970, but in the end they had been unable to get across the line, and as the next 30 years went by this was to become a recurring problem with their cricket. But what a return it had been, even if they had choked at the end.

WEST INDIES v SOUTH AFRICA (Only Test)
At Kensington Oval, Bridgetown, Barbados, on 18–23 April 1992.
West Indies

D.L. Haynes c Wessels b Snell	58	c Richardson b Snell	23
P.V. Simmons c Kirsten b Snell	35	c Kirsten b Bosch	3
B.C. Lara c Richardson b Bosch	17	c Richardson b Donald	64
*R.B. Richardson c Richardson b Snell	44	lbw b Snell	2
K.L.T. Arthurton c Kuiper b Pringle	59	b Donald	22
J.C. Adams b Donald	11	not out	79
†D. Williams c Hudson b Donald	1	lbw b Snell	5
C.E.L. Ambrose not out	6	c Richardson b Donald	6
K.C.G. Benjamin b Snell	1	lbw b Donald	7
C.A. Walsh b Pringle	6	c Richardson b Snell	13
B.P. Patterson run out	0	b Bosch	11
Extras (7 lb, 17 nb)	24	(17 b, 11 lb, 20 nb)	48
Total (all out, 71.4 overs)	**262**	(all out, 81.3 overs)	**283**

1–99 2–106 3–137 4–219 5–240 6–241
7–250 8–255 9–262 10–262

1–10 2–66 3–68 4–120 5–139
6–164 7–174 8–196 9–221 10–283

Bowling, *1st innings*: Donald 20–1–67–2; Bosch 15–2–43–1; Pringle 18.4–2–62–2;
Snell 18–3–83–4. *2nd innings*: Donald 25–3–77–4; Bosch 24.3–7–61–2; Snell 16–1–74–4;
Pringle 16–0–43–0.

South Africa

M.W. Rushmere c Lara b Ambrose	3	(2)	b Ambrose	3	
A.C. Hudson b Benjamin	163	(1)	c Lara b Ambrose	0	
*K.C. Wessels c Adams b Ambrose	59		c Lara b Walsh	74	
P.N. Kirsten c Lara b Benjamin	11		b Walsh	52	
W.J. Cronje c Lara b Adams	5		c Williams b Ambrose	2	
A.P. Kuiper c Williams b Patterson	34		c Williams b Walsh	0	
†D.J. Richardson c Ambrose b Adams	8		c Williams b Ambrose	2	
R.P. Snell run out	6		c Adams b Walsh	0	
M.W. Pringle c Walsh b Adams	15		b Ambrose	4	
A.A. Donald st Williams b Adams	0	(11)	b Ambrose	0	
T. Bosch not out	5	(10)	not out	0	
Extras (4 b, 6 lb, 25 nb, 1 w)	36		(4 b, 3 lb, 4 nb)	11	
Total (all out, 135.5 overs)	**345**		(all out, 72.4 overs)	**148**	

1–14 2–139 3–168 4–187 5–279 6–293
7–312 8–316 9–336 10–345

1–0 2–27 3–123 4–130 5–131
6–142 7–142 8–147 9–148 10–148

Bowling, *1st innings*: Ambrose 36–19–47–2; Patterson 23–4–79–1; Walsh 27–7–71–0;
Benjamin 25–3–87–2; Arthurton 3–0–8–0; Adams 21.5–5–43–4.
2nd innings: Ambrose 24.4–7–34–6; Patterson 7–1–26–0; Benjamin 9–2–21–0;
Walsh 22–10–31–4; Adams 5–0–16–0; Simmons 5–1–13–0.

Close of play, *day 1*: South Africa (1) 13–0 (Rushmere 2*, Hudson 9*); *day 2*: South Africa (1)
254–4 (Hudson 135*, Kuiper 19*); *day 3*: West Indies (2) 184–7 (Adams 23*, Benjamin 6*);
day 4: South Africa (2) 122–2 (Wessels 74*, Kirsten 36*).

Toss: South Africa. Last-innings target: 201 runs.
Umpires: D.M. Archer (WI), S.A. Bucknor (WI).
Man of the Match: C.E.L. Ambrose, A.C. Hudson.

WEST INDIES won by 52 runs.

18

A GLORIOUS EXCEPTION

Australia v South Africa (2nd Test)
2–6 January 1994; Sydney Cricket Ground
South Africa won by five runs.

SINCE South Africa's return to international cricket in November 1991, their main problem had been their inability to win matches in a tight finish. This failing had cost them dear in both Test match and one-day cricket. One glorious exception came at the Sydney Cricket Ground in January 1994 when Allan Border's Australian side failed to score 117 in the fourth innings. Thanks to Shane Warne's genius, it had looked as if Australia would be comfortable winners. The game was then given its final, exciting twist by an inspirational spell of fast bowling by Fanie de Villiers late on the fourth day. He carried on the next morning, when he was superbly backed up by no less an exponent of the art than Allan Donald.

De Villiers's bursting enthusiasm as he sprinted in to bowl was a joy, as was his fresh-faced happiness when he took a wicket. At the time, he gave the impression that it had all come as rather an unexpected surprise, and this was also his first haul of five Test wickets in an innings, in only his second Test match. His appearance when bowling was in marked contrast to his senior partner's. Allan Donald was always such an alarming prospect that he will have helped De Villiers, in that batsmen will have been so grateful no longer to be facing Donald and have lost concentration.

Donald is aggressively fair-haired and his appearance when bowling always reminded me of one of those blond Russians employed by the KGB to exterminate James Bond. He was ruthless, resolute and unrepentant. His arguments in the middle with Michael Atherton at the Wanderers in Johannesburg in 1995, and again at Trent Bridge in 1998, illustrate my point, although on both occasions it was Atherton who won the battle. Donald bowled fast, argued hard and took no prisoners.

The SCG is one of the game's principal holy temples. As with most grounds, the need to increase the capacity for spectators and the importance of generating more money has caused much rebuilding to be carried out. For all that, those in charge have done well to prevent it becoming another anonymous concreted stadium. Although the famous Hill has been submerged by the Doug Walters Stand, the massive old scoreboard at the back of the Hill, which has become a listed building, has been preserved, although it is now hidden behind the new Walters Stand. At the other end, the lovely old pavilion with its green corrugated roofing has been left as it was. Next to it, built only in 1980 but in the same style as the pavilion with its sloping, corrugated roof, is the Brewongle Stand, which was once the old Ladies Stand. 'Brewongle' is the Aboriginal word for a camping place. Sadly, the Paddington Hill has gone, but the ground still retains much of its old atmosphere and it is in all ways still very much a cricket ground, while a number of others have become gigantic featureless sports stadiums.

This second Test match was only the second played between the two countries after South Africa's readmission to Test cricket. It was one of those games which was always interesting, but without any great excitement until Australia set out to make the 117 they needed towards the end of the fourth day. Up until then, the genius of Shane Warne had held centre stage for three days. In South Africa's first innings he had taken 7–56, which he followed up with 5–72 in the second – amazing figures, but run-of-the-mill stuff for him.

Warne, an outrageously extrovert character who, for me, pips Sydney Barnes for the accolade of the greatest bowler of all time, is truly incomparable. He transformed the art of leg-spin bowling and although he had a supremely happy-go-lucky lifestyle, he left nothing to chance when it came to his bowling. He worked relentlessly at his game to perfect the most difficult art of all: wrist-spin. Wrist-spinners have, by their very nature, often been a bit of a luxury. Traditionally, even the best have their bad days when they can be horribly expensive, as well as others when the ball comes out of their hand as they want it to. Warne polished his art to the extent that he continually returned figures which would have been a credit to a finger-spinner, whose job it often is to bowl long and economical spells. Warne was not only the best of attacking bowlers; he also performed this economy role more efficiently than many good finger-spinners were able to do. So Warne effectively fulfilled two functions for his captain. If he could not get the batsman out, he was able to prevent him from scoring runs. Added to that, he was far from being a mug with the bat, without quite being a genuine all-rounder. He was a great deal more than just a useful chap to have in your side.

In this match, while taking 12–128, he also bowled 25 maiden overs. To be able to put so much spin on the ball and, indeed, to have four or even five different deliveries up your sleeve, all of which are so well controlled, argues for the importance of the constant, dedicated, relentless practice which seems to go against the other side of Warne's disparate and intriguing character. Fair-haired, thickset, eternally cheerful, with a keen eye for beauty – and for controversy too – the latter two often combining, he was up to and up for anything and for as much of it as possible. Cricket was only one of the reasons he continually hit the headlines. The game would have been infinitely the poorer if he had never existed.

In South Africa's first innings only Gary Kirsten (67) and Hansie Cronje (41) reached double figures. The rest had no answer to Warne. Their batsmen had not seen him before and as there was a shortage of good leg-spinners in South African domestic cricket, they had little idea how to cope with his bowling. South Africa's strength was the fast bowling of De Villiers and Donald, who took four wickets each in Australia's first innings. Only Michael Slater, Allan Border and Damien Martyn held them up for long in what was becoming a low-scoring match and a lead of 123 was likely to be enough. This was underlined even more when, in their second innings, South Africa managed to make only 239, with Jonty Rhodes, in his usual cheeky way, the only batsman to go past 50. A target of 117 in the final innings looked little more than a formality, but it was now that the game dramatically changed course and became unbelievably exciting.

Michael Slater, who could be such a punishing player, was the first to go, in De Villiers's second over. He received a beauty which, bowled from wide on the crease, pitched on the middle stump and did enough off the pitch to go past the outside edge of the bat and hit the off stump. Mark Taylor and David Boon put on 47 runs, with both of them looking as if they might be out at any moment, but at 51–1, Australia were well placed. Boon then played De Villiers firmly away off his pads and Kirsten held a good catch just in front of square at short leg. Kirsten was standing deeper than most short legs, waiting to catch the ball off the face of the bat, as he did now, rather than coming in closer for the catch that bubbles up off bat and pad. Boon's place was taken by the nightwatchman, Tim May, who played half forward to the next ball, which hit him underneath the knee roll of the front pad and had him lbw. Five runs later, Taylor pushed forward to a perfect leg-cutter to the left-hander and wicketkeeper Dave Richardson held a good low catch wide to his left. Australia were 63–4 at the close of play with a fight on their hands, but one which they would still have expected to win, needing only 54 more with six wickets in hand.

In the first over the next morning, Allan Border's judgement let him down, a rare event. He shouldered arms to a ball from Donald which pitched outside the off stump, came in to the left-hander just a fraction and hit the top of the off stump. This, above all, was the wicket South Africa wanted, for while Border was there the game was never over. Nine runs later, Donald did it again when he produced a yorker which dipped in to Mark Waugh. The ball hit him on the boot and he was plumb lbw, which left Australia reeling at 72–6. One run later, Ian Healy played hurriedly forward to De Villiers with his bat away from his pad and the ball flicked the inside edge before crashing into his off stump. Only two more runs had been scored when, with Warne as his partner, Damien Martyn drove between mid off and extra cover. They ran the first quickly and Warne called Martyn back for the second and was thrown out by a direct hit from Hansie Cronje, acting as the South African captain as Kepler Wessels had had to go off after hurting his hand in the field.

Australia were now 75–8 and surely beaten, but Craig McDermott had other ideas and played some splendid strokes against both De Villiers and Donald. He drove powerfully and hit the ball hard off his legs and suddenly made batting look easier. He hit four spanking fours and he and Martyn, to the great delight of the crowd, put on 35, taking Australia to 110–8, when they needed only seven more. Up until then, Martyn had been happy to defend and give McDermott the strike when he could, but now he tried to join in – and with disastrous results. He drove Donald on the up hard into the covers, where Andrew Hudson held a good catch at shoulder height to his left. Glenn McGrath took his place and managed to score a single before pushing a simple return catch back to De Villiers, who finished with 6–43 in 23.3 overs. In a thrilling finish, South Africa had won by five runs, the fourth-closest margin of defeat in all Test matches until then.

AUSTRALIA v SOUTH AFRICA (2nd Test)
At SCG, Sydney, on 2–6 January 1994.
South Africa

A.C. Hudson lbw b McGrath	0	c Healy b McDermott 1
G. Kirsten st Healy b Warne	67	b McDermott 41
W.J. Cronje c Waugh b McDermott	41	b McDermott 38
D.J. Cullinan b Warne	9	(5) lbw b Warne 2
J.N. Rhodes lbw b Warne	4	(6) not out 76
*K.C. Wessels c and b Warne	3	(4) b Warne 18
†D.J. Richardson c Taylor b Warne	4	lbw b McGrath 24
P.L. Symcox b Warne	7	c Healy b McDermott 4
C.R. Matthews c Taylor b Warne	0	c Waugh b Warne 4
P.S. de Villiers c Waugh b McDermott	18	lbw b Warne 2
A.A. Donald not out	0	c Healy b Warne 10
Extras (1 b, 4 lb, 11 nb)	16	(13 b, 1 lb, 5 nb) 19

Total (all out, 74.1 overs) **169**
1–1 2–91 3–110 4–133 5–134 6–141 7–142
8–142 9–152 10–169

(all out, 109 overs) **239**
1–2 2–75 3–101 4–107 5–110
6–182 7–188 8–197 9–203 10–239

Bowling, *1st innings*: McDermott 18.1–2–42–2; McGrath 19–5–32–1; Warne 27–8–56–7;
May 10–1–34–0. *2nd innings*: McDermott 28–9–62–4; McGrath 14–3–30–1; May 22–4–53–0;
Warne 42–17–72–5; Border 3–1–8–0.

Australia

M.J. Slater b Donald	92	(2) b de Villiers 1
M.A. Taylor c Richardson b Donald	7	(1) c Richardson b de Villiers 27
D.C. Boon b de Villiers	19	c Kirsten b de Villiers 24
M.E. Waugh lbw b Symcox	7	(5) lbw b Donald 11
*A.R. Border c Richardson b de Villiers	49	(6) b Donald 7
D.R. Martyn c Richardson b de Villiers	59	(7) c Hudson b Donald 6
†I.A. Healy c Richardson b Donald	19	(8) b de Villiers 1
S.K. Warne c Rhodes b Symcox	11	(9) run out 1
C.J. McDermott c Cronje b de Villiers	6	(10) not out 29
T.B.A. May not out	8	(4) lbw b de Villiers 0
G.D. McGrath b Donald	9	c and b de Villiers 1
Extras (1 b, 2 lb, 3 nb)	6	(3 lb) 3

Total (all out, 141.2 overs) **292**
1–10 2–58 3–75 4–179 5–179 6–229 7–250
8–266 9–281 10–292

(all out, 56.3 overs) **111**
1–4 2–51 3–51 4–56 5–63 6–72
7–73 8–75 9–110 10–111

Bowling, *1st innings*: Donald 31.2–8–83–4; de Villiers 36–12–80–4; Matthews 28–11–44–0;
Symcox 46–11–82–2. *2nd innings*: Donald 17–5–34–3; de Villiers 23.3–8–43–6; Matthews
6–5–9–0; Symcox 10–3–22–0.

Close of play, *day 1*: Australia (1) 20–1 (Slater 5*, Boon 7*); *day 2*: Australia (1) 200–5 (Martyn
15*, Healy 6*); *day 3*: South Africa (2) 94–2 (Cronje 37*, Wessels 7*); *day 4*: Australia (2) 63–4
(Waugh 4*, Border 7*).

Toss: South Africa. Last-innings target: 117 runs.
Umpires: S.G. Randell (Aus), W.P. Sheahan (Aus).
Man of the Match: P.S. de Villiers.

SOUTH AFRICA won by five runs.

19

IN THE SHADE OF THE MAHOGANY TREES

Zimbabwe v England (1st Test)

18–22 December 1996; Queens Club, Bulawayo

Match drawn with the scores level.

THE first Test match England played against Zimbabwe, and the first they had played on Zimbabwean/Rhodesian soil, became the first Test to end as a draw with the scores of the two sides level. Sadly, it was not the happiest of tours, although this had nothing directly to do with the machinations of Robert Mugabe and his political machine. Indeed, Mugabe himself even turned up to watch some play and have lunch in the committee room on the third day of the second Test in Harare, although he freely admitted that cricket was not his favourite game.

England had been the only Full Member country of the ICC to vote against giving Zimbabwe full Test match status in 1992. This must, at least in part, explain why more than four years went by before England were prepared to play a Test match against them. This reluctance will inevitably have caused some bad feeling. It is no secret that the main reason for Zimbabwe's elevation was the urgent need to encourage the future of the game in the country. After independence, cricket can only have been looked upon by those now in charge of Zimbabwe as a colonial legacy which was not to be encouraged. It was still principally a game for the white population, although there was a large untapped reservoir of talent in the coloured communities which was just beginning to be allowed to come through.

Those who ran cricket in Zimbabwe were doing everything they could to make the game available to everyone. Although it was naturally perceived as a white man's sport, it was catching on too, albeit slowly, and Henry Olonga, a fine fast bowler, was, by right, already in the Zimbabwe side. The government in Zimbabwe was tolerating rather than embracing cricket. The main reason for English cricket's refusal to back Zimbabwe's elevation was a reluctance to see the standard of Test cricket diluted by a side which was not good enough for the game at this level. It was important to try and maintain the standard of Test cricket, but, in the circumstances, it was not unreasonable that Zimbabwe called for special treatment. The irony may have been that this refusal by the English authorities will have made Mugabe feel instinctively that if he was more sympathetic to the needs of cricket in his country, it would be one in the eye for the country at the top of his hate list.

All these things and more will have been going on in some people's minds as the two countries began their first ever Test series, in Bulawayo. Another irony was that the atmosphere that first morning at the Queens Club was more friendly, matter-of-fact and relaxed than I have ever come across anywhere in the world on the first morning of a Test series. It was more like the beginning of a club game than a Test match. Spectators turned up with picnic baskets and strolled about as they wanted. The stewards did not get in their way. The players ambled off to the nets, the ground staff got on with their jobs and no one seemed too worried about anything. The only thing which may have shown that this was a highly significant moment was the presence of a formidable array of journalists in the press tent keeping an eye out for trouble, cricketing or otherwise.

This visit to Zimbabwe was the first part of a tour which moved on to New Zealand. It had been decided that even though Christmas and the New Year were looming in the Zimbabwean leg, wives, girlfriends and children were not welcome on the tour. Even if the players bit their tongues over this, those left at home were likely to have been more outspoken, which will not have helped the peace of mind of the players.

The tour began with a couple of warm-up one-day games and there was also a four-day game in Harare against Mashonaland, whose team included most of the Zimbabwean side, and Mashonaland won by seven wickets. Matabeleland were then beaten in a four-day game at the Bulawayo Athletic Club. This was followed by an exciting one-day international at the Queens Club, which Zimbabwe won by two wickets.

I must now declare my hand. I had been asked by the BBC to commentate on the two Test matches in Zimbabwe and I flew out so that I arrived a few days before the Test series began. I had not been to Zimbabwe before and there is always an extra *frisson* of excitement on one's first visit anywhere. The country had been under the rule of Robert Mugabe for nine years and there had understandably been a great many changes to the old way of life. I spent a night in Harare at the Holiday Inn, where I joined up with Simon Mann, also part of the commentary team and on his first overseas tour.

The next day we drove for well over five hours to Bulawayo and lost our way more than once. We were all staying – the players on both sides too – at another Holiday Inn and, as far as I was concerned, it got off to a particularly bad start. The ruling political party had been holding its annual conference in Bulawayo. The hotel was brim-full of delegates and although the conference had ended that day, they were reluctant to move out. The wait in the hall with my luggage was interminable, and was all I needed after a long aeroplane journey and a distinctly hazardous drive. It got to the point where the receptionists were ringing round to see if they could find another hotel for us. It was then that some of the politicians returned and decided that they would move on after all and we were saved.

The next blow came when Peter Baxter, our intrepid producer, arrived and gleefully asked me if I would care for a glass of Bollinger. Words have not often failed me, but they did now because there was nothing in the world I would have liked more and nothing could have been more unexpected. With a mischievous grin on his face, he produced from behind his back a bottle of the local Zimbabwean beer, called Bohlinger, which at the time seemed a joke in the worst possible taste. Nonetheless, once I had got over the initial shock, I found that first half pint a considerable step in the right direction. In fact, by the time I had finished it, my tongue was almost hanging out for more.

The Queens Club would never have been mistaken for the Melbourne Cricket Ground, but it was charming in its delightfully countrified way. There were lots of grassy banks, a few temporary stands held in place by scaffolding and a low, rambling clubhouse and pavilion in one corner. There was, too, a wonderful display of Natal mahogany trees stretching out on either side of the sightscreen at the far end. These evergreens provided welcome shade for spectators.

Our *Test Match Special* team consisted of Simon Mann, Peter Baxter and me as commentators, Trevor Bailey and Christopher Cowdrey as summarisers and Jo King as our patient and long-suffering scorer. Jonathan Agnew, the BBC cricket correspondent, had the Zimbabwe leg of the tour off, but would join the party later on in New Zealand. Our commentary box was in an open tent at long on at the pavilion end of the ground. It also turned out to be the ground's most popular meeting point, which became something of a problem. The trouble was that people always met their friends in front of the tent rather than behind it, which made it difficult for us to see the cricket. Then, after much negotiation, we were loaned a solitary steward. With people coming from both sides, he did not know where to stand and in the end took up his position in the middle, just in front of the commentator – which was no help either, until we managed to secure a second steward so one could stand on each side of our tent.

By the time the match began, our electronics were working reasonably well, in spite of its Heath Robinson appearance, although inevitably there were times when all contact with the outside world was lost. There is a certain pioneering spirit of adventure in broadcasting from grounds such as this and, at times, it can be extremely funny. I have to say that on this occasion these moments of high humour were not fully appreciated by our splendid producer. He had a tricky time coping with the sundry naked and unidentified wires which kept making sudden appearances. He was not helped either by the local telecom chaps who, in spite of their unquenchable enthusiasm, had about as much idea of how it all worked as the rest of us.

Everything about this groundbreaking game seemed to be in the lowest possible key. It was a wonderfully peaceful atmosphere, which was raucously disturbed for much of the match by the presence of the Barmy Army. It was the first time I had knowingly come across them and from under the mahogany trees at the far end from us, their monotonous and endless chanting of 'Barmy Army, Barmy Army, Barmy Army' was anything but melodic and became gratingly intrusive. Of course, we all learned to live with it and the Barmy Army was soon to become an integral and jolly part of England's cricket. Any initial irritation on the part of home spectators in other countries – the Barmy Army was at their best and noisiest abroad – was soon dissolved by both their friendliness and their not inconsiderable spending power, which will have done no harm whatever to the local economy. They were in good voice throughout this match, but on the dramatically exciting last day they excelled themselves.

A Test match which by the time it finished had become statistically unique began with Zimbabwe winning the toss and deciding to bat on the flattest of pitches. As often happens with matches with dramatic climaxes, the early exchanges between the two sides gave little hint of what was to come. It began with an old-fashioned day's Test cricket and at the end of it Zimbabwe had reached 256–6. Two newcomers to Test cricket were soon in the thick of it. Zimbabwe's future coach-cum-manager Andy Waller, a middle-order batsman who had played in many one-day internationals, was a 37-year-old farmer and had been chosen for his first Test match. He made only 15 in the first innings but an important 50 in the second innings on the last day, while England's debutant, Chris Silverwood, who subsequently became England's coach, took his first wicket when he had Grant Flower caught at slip. Zimbabwe's captain, Alistair Campbell, made 84 and Andy Flower had reached a good half-century before the close, with Robert Croft picking up three wickets with his off-spin. Flower reached his hundred the next morning, while Paul Strang helped him in an important seventh-wicket partnership of 79.

Zimbabwe were all out for 376 before hundreds by Nasser Hussain, who was dropped at short leg off his first ball, and John Crawley took England to 406 and a lead of 30. Paul Strang's tossed-up leg-breaks brought him 5–123. The most exciting moment of the innings came early on the fourth day. Hussain hooked Heath Streak and it looked to be going for six. Bryan Strang, on the backward-square-leg boundary, standing with his heels almost touching the boundary rope, pushed his left hand up high above his head and not only did the ball stick in his hand, but even more surprisingly, the impetus did not knock him back over the boundary. It was a remarkable catch.

Zimbabwe began their second innings 45 minutes before tea on this fourth day and immediately lost both openers. At 6–2, they were looking at defeat and the innings was a struggle from then on. Zimbabwe had reached 107–5 at the end of the day, only 77 runs ahead, and England will have fancied their chances. The next morning, Andy Waller and Guy Whittall put on 67 in a crucial seventh-wicket stand. Waller hit the ball hard, with two huge sixes off the spinners, Croft and Phil Tufnell. Both batsmen reached 50 and then perished, the innings ending in mid-afternoon on the last day. In the final equation, England were left to score 205 in a minimum of 37 overs, which worked out at five and a half runs an over.

The question was would they go for it? This was answered most emphatically in the first over when Nick Knight came charging down the wicket to Streak's fourth ball and, with a flat bat, hit it through midwicket for four. And didn't the Barmy Army enjoy that one. Now, suddenly everything had changed. It had become a limited-overs match, with all the attendant excitement. Zimbabwe got their breakthrough when captain Mike Atherton dragged a ball from Olonga into his stumps, but they did not have their own Barmy Army to offer vociferous celebrations. Alec Stewart now joined Knight, an ideal combination of right-hander and left-hander, and Campbell, Zimbabwe's captain, decided that Zimbabwe should defend. There were plenty of places to look for singles and the odd bad ball also came along. At tea, England were 36–1 off five overs. Zimbabwe had made little attempt to take wickets and were content only to try and defend the boundaries.

They also began to bowl wide down the leg side and the umpires, particularly Ian Robinson, the home umpire, were surprisingly lenient in their opinion of what constituted a wide. In my opinion Robinson would have found it difficult to refute the charge that he was displaying home-town bias. In those days only one neutral umpire was required and on this occasion it was Steve Dunne from New Zealand, who was himself not always the surest of umpires. Heath Streak, bowling at fast-medium, was extremely lucky to get away with it as he did, and although he was the principal culprit, he was not alone. Only three wides were called in the innings, which was absurd. The irony was that when Streak later said he was lucky not to have been called for a wide in the final over, the match referee, former Indian batsman Hanumant Singh, fined him 15 per cent of his match fee for implied criticism of the umpires.

The other unusual occurrence that afternoon took place in the *TMS* commentary box, when I am ashamed to say I was the villain of the piece. Peter Baxter had done the rota for the commentators up until the start of the last hour, in which 15 overs had to be bowled regardless of time, which as a result became irrelevant. I took up my position at the microphone 20 minutes before the start of the last hour and my name was the last Backers had put down on the rota, although he had left room for additions to be made. There was a lot going on, it was getting pretty exciting and I went for it. My 20-minute spell ended, but 'HB' was still the last entry on the rota and mischievously I kept going.

At the end of each over, Simon Mann, later to become known most affectionately as Grumps, which was an early and always affectionate nickname for him back in London's Broadcasting House, and Backers himself kept peering at me in hope. I was hugely enjoying it and was in no mood to give up, while Trevor Bailey, a trifle perplexed by my reluctance to leave the microphone, and Chris Cowdrey alternated alongside me as summarisers. Jo King, scoring beside me, never let on that I was being chivvied from all sides. I have to say, I heard a certain amount of coughing and probably felt a bit of nudging too, but I was immune to it and kept banging on to the thrilling end. It had to be the most supremely selfish moment, from me or anyone else, in all my years in the commentary box. I am not sure why Backers or Grumps ever spoke to me again. One thing was for sure, I don't remember Backers coming up with another bottle of Bohlinger in the hotel that evening, but Grumps, to his great credit, made no attempt to live up to his nickname.

Since then commentators who overstay their time at the microphone have always been accused of 'doing a Bulawayo'. Maybe it has become my only lasting legacy to the *TMS* box. The awful truth is that I have never regretted it for a single moment: it was such fun.

When those final 15 overs began, England were 118–1, needing 87 more. This was reduced to 51 in eight overs when, after putting on 137 in 26 overs with Knight, Alec Stewart skied an attempted pull against Strang and Campbell judged the catch well. To the noisy dismay of the Barmy Army, England now lost their way. Two runs later, Hussain was well caught low down at cover, trying to make room to cut Paul Strang, and Zimbabwe now did all they could to keep Knight off strike. Strang, the leg-spinner, bowled over the wicket to the left-hander, pitching the ball a yard outside his leg stump, with the ball turning even further away down the leg side. John Crawley came charging down the wicket to Guy Whittall and skied the ball to deep cover, where Stuart Carlisle, who had not had a good match, held an outstanding catch. In the next over, an out-of-sorts Graham Thorpe was caught at cover off a leading edge against Streak, while Knight soldiered on as best he could at the other end.

England were now 184–5, needing 21 more off the last two overs, and Darren Gough had joined Knight. Eight desperate runs were scrambled in the penultimate over and 13 more were needed from the last, bowled by Streak. Knight could not get the first ball away, and when he off-drove the second only for a furiously run two, it looked as if Zimbabwe were now sure of a draw, with 11 wanted from four balls. The third ball was on the stumps and Knight had a tremendous swing, picked it up beautifully and it disappeared over the leg-side boundary for six. Streak's next ball was way down the off side and was surely a wide but, no, umpire Robinson did not move a muscle, and five were needed from the last two.

Knight played the first ball away to long off and somehow they scampered two, with Gough diving in at the bowler's end. With three needed from the last, there were nine men on the boundary. Knight drove it away square on the off side and off they went.

Carlisle fielded the ball quickly and well on the boundary and the batsmen, after running two, had just started on what would have been the third and winning run when Andy Flower lunged at the stumps. The batsmen had not even crossed when he broke the wicket. Gough was given out at first, but the decision was later revised and Knight was the one who had to go. The scores were level and the match was drawn.

In all the circumstances, perhaps this was the best possible result for Zimbabwe's first Test against England. It was too much for England's hugely patriotic and emotional coach, David Lloyd, who pronounced loudly and often, 'We flippin' murdered 'em.' Which may not have been an ideal choice of words. When the chairman of the Test and County Cricket Board, Lord MacLaurin, arrived in Zimbabwe a day or two later, he wagged a meaningful finger in Lloyd's direction. History had been made in Bulawayo in more ways than one.

ZIMBABWE v ENGLAND (1st Test)

At Queens Sports Club, Bulawayo, on 18–22 December 1996.

Zimbabwe

G.W. Flower c Hussain b Silverwood	43		lbw b Gough	0
S.V. Carlisle c Crawley b Gough	0		c Atherton b Mullally	4
*A.D.R. Campbell c Silverwood b Croft	84		b Croft	29
D.L. Houghton c Stewart b Croft	34		c Croft b Tufnell	37
†A. Flower c Stewart b Tufnell	112		c Crawley b Tufnell	14
A.C. Waller c Crawley b Croft	15		c Knight b Gough	50
G.J. Whittall c Atherton b Silverwood	7	(8)	c Croft b Tufnell	56
P.A. Strang c Tufnell b Silverwood	38	(9)	c Crawley b Croft	19
H.H. Streak b Mullally	19	(10)	not out	8
B.C. Strang not out	4	(7)	c Mullally b Tufnell	3
H.K. Olonga c Knight b Tufnell	0		c Stewart b Silverwood	0
Extras (4 lb, 13 nb, 3 w)	20		(4 b, 6 lb, 2 nb, 2 w)	14
Total (all out, 137.5 overs)	**376**		(all out, 101 overs)	**234**

1–3 2–130 3–136 4–206 5–235 6–252
7–331 8–372 9–376 10–376

1–6 2–6 3–57 4–82 5–103 6–111
7–178 8–209 9–233 10–234

Bowling, *1st innings*: Mullally 23–4–69–1; Gough 26–4–87–1; Silverwood 18–5–63–3; Croft 44–15–77–3; Tufnell 26.5–4–76–2. *2nd innings*: Gough 12–2–44–2; Mullally 18–5–49–1; Croft 33–9–62–2; Silverwood 7–3–8–1; Tufnell 31–12–61–4.

England

N.V. Knight lbw b Olonga	56		run out (A. Flower)	96
*M.A. Atherton lbw b P.A. Strang	16		b Olonga	4
†A.J. Stewart lbw b P.A. Strang	48		c Campbell b P.A. Strang	73
N. Hussain c B.C. Strang b Streak	113		c Carlisle b P.A. Strang	0
G.P. Thorpe c Campbell b P.A. Strang	13	(6)	c Campbell b Streak	2
J.P. Crawley c A Flower b P.A. Strang	112	(5)	c Carlisle b Whittall	7
R.D.B. Croft lbw b Olonga	7		did not bat	
D. Gough c G.W. Flower b Olonga	2	(7)	not out	3
C.E.W. Silverwood c Houghton b P.A. Strang	0		did not bat	
A.D. Mullally c Waller b Streak	4		did not bat	
P.C.R. Tufnell not out	2		did not bat	
Extras (4 b, 4 lb, 24 nb, 1 w)	33		(2 b, 13 lb, 1 nb, 3 w)	19
Total (all out, 151.4 overs)	**406**		(6 wkts, 37 overs)	**204**

1–48 2–92 3–160 4–180 5–328 6–340
7–344 8–353 9–378 10–406

1–17 2–154 3–156 4–178 5–182
6–204

Bowling, *1st innings*: Streak 36–8–86–2; B.C. Strang 17–5–54–0; P.A. Strang 58.4–14–123–5; Olonga 23–2–90–3; Whittall 10–2–25–0; G.W. Flower 7–3–20–0. *2nd innings*: Streak 11–0–64–1; Olonga 2–0–16–1; P.A. Strang 14–0–63–2; G.W. Flower 8–0–36–0; Whittall 2–0–10–1.

Close of play, *day 1*: Zimbabwe (1) 256–6 (A. Flower 58*, P.A. Strang 0*); *day 2*: England (1) 48–1 (Knight 29*); *day 3*: England (1) 306–4 (Hussain 101*, Crawley 51*); *day 4*: Zimbabwe (2) 107–5 (Waller 14*, B.C. Strang 0*).

Toss: Zimbabwe. Last-innings target: 205 runs.
Umpires: R.S. Dunne (NZ), I.D. Robinson (Zim).
Man of the Match: N.V. Knight.
MATCH DRAWN.

20

SO MUCH MORE THAN JUST CRICKET

India v Pakistan (1st Test)
28–31 January 1999; Chepauk Stadium, Chennai
Pakistan won by 12 runs.

POLITICS and religion have combined to makes series between India and Pakistan an endangered species. In 1998–99, Pakistan visited India to play two Test matches which were remarkable for the quality of the cricket and the excitement both matches generated, on the field and off it. Inevitably, they were played amidst intense security, with the local fundamentalist Hindu population objecting strongly to the presence of the Pakistan cricketers. Pakistan won the first match in Chennai, which was the first Test the two countries had played for nine years, by the narrow margin of 12 runs after a brilliant hundred by Sachin Tendulkar had so nearly seen India home. In the second, in Delhi, India would gain revenge by 212 runs. A third match was then played in Kolkata which was won by Pakistan, but this was counted as part of the Asian Test Championship and so the Test series was officially drawn.

The right-wing Hindu fundamentalists, led by an independently minded politician, Bal Thackeray, did everything they could to stop the tour. Shortly before the Pakistan players arrived in India, protesters dug up the pitch in Delhi where the first Test was due to have been played. The match was moved to Chennai.

Then the offices of the Indian Board of Control in Mumbai were ransacked, but the Indian government promised the maximum security for the Pakistan players, amid much public support. Seeing that public opinion was not with them, Bal Thackeray's party backed down and the tour went ahead.

For all that, the Pakistan players had to be closely guarded by commandos and all the other forces of law and order. It was greatly to the credit of the Pakistan manager, the former foreign minister Shaharyar Khan, and the captain, Wasim Akram, that the series not only went ahead but was also such a success. Crowds of 45,000 watched each day's play in Chennai and there were almost as many for the second in Delhi, after the ground had been repaired. It was still a far from happy situation for the players and, considering everything, it was remarkable the cricket was of such a consistently high standard.

Of course, cricket matches, or indeed any sporting contests between these two countries, assume a huge local significance. While the Pakistan players must be congratulated for being prepared to come to India in the first place, the big crowds at the two grounds must be congratulated on the way they made them welcome and on their open-mindedness when it came to appreciating the quality of the cricket. At the end in Chennai, when Pakistan had won, their players did a lap of honour around the ground and received a standing ovation, even though most of the crowd will have been deeply disappointed.

After winning the toss, Wasim Akram decided to bat and maybe it was the tenseness of the situation which, on a lifeless pitch, caused them to lose their first five wickets for 91. Three of them fell to Javagal Srinath, a lively and consistent bowler who became the second Indian fast bowler after Kapil Dev to take more than 200 Test wickets. The other two fell to the redoubtable Anil Kumble, who in the list of recent leg-spinners must come as second only to Shane Warne, although a different type of bowler. Kumble, with a cheerful, open, unchanging expression, is tall with a long run-up for a spinner and an upright, rangy action. He was not a big spinner of the ball, but he was brisk for a leg-spinner and had excellent control. It was in the second Test, on a repaired Delhi pitch, that he took all ten wickets in Pakistan's second innings. England's Jim Laker was the only other bowler to do that when he took an incredible 19–90 against Australia at Old Trafford in 1956. Like all successful leg-spinners, Kumble has a good sense of humour, something wrist-spinners need to protect them against those dreadful days which occasionally come along when nothing pitches in the right place.

At Chennai, Pakistan were saved from batting ignominy by Yousuf Youhana, who when he converted from the Christian faith to Islam in 2005 became known as Mohammad Yousuf, and wicketkeeper Moin Khan, who made good fifties and, with the help of a robust contribution from Wasim, took their first-innings score to 238. India will have been extremely happy to dispose of Pakistan for such a small total, but they now had to cope with the wiles of Saqlain Mushtaq, which of course included his own invention, the doosra. This is the ball which enables the off-spinner to turn the other way, from leg to off, and it has always been a controversial delivery. It is an unnatural ball for an off-spinner and it is extremely difficult to bowl one without straightening a bent elbow at the point of delivery, which turns it into a throw.

Saqlain himself is one of the most delightful cricketers I have met and since he retired, I have been lucky enough to watch him bowl in many charity games for the Lashings World XI. He has more than once gone through the mechanics required for bowling a doosra. When it is done the Saqlain way in slow motion, it does not look like a throw. When he quickens up and bowls it for real, he assures me there is no straightening of the arm and, knowing Saqlain as I do, I am happy enough with that. But undoubtedly there are would-be imitators who have to resort to straightening the elbow at the point of delivery. It is easy to say that all doosras must be thrown, but I am not sure that it is as simple as that.

There is no doubt that Saqlain has been able to develop this particular personal skill to a high level of perfection, as he was now to demonstrate to the Indian batsmen. He took five wickets in each of the four innings in this series and the combination of his beguiling flight and the doosra was devastating. Maybe the impetus of a series against India turned him into an even better bowler.

In India's first innings in Chennai, both openers were despatched by Wasim Akram, one of the greatest of modern fast bowlers, and the best of all those who bowled left arm over the wicket. The score was 71–2 and Saqlain was bowling when the diminutive figure of Sachin Tendulkar came out to join Rahul Dravid. Tendulkar was surely Saqlain's technical equal in the batting department. He is a small man, always modest and unobtrusive to a fault, and when he came out to bat, there was something delightfully inconsequential about his appearance. His walk would not naturally attract a fanfare of trumpets. It always left me mildly surprised to find that this really was Tendulkar, a truly great batsman and one who was never tripped up by his own ego.

One more run was scored and the great man took guard to face Saqlain. After a careful look round the field, he took up his stance. Saqlain's feet twinkled quickly as they brought him up to the crease to bowl. His arm came over smoothly and another ball was on its way, setting its own problems – first in the air with its flight, before pitching on the probing length Saqlain had chosen. No one will have been more aware than Tendulkar of the likely impact of Saqlain's bowling on this series. He will have known how important it was for him to show the spinner right from start who was in control. Tendulkar came down the wicket to him, almost like a sprinter out of the blocks. Like so many before and after him, he was beaten in the air and mistimed his drive, which flew straight to Saleem Malik at backward point. It was his third ball, he was not yet off the mark and Saqlain had taken the first of those 20 wickets – one he will always treasure. Indian crowds are never silent, but this was now as near as one will ever get to silence as Tendulkar began the long walk back to the pavilion. It was a moment of almost unreal drama, and the only person not to be as dumbfounded as everyone else was Saqlain Mushtaq himself, although I am sure he will have allowed himself a brief smile of satisfaction at winning this particular battle.

Dravid and Sourav Ganguly both passed 50 and took India to a first-innings lead of 16. Nerves had clearly played quite a part in this match so far – and maybe even Tendulkar had not been immune. Pakistan's second innings centred around Shahid Afridi, a highly talented batsman and a more-than-useful leg-spinner. He has a joyful character, which may not have allowed him, in either capacity, to produce the figures his talent suggested he should have done. It came as no surprise when, in 2006, Afridi decided to turn his back on Test cricket and throw in his lot with the one-day game. If ODIs became his staple diet, Twenty20 provided the icing on the cake.

He showed in Chennai, in only his second Test match, what he might have brought to Test cricket, although the longer form of the game was not in keeping with his temperament. Maybe these matches between Pakistan and India provided the inspiration he needed. In India's first innings, he had taken three wickets and when Pakistan went in again, he batted for more than five hours for 141. He has always said it was the best innings he ever played and, although he was still only 18 years old, it was surely the most mature. In 1996, when Afridi was 16, he had made the fastest ever hundred to date, in an ODI against Sri Lanka in Nairobi. It took him only 37 balls and his batting then was pure, untrammelled instinct. Now in Chennai, the instinct was there, but it was tempered with the discretion a consciously studied technique should have brought to his batting more often.

In this game, against such a capable bowling attack, he would not have got away with his usual devil-may-care approach. Maybe he will have learned from seeing Tendulkar's dismissal in India's first innings and realised that the path of discretion was, temporarily, at any rate, the only one to follow. It was not that he forgot about his strokes so much as he suddenly became uncharacteristically selective in playing them. If the bowlers gave him the chance, he lived up to his nickname of 'Boom Boom'. Of course, he could not entirely control himself and when he did not, his supreme natural talent protected him. When the Indians turned to spin, Afridi's strokeplay was more obviously lured on by temptation and the spinners will surely have felt they had a better chance than their faster team-mates. For example, slog-sweeping a leg-spinner of Kumble's pace is hazardous, but Afridi went for it. When they overpitched, Kumble and Tendulkar were both driven powerfully through the covers.

Throughout this innings, it was clear that Afridi, with that cheeky-chappie look of his, was enjoying every moment, even if he had continually to bite his lip. He hit 21 fours and three sixes and made his runs from 191 balls. He reached his first Test hundred by driving a ball off his middle stump through midwicket as if it was the easiest thing in the world – just a bit of fun on a day out. After Pakistan had lost two early wickets, Afridi received useful support from Inzamam-ul-Haq, Yousuf Youhana, as he was then, and Saleem Malik, before being seventh out himself at 279. The other hero in this Pakistan second innings was the Indian fast-medium bowler Venkatesh Prasad, who took 6–33 in 10.2 overs. To be at his best, he ideally wanted a pitch which helped seam bowling, but now he produced his best ever Test bowling figures on a slow and unhelpful pitch. One of his main weapons was an extremely well-concealed slower ball, as well as impeccable control.

After Afridi departed, the last three Pakistan wickets added only seven more runs and India were left to score 271 to win, with more than two days left. They began badly when Waqar Younis – on his day, as dangerous a fast bowler as any – removed both openers for six, but by the end of this third day, Dravid and

Tendulkar were beginning to develop a promising partnership. Just before the close of play, Tendulkar hit three fours, including one perfect cover drive off Wasim.

When stumps were drawn, with two of their demi-gods together at the crease, Indian supporters will have been breathing the more easily. But not for long. Tendulkar glanced the first ball of the fourth morning, from Wasim Akram, for four, but on this pitch, which was showing signs of wear, runs were never going to be easy to make and survival alone was quite a problem. Only ten had been added when Dravid received a beauty from Wasim. The ball, which was well up to the bat, started on the leg stump before swinging across the right-hander and removing his off bail. With anything possible on this fourth day the ground was full long before the start and it was difficult to escape the feeling that the virility of both countries was at stake. Only games between Pakistan and India can produce this atmosphere.

This was not a pitch for Azharuddin's lovely wristy, angular strokeplay. He struggled for an hour before he was beaten in the air by Saqlain and, misjudging the length, was leg before, although there were those who felt it may have been going down the leg side. Umpire Steve Dunne from New Zealand thought otherwise. There were a number of doubtful decisions given in this match and umpire Dunne did not have a particularly happy time. Arguably, the worst of all came nine runs later when Sourav Ganguly drove Saqlain hard to silly point. The ball reached the fielder on the bounce and rebounded to wicketkeeper Moin Khan – there were even those who thought it bounced again on the way to Moin. The two umpires – the other was the Indian V.K. Ramaswamy – conferred before Ganguly was given out by Dunne.

By now, the crowd were despondent, for it seemed that nothing could save India, who had sunk to 82–5. Saqlain was weaving his magic at one end and that formidable pair of fast bowlers, Wasim and Waqar, were taking it in turns at the other. It was now all up to Tendulkar, with wicketkeeper Nayan Mongia as his new partner. He immediately pulled a shorter one from Saqlain to the midwicket boundary and, at lunch, India were 86–5, with Tendulkar 44 not out. He relieved Indian anxiety a fraction after lunch when he square-cut Saqlain for four and steered Wasim to third man for another, which took him to 50. At the other end, Mongia somehow managed to hold on while Tendulkar played a paddle sweep for four off Saqlain. The crowd loved every stroke Tendulkar played, but it still looked as if he was fighting a losing cause.

Wasim now turned to Nadeem Khan and Afridi, who both kept things tight on a pitch which gave them some help. It was Test cricket at its best and it all made for a thrilling spectacle. You could almost feel the intensity of the battle and the singleness of purpose of the individual players. Mongia fought gallantly and nudged his way to 12 in 87 balls and then he slashed a short one from Afridi past cover for four for his first boundary. India were 152–5, with Tendulkar on 83 and in obvious discomfort from his back, when Saqlain began the 78th over of the innings. The first ball was a fraction short and Tendulkar pulled it over midwicket for four and this was followed by another well-executed paddle sweep which also went for four. The third ball was Saqlain at his best. He gave it some air. Tendulkar came haring down the pitch to drive it back over Saqlain's head and, like so many of his victims, was beaten in the air. The ball hit the inside edge of the bat and Moin not only dropped a difficult catch, but also missed the stumping chance. Saqlain knelt down on the pitch in his disappointment, which can only have been intensified when his fifth ball was paddle-swept for four and the last pulled to the midwicket boundary. A single to square leg in Saqlain's next over took Tendulkar to perhaps the best of all his Test hundreds.

The new ball was now taken and in Wasim's first over, he was driven through the covers for four and then, in his first, Waqar was straight-driven to the boundary with what was no more than a perfectly timed forward-defensive stroke. The crowd, in great voice, was being given something to hope for. Mongia felt the time had come to join in and he hoisted Waqar over mid on for four. When Saqlain came back to try his hand with a harder ball, Mongia despatched his first over midwicket for six. This brought him to his half-century, which may have filled him with a misplaced confidence. He now had a crude swipe at Wasim and the ball spiralled to mid off, where Waqar waited a long time before taking the catch. There came a surprise when the new bats-man, Sunil Joshi, suddenly whacked Saqlain over mid on for six. At this point it was obvious that Tendulkar's back was giving him a lot of pain, but for all that, he drove Wasim for four more before the start of another memorable over from Saqlain.

Tendulkar began with a paddle sweep, which was cleverly anticipated by Ijaz Ahmed moving from slip across to the leg side. He straight-drove the next ball for four and this really seemed to hurt his back, with the effect, perhaps, of making him in an even greater hurry to finish off the match. The next ball was pulled to the midwicket boundary and India needed 17 more with four wickets left. The crowd was bubbling over as they began to feel that nothing could surely stand in the way of an Indian victory. Then it was Saqlain again and along came the doosra, enticingly floated up. Tendulkar did not read it and made to hit it straight back over the bowler's head. The ball struck the leading edge of his bat and lifted into the covers, where Wasim made no mistake with the catch. Tendulkar could not believe what he had done and walked back, head down, into the pavilion. You could see it all: he thought he had let down his country; it was as bad as that. Tendulkar had faced 273 balls and been in for 405 minutes for his 136, and few players in the history of the game could have played that innings, and yet, in the end, his immediate feeling will have been of overwhelming failure.

For the record, Kumble then had no answer to Wasim's pace, while Joshi, another beaten in the air, pushed a catch back to Saqlain, who picked up his fifth wicket of the innings when, two runs later, he completely flummoxed and bowled Srinath. The last three wickets fell for two runs and Pakistan had won by 12 runs, Saqlain having taken 5–93 in the innings and 10–187 in the match. The Man of the Match award was given to Tendulkar, however, and Saqlain, who dismissed him twice, knew where he was and will have understood why.

The significance of the match had brought out something extra in Saqlain, just as it had from Tendulkar and Afridi. The Chennai crowd was stunned into a despairing silence, before recovering itself to give the Pakistanis a standing ovation as they did a lap of honour – a fitting and generous tribute. It had been an incredible game of cricket between two sides who, when they play each other, bring pressures to the contest which may not be found in any other. Throughout these four days in Chennai, it had felt as if this match was about something more than just cricket.

INDIA v PAKISTAN (1st Test)

At Chepauk Stadium, Chennai, on 28–31 January 1999.

Pakistan

Saeed Anwar lbw b Srinath	24	lbw b Prasad	7
Shahid Afridi c Ganguly b Srinath	11	b Prasad	141
Ijaz Ahmed lbw b Kumble	13	c and b Kumble	11
Inzamam-ul-Haq c and b Kumble	10	c Laxman b Tendulkar	51
Yousuf Youhana lbw b Tendulkar	53	b Tendulkar	26
Saleem Malik b Srinath	8	c Dravid b Joshi	32
†Moin Khan c Ganguly b Kumble	60	c Mongia b Prasad	3
*Wasim Akram c Laxman b Kumble	38	c Joshi b Prasad	1
Saqlain Mushtaq lbw b Kumble	2	lbw b Prasad	0
Nadeem Khan c Dravid b Kumble	8	not out	1
Waqar Younis not out	0	c Ramesh b Prasad	5
Extras (5 lb, 6 nb)	11	(1 b, 4 lb, 3 nb)	8
Total (all out, 79.5 overs)	**238**	(all out, 71.2 overs)	**286**

1–32 2–41 3–61 4–66 5–91 6–154 7–214
8–227 9–237 10–238

1–11 2–42 3–139 4–169 5–275
6–278 7–279 8–279 9–280 10–286

Bowling, *1st innings*: Srinath 15–3–63–3; Prasad 16–1–54–0; Kumble 24.5–7–70–6; Joshi 21–8–36–0; Tendulkar 3–0–10–1. *2nd innings*: Srinath 16–1–68–0; Prasad 10.2–5–33–6; Kumble 22–4–93–1; Joshi 14–3–42–1; Tendulkar 7–1–35–2; Laxman 2–0–10–0.

India

S. Ramesh lbw b Wasim Akram	43		c Inzamam-ul-Haq b Waqar Younis	5
V.V.S. Laxman lbw b Wasim Akram	23		lbw b Waqar Younis	0
R.S. Dravid lbw b Saqlain Mushtaq	53		b Wasim Akram	10
S.R. Tendulkar c Saleem Malik			c Wasim Akram	
b Saqlain Mushtaq	0		b Saqlain Mushtaq	136
*M. Azharuddin c Inzamam-ul-Haq				
b Saqlain Mushtaq	11		lbw b Saqlain Mushtaq	7
S.C. Ganguly c Ijaz Ahmed b Shahid Afridi.	54		c Moin Khan b Saqlain Mushtaq	2
†N.R. Mongia st Moin Khan b Saqlain Mushtaq	5		c Waqar Younis b Wasim Akram.	52
A. Kumble c Yousuf Youhana b Saqlain Mushtaq	4	(9)	lbw b Wasim Akram	1
S.B. Joshi not out	25	(8)	c and b Saqlain Mushtaq	8
J. Srinath c Ijaz Ahmed b Shahid Afridi	10		b Saqlain Mushtaq	1
B.K.V. Prasad st Moin Khan b Shahid Afridi	4		not out	0
Extras (2 b, 2 lb, 18 nb)	22		(8 b, 10 lb, 18 nb)	36
Total (all out, 81.1 overs)	**254**		(all out, 95.2 overs)	**258**

1–67 2–71 3–72 4–103 5–156 6–166 7–188
8–229 9–246 10–254

1–5 2–6 3–50 4–73 5–82 6–218
7–254 8–256 9–256 10–258

Bowling, *1st innings*: Wasim Akram 20–4–60–2; Waqar Younis 12–2–48–0; Saqlain Mushtaq 35–8–94–5; Shahid Afridi 7.1–0–31–3; Nadeem Khan 7–0–17–0. *2nd innings*: Wasim Akram 22–4–80–3; Waqar Younis 12–6–26–2; Shahid Afridi 16–7–23–0; Saqlain Mushtaq 32.2–8–93–5; Nadeem Khan 13–5–18–0.

Close of play, *day 1*: India (1) 48–0 (Ramesh 30*, Laxman 18*); *day 2*: Pakistan (2) 34–1 (Shahid Afridi 16*, Ijaz Ahmed 11*); *day 3*: India (2) 40–2 (Dravid 8*, Tendulkar 20*).

Toss: Pakistan. Last-innings target: 271 runs.
Umpires: R.S. Dunne (NZ), V.K. Ramaswamy (Ind).
Man of the Match: S.R. Tendulkar.

PAKISTAN won by 12 runs.

21

MIDSUMMER MADNESS

Australia v South Africa (World Cup semi-final)
17 June 1999; Edgbaston, Birmingham
Match tied.

A T the time, this match, one of the semi-finals in the 1999 World Cup, was regarded as the greatest one-day international ever to have been played, perhaps even the greatest game of one-day cricket. At the very end, a lunatic piece of cricket by Lance Klusener, whose brilliant batting had taken South Africa to within one run of victory, was responsible for enabling Australia to reach the final. This game at Edgbaston was tied and a superior run rate in the early stage of the competition ensured that Australia finished as the greater of two equals. The scores were level, South Africa's last pair were together, there were four balls left and Lance Klusener, who had made 31 in 14 balls, was on strike. Surely South Africa would not fail now, but under the intense pressure which these moments produce, brains become scrambled.

The thought that a tie would give the match to Australia may have been playing on Klusener's mind as Steve Waugh brought in his fielders so they were all saving the single. Having driven Damien Fleming's first two balls for thunderous off-side fours, I would have thought Klusener would have been calm enough. He mistimed a drive to the second of these last four; it went to mid on and he set off, head down, like a runaway train, for the other

Garry Sobers (152) miscues at Bourda in 1968, but Knott and Cowdrey are not quick enough.

But Clive Lloyd manages to get there when Ken Barrington miscues in England's second innings.

Ian Botham dispatches Dennis Lillee to the backward-point boundary at Headingley in 1981.

The *coup de grâce*: Bob Willis removes Ray Bright's middle stump. England win by 18 runs.

17

TERRIFIC THOMMO

G J S Company

Above: Chris Tavaré has dropped Jeff Thomson, but Geoff Miller holds the rebound and England win by three runs in 1982.

Right: Test cricket's second tie, in 1986. Maninder Singh queries the final lbw decision.

Andrew Hudson on his way to 163 in South Africa's first Test match in the Caribbean, in 1992.

Shane Warne, not in prayer, but celebrating a return catch against South Africa in Sydney in 1994.

Courtney Walsh celebrates the all-important wicket of Kepler Wessels early on the last morning.

Fanie de Villiers catches Glenn McGrath and wins the Sydney Test for South Africa.

Nick Knight swings Heath Streak for six in the last over in Bulawayo in 1996.

Sachin Tendulkar reaches his century against Pakistan in Chennai in 1999: perhaps his finest innings.

Pakistan, and principally Saqlain Mushtaq, celebrate their famous victory in Chennai.

Above: Freddie Flintoff consoles the not-out Brett Lee after Australia's two-run defeat at Edgbaston in 2005.

Left: Steve Harmison flicks Michael Kasprowicz's glove and England have won.

Below: South Africa's Allan Donald is comprehensively run out and Australia reach the 1999 World Cup final.

Doug Bracewell has just taken the wicket of Nathan Lyon to give New Zealand victory in Hobart in 2011.

Anya Shrubsole's purposeful action, which took England to a thrilling victory in the 2017 World Cup.

New Zealand's Ajaz Patel has Azhar Ali leg before on their way to victory over Pakistan.

Trent Boult catches Ben Stokes in the 2019 World Cup final, but his foot is on the boundary rope.

England win their first World Cup. Jos Buttler runs out Martin Guptill from the last ball.

Ben Stokes again. A magnificent reverse sweep for six against Australia in the 2019 Headingley Test.

end. Allan Donald, an experienced number eleven if ever there was one, realising the danger of being run out at the non-striker's end, started so late that he was left stranded in his own half of the pitch when Adam Gilchrist removed the bails. Australia went on to beat Pakistan by eight wickets in the final at Lord's.

Four days earlier, at the end of the Super Sixes, Australia had beaten South Africa at Headingley, which had obviously given them an important psychological boost for the semi-final. That was the match in which Steve Waugh, when he had made 56, was caught at short midwicket by Herschelle Gibbs, who cele- brated, as usual, by throwing the ball up in the air, but in so doing let it slip through his fingers before he had brought it properly under control. Waugh is purported to have told him, 'Hersch, you have just dropped the World Cup.' Waugh, who went on to make 120 not out, later denied saying this, and knowing him, he will almost certainly have come up with something much more fruity.

When the two sides met again here at Edgbaston in the second of the semi-finals, South Africa were desperate to reach the final for the first time, knowing that they had on their back a reputa- tion for choking when the pressure was at its greatest, especially in tight finishes. It was an accusation they did not appreciate, but it was born out by the facts since their return to international cricket. It was never better illustrated, as we have seen, than in their first Test match on their return, against the West Indies in Barbados in 1992.

It was a cloudy morning in Birmingham, which was already having to live with the news that if Australia failed to qualify for the final, this might turn out to be Shane Warne's last appearance for them. Warne has always loved to create a drama out of noth- ing if he can. The next excitement came when Hansie Cronje won the toss and put Australia in to bat. When a side has been put in, it quickens the collective pulse a touch. The South Africans will have been happier than Warne at the way the first part of the day went. They kept Australia to 213, which they will have regarded as a more-than-acceptable target.

It was gripping stuff all the way through. In the first over Mark Waugh tried to flick away a lifter from Shaun Pollock down the leg side, got a bat on it and wicketkeeper Mark Boucher held the catch. It took Ricky Ponting a little time to settle in before he announced himself with successive pulls against Steve Elworthy, which went for six and four. At the other end, Adam Gilchrist, who usually sets off at a spanking pace, did not find it easy to play his strokes. The 50 arrived in the 13th over and Allan Donald, the fourth bowler to be used, came on to bowl the 14th. Donald was both an inspiring and a frightening sight when he ran in, some-how embodying his nickname of 'White Lightning'. Apart from that predatory run-up and a fiercely controlled and hostile action, there was an ice-cold deadliness in the manner of it all. No one will have wanted to see South Africa get into the final more than Donald, a fierce patriot who, to his dismay, had seen the side fail to press home their advantage on a number of occasions. Little did he know what lay just around the corner. He now bowled at Ponting, who looked as if he may have been surprised by the pace of his first ball, which he probably expected to be a warm-up delivery, and he pushed it into cover's hands. The sixth, if anything even faster, then found the edge of Darren Lehmann's bat. Three overs later, Gilchrist steered a short one from Jacques Kallis into Donald's hands at third man and Australia were 68–4 from 17 overs, three wickets having fallen in four overs. Cronje will have been more than happy with his decision to field first. With the cloud cover, it had looked a bowling morning.

Michael Bevan and Steve Waugh, who was already lucky not to have been run out, now had to rebuild the innings and therefore bat more carefully than they will have wanted. 'Sometimes you have to do less than your conscience is nagging you to do,' was how Bevan put it. At one point they added six runs in 8.4 overs, and although they quickened up, at no stage were they near to moving the scoreboard along at a reckless speed. In limited-overs cricket, Bevan had played any number of hectic match-winning innings when his side was batting second. In the end, this too could be considered to be a match-winning effort, although it was a very different type of innings. He faced 101 balls for his 65 and hit only six fours.

Both these two were admirably circumspect, although it was never less than vibrantly exciting. Waugh and Bevan had added 90 when Waugh was caught behind off the tireless Pollock, whose accuracy, like Donald's, caused the Australians great problems. Three balls later, Tom Moody was caught on the crease by Pollock and was plumb in front. Bevan now found another worthy partner in Shane Warne, always a difficult man to get out. They put on 49 invaluable runs in eight overs before the innings fell in a heap. At 207, Warne was out to a tumbling catch by Cronje off Pollock at midwicket, and in a flurry of excitement the last three wickets then fell for six runs in eight balls. Australia were all out for 213, Pollock finishing with 5–36 and Donald with 4–32, and both were magnificent. It had been a thrilling first half of the day, but with all the drama to come, these details were at the back of everyone's minds by nightfall.

By the time South Africa began their innings, the sun was shining and the pitch seemed blameless. Gary Kirsten and Herschelle Gibbs batted comfortably against Australia's three seam bowlers, Glenn McGrath, Damien Fleming and Paul Reiffel. With Gibbs hitting six lovely fours, they had put on 48 in 12 overs when Steve Waugh turned to Shane Warne, who wanted victory for Australia almost as much as Donald wanted it for South Africa. He now bowled his second over to Gibbs. He gave the second ball a real flip, it pitched well wide of the leg stump and, just like that defining first ball to Mike Gatting at Old Trafford in 1993, it spun viciously all the way across Gibbs and hit the top of the off bail. Like Gatting, it took Gibbs a moment or two to realise what had happened, although Warne's celebrations cannot have left him in much doubt.

It was a moment which could only have made the South African dressing room quiver with apprehension. That one ball instantly changed the fabric and the perception of a match which had seemed to be heading for a comfortable South African victory. Suddenly the ground and the huge television audience was gripped with tension. On a tour of the West Indies, Steve Waugh had once dropped Warne from the Australian side, after which they did not send each other Christmas cards, but they will have respected each other hugely as players. Steve Waugh could not have summed up better the importance of this moment when he said of Warne, 'His drive and will were literally scary, but he sparked life into others who were tensing up under the South African onslaught and got us back into the game.' Warne's own take on that moment was, 'I thought that if this was going to be my last chance to win the World Cup, I was going to give it a red-hot dip.'

The effect was immediate. Kirsten, who had been playing with his usual calmness, suddenly launched himself into a wild slog-sweep against Warne and was bowled. It was a stroke inspired by the mesmerising influence Warne now had over the game. Two balls later, Hansie Cronje was given out caught at slip when the ball looked as if it may have come off his boot. Perhaps even umpire David Shepherd had been infected by Warne's midsummer madness. Now, Daryll Cullinan started late when called for a single by Kallis and was run out by Bevan and in nine overs South Africa had gone from 48–0 to 61–4. There was a marked similarity between the two innings. Australia had earlier been 68–4, and now Kallis and Jonty Rhodes put together a stand of 84, just as Steve Waugh and Michael Bevan had put on 90 for Australia.

For a while South Africa's innings stagnated and no boundaries came in 17 overs, which was another side effect of the threat of Warne. The batsmen were frightened of him and did not want to take the slightest risk, as all they were interested in was surviving until the end of his ten overs. The bowlers at the other end profited from this mindset. As one of the batsmen was Rhodes, a brilliant runner between the wickets, South Africa collected a good number of short singles, such an important way of keeping the score moving. Even so, to confuse the final equation, the required run rate now came into play and South Africa did not want to fall too far behind. Kallis, no slouch himself, will have made Rhodes a willing partner in this.

The stage had now been reached when Steve Waugh had to bring on his other bowlers, Tom Moody and Mark Waugh, and so the scoring rate inevitably increased, and when, in the 40th over, Rhodes hooked Waugh for six, the balance of the game was again leaning towards South Africa. Seventy runs were needed from the last ten overs, with Rhodes and Kallis in control and Klusener and Pollock, both powerful strikers of the ball, still to come. Then, in the 41st over, Rhodes pulled Reiffel and Bevan came racing in off the leg-side boundary and held a superb catch. Once again all predictions were off.

Rather surprisingly, it was Shaun Pollock and not Lance Klusener who came in now. Klusener's performance with the bat in the whole tournament had been exceptional. At times, he had batted as high as number five and he averaged 140.50 in this World Cup, with a strike rate of 122.17. At this point, Warne had two overs left, which was perhaps why they held Klusener back. Warne again. When the leg-spinner began his last over, South Africa needed 53 runs from 36 balls, and from his first ball, Kallis was dropped from a difficult chance by Reiffel running in from long off. Pollock hit Warne's next two balls for six and four, the first boundaries he had conceded. His first nine overs had cost 14 runs and 14 had come off the first four balls of his last over. Warne deliberately took his time before bowling the fifth ball of the over, to Kallis. He sent down a slower, flighted ball and Kallis pushed a simple catch to Steve Waugh in the covers.

Klusener, nicknamed Zulu because he spoke their language perfectly, now emerged from the pavilion and took a single off

Warne's last ball, before hammering his second, from Fleming, to the boundary. Later in the same over, Pollock dragged a ball back into his stumps, having hit 20 from 14 balls. For South Africa, it was now Klusener or nothing. The tension, the noise and the suspense around the ground was extraordinary. In their special enclosure, even the girlfriends and wives of the two sides had a run-in. It was as tight as that.

The young wicketkeeper, Mark Boucher, came next and had a difficult time trying to give Klusener the strike. When he was bowled by McGrath, they needed 18 runs from 10 balls, with only Steve Elworthy and Allan Donald to come. Before Elworthy arrived, Klusener had only faced five of the last 16 balls and the new batsman's sole objective was to give his partner the strike. He was successful in that, before having to sacrifice himself when Klusener set off for an unlikely second run. Donald, the last man, now took up his position at the non-striker's end. 'I've never been so nervous in my life,' he said when it was all over. 'It was like flying with one wheel off and waiting for the crash landing.' He did not have to wait too long.

Sixteen were needed from eight balls. The next, a low full toss from McGrath, was struck powerfully by Klusener towards long on, where Reiffel was fielding. He instinctively came a pace or two forward, found the ball had been hit harder than he thought and was arriving quicker than he expected. He got both hands up in front of his face, but it burst through them and went over the boundary for six. Klusener picked up the single he wanted off the last ball of the over and the target was down to nine from the last six balls of the match, which were to be bowled by Fleming, who had experience of this. He had bowled the last over in the World Cup semi-final against the West Indies in 1996, which Australia had won by five runs.

The Australians had talked the day before about the possibility of bowling at the end to the powerful left-hander, who looked exactly like the robust and powerful Natal farmer that he was as he stood there with the heaviest bat in the tournament in his hands. The plan was to bowl wide yorkers outside the off stump from round the wicket. There had been no time to practise this manoeuvre, but Fleming was up for it. There were five men back, so that Klusener could take a single if he wanted.

The first ball, Fleming said later, was perfect in every way. Klusener thought so too, and smashed it through extra cover with bewildering power. Moody, at deep cover, was sure he could prevent two runs, but he had hardly moved when the ball crossed the boundary. The noise from the South African supporters in the crowd was unbelievable. In the middle, Klusener stood still and expressionless. The ball was back with Fleming. He settled over his bat. The second ball was another pretty good yorker and with even greater power 'Zulu' dispatched it through mid off for four more and South Africa's target was one run from four balls.

Bedlam broke out and now surely South Africa would take their place in their first ever World Cup final. Klusener had made 31 from 14 balls and for the first time Australia looked beaten. Fleming went back over the wicket and attempted to bowl another yorker, but it landed in the middle of the pitch, no doubt surprising Klusener too. All he could do was pull it towards Lehmann at mid on. Donald was on his toes and was backing up well down the pitch. Lehmann's short underarm throw, which missed the wicket by a fraction, would have run him out by feet.

Again, Fleming was quickly back to his mark, although it was extraordinary the two batsmen did not now have a chat. This time, Fleming got the yorker right and Klusener miscued back down the off side of the pitch towards Mark Waugh, who was at mid off. Klusener set off for a run almost before the ball had left the bat. It looked as if Donald had seen him start but then remembered what had happened the ball before and started to follow this one as it went past him, so as not to be run out at the non-striker's end. Klusener kept going for all he was worth and suddenly Donald looked round and found him almost in the crease beside him.

Waugh picked up the ball and flicked it out of the side of his hand the few yards towards the stumps at the bowler's end. If he had hit the wicket, either batsman might have been out, for neither was in the crease. The ball missed the stumps and was collected by Fleming about five yards down the pitch. He could see Donald just starting for the run. He kept wonderfully calm and rolled the ball along the pitch to Gilchrist at the other end, who removed the bails and Australia were through to the final.

Donald had managed to drop his bat before starting forlornly off on what has by now become the most famous ridiculous single in the history of international limited-overs cricket. The agony in the South African dressing room may perhaps have been equalled by that of the New Zealanders in the dressing room at Lord's after the World Cup final in 2019. But then again, perhaps not. At Edgbaston that evening, strong men wept.

AUSTRALIA v SOUTH AFRICA
ICC 1999 World Cup (semi-final)

At Edgbaston, Birmingham, on 17 June 1999.

Australia

†A.C. Gilchrist c Donald b Kallis		20
M.E. Waugh c Boucher b Pollock		0
R.T. Ponting c Kirsten b Donald		37
D.S. Lehmann c Boucher b Donald		1
*S.R. Waugh c Boucher b Pollock		56
M.G. Bevan c Boucher b Pollock		65
T.M. Moody lbw b Pollock		0
S.K. Warne c Cronje b Pollock		18
P.R. Reiffel b Donald		0
D.W. Fleming b Donald		0
G.D. McGrath not out		0
Extras (1 b, 6 lb, 6 nb, 3 w)		16
Total (all out, 49.2 overs)		**213**

1–3 2–54 3–58 4–68 5–158 6–158 7–207 8–207 9–207 10–213

Bowling: Pollock 9.2–1–36–5; Elworthy 10–0–59–0; Kallis 10–2–27–1; Donald 10–1–32–4; Klusener 9–1–50–0; Cronje 1–0–2–0.

South Africa

G. Kirsten b Warne		18
H.H. Gibbs b Warne		30
D.J. Cullinan run out (Bevan)		6
*W.J. Cronje c M.E. Waugh b Warne		0
J.H. Kallis c S.R. Waugh b Warne		53
J.N. Rhodes c Bevan b Reiffel		43
S.M. Pollock b Fleming		20
L. Klusener not out		31
†M.V. Boucher b McGrath		5
S. Elworthy run out (Reiffel→McGrath)		1
A.A. Donald run out (M.E. Waugh→Fleming→Gilchrist)		0
Extras (1 lb, 5 w)		6
Total (all out, 49.4 overs)		**213**

1–48 2–53 3–53 4–61 5–145 6–175 7–183 8–196 9–198 10–213

Bowling: McGrath 10–0–51–1; Fleming 8.4–1–40–1; Reiffel 8–0–28–1; Warne 10–4–29–4; M.E. Waugh 8–0–37–0; Moody 5–0–27–0.

Toss: South Africa.
Umpires: D.R. Shepherd (Eng), S. Venkataraghavan (Ind).
Man of the Match: S.K. Warne

MATCH TIED (Australia won on better record in qualifying).

22

AN AGONISINGLY SYMPATHETIC ARM

England v Australia (2nd Test)
4–7 August 2005; Edgbaston, Birmingham
England won by two runs.

ENGLAND, who had last won the Ashes in Australia in 1986–87, arrived at Edgbaston for the second Test match in 2005 after they had been bowled out, principally by Glenn McGrath, and lost the first at Lord's by 239 runs. For three days in Birmingham, everything went according to plan and England were on course for a convincing victory, but English cricket-lovers are brought up on stories of how Australian tail-end batsmen have always been irritatingly adhesive and, on occasions, alarmingly productive. When Michael Clarke was out on the third evening, Australia were 175–8, needing 107 runs to win. The next morning, Shane Warne, Brett Lee and Michael Kasprowicz took them to within three runs of what would have been an astonishing victory, in one of the most exciting Test matches I have seen, and my vantage point was the *Test Match Special* commentary box.

The drama began before a ball had been bowled. At 9.15 on the first morning, while the players were going through their warm-up exercises on the outfield, McGrath inadvertently trod on a stray ball and tore the ligaments in his right ankle. He was in pain and had to be wheeled into the pavilion in the groundsman's cart and Kasprowicz took his place in the side. This massive blow for

Australia was followed by a curious decision from their captain, Ricky Ponting. When he won the toss, contrary to local advice, he put England in to bat on a pitch which looked a good one. So it proved when the England score at lunch stood at 132–1 and they went on to reach 407 just before the end of an extraordinary day's cricket. This was a game, too, where Andrew Flintoff and Kevin Pietersen, playing his first series for England, both revealed their respective talents, most especially in a fifth-wicket stand of 103 on this first afternoon. Inevitably, Shane Warne, who took ten wickets in the match, played a major part for Australia with the ball, but in their second innings, he did so with his bat as well. His 42 then put them on course for what would have been a remarkable victory.

Thirty years before, even the most enthusiastic cricket supporter would never have dreamt of such an exciting opening day. This was the first time 400 runs had been scored on the first day of a Test against Australia since 1938. For the first two hours, the two left-handed England openers, Marcus Trescothick and Andrew Strauss, gave the innings an explosive start against bowling which badly missed McGrath's impeccable control. Trescothick's cover-driving was at its best and Strauss really came into his own when Warne came on. Then, just before lunch, when Strauss tried to cut Warne, the ball spun back a huge distance and bowled him.

After lunch, Australia took the wickets of Trescothick, Ian Bell and Michael Vaughan, and with England 187–4 they will not have been too disheartened. At this point, Pietersen was joined by Flintoff and in the next 74 minutes they put on 103 runs in 17 overs with a remarkable display of strokes, each one of which was deafeningly cheered by an amazed crowd. Flintoff and Pietersen are both big men and crowds are naturally attracted to big men who hit the ball hard. They now hit it with such power and certainty that even the slogs were made to look as if they were authentic cricket strokes. Apart from the odd Australian, no one will have wanted this stand to end. Pietersen played one extraordinary stroke I shall not forget when he whipped a ball from Brett Lee from outside the off stump to the mid-on boundary. Lee tried to bounce Flintoff, who kept hooking and pulling him further and further into the stand at square leg. England scored 157 in the two hours between lunch and tea, which is an unthinkable rate of scoring for the first day of any Test match, let alone one between England and Australia.

Flintoff, massively built, with a lovely open boyish face, is, *par excellence*, the homespun hero from Preston. He has such an easy-going manner, as well as a bubbling enthusiasm, which is now seen regularly on television and makes so many of those who watch him feel that they know him. He could easily be the chap living in the next street and we can all identify with him. He was in sharp contrast to his more remote partner that day at Edgbaston. Pietersen has an imperious manner, walks his own path and will not be distracted. There is a slight Machiavellian look to him, for what sense of humour he has, he masks extremely successfully, and he is not a man who indulges easily in light banter either. He attracts controversy, which is not to say that he deliberately seeks it. He certainly does not crave popularity and is true to his feelings. He has never been a team man and as a person he does not often think he may have been in the wrong. It is a moot point whether financial reward, *esprit de corps* or an urge to be one of the boys was his main motivating factor. At his best as a batsman, it was hard to imagine that anyone could ever have been much better. But he was never an easy man to share a dressing room with.

Both Pietersen and Flintoff hit the ball uncommonly hard that day, but their batting styles, just like their ways of life, could scarcely have been more different. Flintoff hit five rumbustious sixes and six fours in his 68 and at all times looked blond and cuddly and homely, while Pietersen, in his more polished way, seemed to be an actor on a distant stage. He contributed one six and ten fours, all memorable strokes, but there was no humour in them. Their contrasting characters were beautifully and cleanly depicted in their respective styles. The crowd will not have cared about this; they revelled in the irrepressible slaughter of the Australian bowling. You could almost feel them drawing in their breath in anticipation each time the bowler's arm came over.

Soon after tea on this first day, when the score had reached 290, Flintoff tried to cut Jason Gillespie and was caught behind. The last four batsmen reached double figures and helped Pietersen – who was eighth out at 348, caught deep on the leg side off Brett Lee – build up the remarkable score of 407 on the first day after being put in. Warne was the most successful bowler, with 4–116, but will have been more than surprised at the indignity of such an assault. Before the innings was over, all the England bowlers had made some telling blows with their bats.

The next day, the game continued at the same cracking pace, even though Matthew Hayden, who never hangs around, was not involved. He was out before a run had been scored, hitting his first ball straight to cover. Ricky Ponting looked in great form, however, playing his strokes on both sides of the wicket. Runs continued to come at a furious pace, but although most of their batsmen made a start, Australia were unable to put together the big partnership they needed. At 88, Ponting swept at Ashley Giles and gave Michael Vaughan a straightforward catch off the top edge at short fine leg, which he accepted with considerable relish. Damien Martyn then played himself in before misjudging a single and being thrown out by Vaughan. Michael Clarke was another who began well, but having reached 40, he carelessly followed one which Giles pushed through a bit faster outside the off stump and was caught behind. Justin Langer was sixth out, having occupied one end for more than four and a half hours. He had made 82 when Simon Jones beat him for pace and had him lbw. After that, only Adam Gilchrist made any impression against some excellent bowling and he was left not out, one short of his fifty. Flintoff took the last two wickets with successive balls and Australia were bowled out for 308, giving England a lead of 99.

They were in a wonderful position, although with just over three days left, they needed to make sure they set Australia a big enough target. Strauss was out that evening, bowled by Warne's second ball, which spun a prodigious distance across the left-hander. The merry course of this match continued the next morning when, to the crowd's bewilderment, England's top order fell in a heap to Warne and Lee. Only two runs had been added to the overnight score of 25–1 when Trescothick played airily at Lee outside the off stump and was caught behind. The score became 29–3 when Lee caught Vaughan on the crease with one which moved in a fraction and removed his off stump. Lee's third wicket of the morning came two runs later when Matthew Hoggard, the nightwatchman, steered a short one to gully. At this moment, England seemed to be losing a match which from the very first ball had moved at an astonishing pace in unexpected directions. Bell and Pietersen took the score somewhat anxiously into the seventies before Pietersen swept at Warne and Gilchrist took a good one-handed catch when the ball ballooned up on the leg side after hitting the edge of the bat or the glove. It became 75–6 when Bell pushed at another from Warne which pitched outside the leg stump and was also caught by Gilchrist.

There was no more important player in this Australian side than Adam Gilchrist. As a batsman, he was one of the main reasons that Test cricket at this time suddenly became a much faster game – Flintoff was another. Runs generally were now coming at a more hectic pace down the batting order and those interminable five-day draws which used to be such a part of the Test scene are now few and far between. Gilchrist opened the innings for Australia in one-day matches and usually batted at number seven in the Test side. It is in the lower middle order that his withering strokeplay has had such a profound effect on the way the game has changed. In the 1950s and 1960s, sides would win the toss and bat and have about 230 or 240 for three or four on the board by the end of the first day. They would have been thought to have done reasonably well. No one in their wildest dreams would have envisaged a score of over 400 on the first day of a match. At the end of the second day here at Edgbaston, England had already begun their second innings.

Among the other principal figures who contributed enormously to this changing scene were Brendon McCullum of New Zealand, A.B. de Villiers of South Africa and Rahul Dravid of India. But Gilchrist was more than just a batsman. He took over from Ian Healy as the Australian wicketkeeper, in which position he has also been outstanding. He was certainly at least Healy's equal standing up to Warne, and as we saw in the day's play I have just described, Gilchrist's reflexes enabled him to hold remarkable diving catches coming off bat and pad in front of the wicket. He is also, as you can see from his face, one of the nicest men, a real sportsman and, like Flintoff, everyone's friend. He has now made himself into one of the least pompous and patronising of television commentators and is always well worth listening to.

Back at Edgbaston, it did not take Warne and Lee long to pick up the next three England wickets, although, at the other end, Flintoff was beginning to play another extraordinary innings. He was joined by Simon Jones at 131–9, when England's lead was 230 – Australia will have fancied their chances of making this sort of score in the final innings – and it was now that he really went to town. He bludgeoned four more sixes, taking his tally for the match to nine, beating Ian Botham's six against Australia at Old Trafford in 1981. Even though most of the fielders were back on the boundary, Flintoff took 20 off one over from Kasprowicz, and then Lee, who at the start of the day had seemed almost unplayable, disappeared for 18 in another. One of the two sixes in the over had to be fished out from among the television cables on the roof of the pavilion by former England captain Graham Gooch, who was himself no slouch with the bat. It was a mesmerising assault and I don't think any of us who had the luck to be there that day will ever forget his innings. On these occasions, the batsman at the other end is usually forgotten, and so it was with Jones. Nonetheless, he produced some good strokes of his own and contributed 12 useful runs to the partnership of 51. In a match which had fluctuated in accordance with the best traditions of Test cricket, the game looked as if it was now almost out of Australia's reach.

The stand ended predictably enough with Flintoff, having made 73 in 85 balls, charging down the wicket, looking for another six against Warne's googly, but failing to make contact. Warne had taken 6–46 in 23.1 overs. These figures perfectly illustrate the unusual control which Warne brought to the art of wrist-spin bowling. By their nature, wrist-spinners are profligate; not so Warne, who continually produced figures which finger-spinners would have envied. Post-First World War Australian leg-spinner Arthur Mailey, always said to be a wonderful bowler, played for New South Wales against Victoria in Melbourne in 1926 and took 4–362 in 64 overs as Victoria made 1,107, still the highest first-class total ever to have been made. Mailey was always rather amused by this; if Warne, always happy to laugh, had suffered a similar fate, I rather think he would have smiled too. The other successful Australian bowler was Lee, a large, robust man with a cheerful head of fair hair who was a wonderfully wholehearted cricketer – a sort of Australian Flintoff, in character if not quite in performance. He had given his all now, taking 4–82 in 18 overs, and these figures may have been a little unfairly dented by Flintoff at the end.

Australia began their second innings in an interminable session after tea on the third day which lasted for three and a half hours in order to make up time which had been lost earlier in the match. Langer and Hayden gave them the perfect start too, when they put on 47 in the first 12 overs. In the next over, Langer, who for once had been outscoring his much more flamboyant partner, played forward to Flintoff with bat slightly away from his body and edged the second ball of the over into his stumps. Flintoff now tested Ponting with a series of inswingers in one of the greatest overs I have ever seen, and Ponting did extremely well to survive four balls. The last ball of that over was a perfectly placed shorter one which left the bat off the seam and lifted nastily. It flicked Ponting's outside edge, which was irresistibly drawn to it.

Flintoff took seven wickets in the match and his bowling was every bit as heroic as his batting. Towards the end, in the second innings, he was suffering from a sore shoulder, but you would never have guessed it. It was sheer willpower that kept him going, and the over in which he sent back Ponting was as fearsome a piece of bowling as you could wish to see. The former Australian captain Ian Chappell said that during this series Flintoff produced some of the most dangerous fast bowling he had ever seen. Having captained Jeff Thomson and Dennis Lillee and faced Andy Roberts, Michael Holding and a few other West Indians, Chappell knew a thing or two about fast bowling.

Australia were now 48–2, with England back on an even keel. Hayden and Martyn added 34 in the next ten overs – the run rate never slackened – before Hayden drove at a wide one from Simon Jones and Trescothick held a fine catch falling to his left at third slip. Jones waved goodbye to Hayden with such extravagance it cost him 20 per cent of his match fee. At 107, Martyn lost concentration and was fourth out when he chipped Hoggard straight to Bell at midwicket. The game was swinging England's way and the Edgbaston crowd was giving it everything. They had to wait until the score had reached 134 before they could salute another wicket. It was then that Simon Katich came forward and played inside a ball from Ashley Giles which went straight on and Trescothick juggled with the catch at slip but held on.

Two runs later Gilchrist came down the wicket to Giles and pushed the easiest of catches to Flintoff at mid on. This was such an important wicket for England because Gilchrist is a batsman who can wreak havoc in this sort of situation. Flintoff immediately got rid of Gillespie with a nasty yorker and England claimed the extra half an hour, thinking they could win the game that evening. As it was, Michael Clarke and Shane Warne batted through almost until the end of the day with some composure. Warne was most determined and gave a hint of what was to come the following morning when he hit two thumping sixes in an over from Giles. Then Clarke was eighth out in the last over, when he was deceived by a brilliantly disguised slower ball from Steve Harmison which hit his middle stump. Even so, with Australia 175–8, needing another 107 more, there cannot have been many people who left that night thinking that Australia might win the match.

There was another big crowd the next morning, even though it might have been all over in five minutes. It was surprising, too, that there should have been such a feeling of tension around the ground. The only two who seemed entirely unaffected were Warne and Lee, who in nine overs proceeded to add 45 runs with a mixture of orthodox strokes together with a few lucky edges. While this was going on, the crowd became distinctly nervous. Then Flintoff, who else, seemed to find the answer when he forced Warne to tread on his own stumps. This brought in Kasprowicz, who was certainly nothing like an exact substitute for McGrath's bowling skills, but with the bat he was averaging ten runs more an innings than McGrath and we soon saw why. He and Lee met and agreed to 'relax and have fun': shades of Botham and Dilley at Headingley in 1981. England's bowlers now got it wrong. As Kasprowicz said later, 'They kept trying to get us out each ball with bouncers and yorkers. It was not until we got down to nine runs that they started bowling good line and length.' The longer it went on, the harder they tried, and that often becomes counterproductive too.

Probably the best stroke of all in this stand was a drive over mid off by Kasprowicz off Giles in an over which produced three fours.

As each one crossed the boundary you could feel the increasing despair in the crowd. In the *TMS* box, we did our best to be fair and unbiased, but it was extremely difficult, just as Jim Maxwell, our Australian colleague, found it difficult to keep the excitement out of his voice. It was impossible to blame him. I remember thinking that nothing is going to stop Australia now. They will be 2–0 ahead in the series and the Ashes have effectively gone.

This gloomy feeling was reinforced five overs later when Kasprowicz flailed at Flintoff outside the off stump and the ball spiralled off the top edge towards Simon Jones at third man. He came in off the boundary, hesitantly at first, and then accelerated and dropped what had by then become a difficult catch low down in front of him. Later, Jones summed it up admirably: 'It's probably the worst I've felt in my life. I lost the ball in the crowd and I just had to guess where it was going. I thought I'd dropped the Ashes.' So did the crowd. Flintoff, now trying to bowl a yorker, slanted it down the leg side and away it went for four byes. To compound the felony, it was also a no-ball.

Meanwhile, Lee had been hit painful blows by Flintoff, on the shoulder and the left hand, but the adrenaline surge kept him going and those five extras will also have helped. Four runs were needed as Harmison began another over from the pavilion end. Sod's Law now struck in the commentary box. As is customary when a visiting side is about to win a Test match in England, the microphone was passed to the visiting commentator, Jim Maxwell, to see Australia home. Harmison bowled a low full toss, which Lee timed beautifully through the covers and had the bad luck to find the only man in the deep on the off side, Simon Jones. They ran a single and three more were needed. Two balls later, Harmison bowled one short of a length which lifted awkwardly and flicked Kasprowicz's glove as he tried to fend it away on the leg side. Geraint Jones, behind the wicket, went sprawling across and took the catch and you could have heard the appeal down at Lord's. Billy Bowden, the New Zealand umpire, raised his favoured bent finger and poor old Jim Maxwell, poised to give news, to Australia especially, of an extraordinary Australian victory, now had to describe their two-run defeat, which was the narrowest margin of victory in any Ashes Test match.

The tremendous cheering from the crowd signalled relief from torment as much as it celebrated one of the most exciting Test matches ever played and, of course, an England victory. For all that, when the match finished, only the most partisan could have failed to notice the forlorn figure of Brett Lee squatting on his haunches in the crease at the non-striker's end. He had fought with all he had got, for an hour and 39 minutes, to take Australia to what would have been an incredible victory, only to see it disappear when it was just an agonising three runs from his grasp.

One can imagine the jumble of thoughts going through his mind. The only person to act upon it and show humility in victory, as well as the true brotherhood of cricket, was Freddie Flintoff, England's main hero in this magnificent topsy-turvy game. Flintoff, who struggled with severe and damaging depression, will have understood Lee's plight all too well. He had been fielding in the slips and when he drew level with Lee, he stooped and put his hand on Lee's shoulder and spoke to him for a moment or two. What was said is their business, but it was clear that Flintoff made time to try and console the miserable Lee, who a few minutes before had been England's number one enemy. It was a wonderful moment.

The final irony of the match was even now unfolding off the field of play. On close examination of the replays on television, it transpired that Kasprowicz's hand had been off his bat at the moment it was struck by the ball. It was therefore not out. Umpire Bowden would have needed superhuman eyesight and reflexes to have been able to spot that and no great fuss was made. The big advantage of Kasprowicz's dismissal was that the series now stood at 1–1, with three dramatically exciting Test matches to come. Going into the fifth Test at The Oval with a 2–1 lead, England just managed to salvage a draw and this brought the Ashes back to England for the first time for almost twenty years – since Mike Gatting's side was victorious in Australia.

ENGLAND v AUSTRALIA (2nd Test)

At Edgbaston, Birmingham, on 4–7 August 2005.

England

M.E. Trescothick c Gilchrist b Kasprowicz...	90		c Gilchrist b Lee	21
A.J. Strauss b Warne	48		b Warne	6
*M.P. Vaughan c Lee b Gillespie	24	(4)	b Lee	1
I.R. Bell c Gilchrist b Kasprowicz	6	(5)	c Gilchrist b Warne	21
K.P. Pietersen c Katich b Lee	71	(6)	c Gilchrist b Warne	20
A. Flintoff c Gilchrist b Gillespie	68	(7)	b Warne	73
†G.O. Jones c Gilchrist b Kasprowicz	1	(8)	c Ponting b Lee	9
A.F. Giles lbw b Warne	23	(9)	c Hayden b Warne	8
M.J. Hoggard lbw b Warne	16	(3)	c Hayden b Lee	1
S.J. Harmison b Warne	17		c Ponting b Warne	0
S.P. Jones not out	19		not out	12
Extras (9 lb, 14 nb, 1 w)	24		(1 lb, 9 nb)	10
Total (all out, 79.2 overs)	**407**		(all out, 52.1 overs)	**182**

1–112 2–164 3–170 4–187 5–290 6–293
7–342 8–348 9–375 10–407

1–25 2–27 3–29 4–31 5–72 6–75
7–101 8–131 9–131 10–182

Bowling, *1st innings*: Lee 17–1–111–1; Gillespie 22–3–91–2; Kasprowicz 15–3–80–3; Warne 25.2–4–116–4. *2nd innings*: Lee 18–1–82–4; Gillespie 8–0–24–0; Kasprowicz 3–0–29–0; Warne 23.1–7–46–6.

Australia

J.L. Langer lbw b S.P. Jones	82		b Flintoff	28
M.L. Hayden c Strauss b Hoggard	0		c Trescothick b S.P. Jones	31
*R.T. Ponting c Vaughan b Giles	61		c G.O. Jones b Flintoff	0
D.R. Martyn run out (Vaughan)	20		c Bell b Hoggard	28
M.J. Clarke c G.O. Jones b Giles	40		b Harmison	30
S.M. Katich c G.O. Jones b Flintoff	4		c Trescothick b Giles	16
†A.C. Gilchrist not out	49		c Flintoff b Giles	1
S.K. Warne b Giles	8	(9)	hit wkt b Flintoff	42
B. Lee c Flintoff b S.P. Jones	6	(10)	not out	43
J.N. Gillespie lbw b Flintoff	7	(8)	lbw b Flintoff	0
M.S. Kasprowicz lbw b Flintoff	0		c G.O. Jones b Harmison	20
Extras (13 b, 7 lb, 10 nb, 1 w)	31		(13 b, 8 lb, 18 nb, 1 w)	40
Total (all out, 76 overs)	**308**		(all out, 64.3 overs)	**279**

1–0 2–88 3–118 4–194 5–208 6–262 7–273
8–282 9–308 10–308

1–47 2–48 3–82 4–107 5–134
6–136 7–137 8–175 9–220 10–279

Bowling, *1st innings*: Harmison 11–1–48–0; Hoggard 8–0–41–1; S.P. Jones 16–2–69–2; Flintoff 15–1–52–3; Giles 26–2–78–3. *2nd innings*: Harmison 17.3–3–62–2; Hoggard 5–0–26–1; Giles 15–3–68–2; Flintoff 22–3–79–4; S.P. Jones 5–1–23–1.

Close of play, *day 1*: England (1) 407 all out; *day 2*: England (2) 25–1 (Trescothick 19*, Hoggard 0*); *day 3*: Australia (2) 175–8 (Warne 20*).

Toss: Australia. Last-innings target: 282 runs.
Umpires: B.F. Bowden (NZ), R.E. Koertzen (SA).
Man of the Match: A. Flintoff.

ENGLAND won by two runs.

23

KEEPING COOL IN COLOMBO

Sri Lanka v South Africa (2nd Test)
4–8 August 2006; P. Saravanamuttu Stadium, Colombo
Sri Lanka won by one wicket.

THIS was a remarkable two-match Test series which may never have received the attention it should have done from the cricketing world. In the first Test those two supreme batting stylists, Mahela Jayawardene and Kumar Sangakkara, who has just finished his two-year term as a most impressive president of the MCC, put together a stand of 624 for the third wicket which was the highest stand ever in all first-class cricket, let alone Test cricket. It is not often that great batsmen both play at their best when they are in together, but these two certainly did now. The greatest example of this that I ever saw was at Kingsmead in Durban in the second Test between South Africa and Australia in 1969–70, when Graeme Pollock and Barry Richards put on almost a hundred in the hour after lunch with as remarkable an exhibition of strokeplay as one could wish to see, although now rivalled by these two Sri Lankans.

Now, the second Test in Colombo, when Sri Lanka made 352–9 in the last innings to win the match, did its best to live up to the first. At the time, this was the sixth highest successful run chase in Test cricket. An innings of 123 by Mahela Jayawardene, taking his tally for the two-match series to a princely 510, led the way, but in the end Sri Lanka reached their target with the last pair together.

One danger with thrilling finishes is that they tend to blot out the cricket played earlier in the game before it rises to its climax. Muttiah Muralitharan, bowling as mysteriously as ever, took 12–225 in the match, which was an immense achievement. These are the sort of figures one came to expect from Muralitharan too, who ended his career with 800 Test wickets, 92 ahead of Shane Warne's 708. Of course, the arguments about the legitimacy of Murali's action will go on for ever. It was an extraordinary action, full of all sorts of kinks, but its product remains in the record books and I shall leave it at that. He was an incredible performer and the nicest man ever to lace on cricket boots, with a wonderful mischievous look to him, which was, perhaps, appropriate.

The fact that more than 300 runs were scored in all four innings of this second Test shows that there was nothing badly wrong with the wicket. A.B. de Villiers, Ashwell Prince, Herschelle Gibbs and Mark Boucher all played important innings for South Africa. All of Sri Lanka's specialist batsmen made useful contributions, while in the last innings Jayawardene made the only century in the match. Dale Steyn and Makhaya Ntini were South Africa's two most successful bowlers and they were seriously handicapped when Ntini, at the time rated number two in the world, pulled a hamstring after bowling 7.2 typically energetic and demanding overs in Sri Lanka's second innings and took no part on the last day.

South Africa had won the toss and were bowled out just before the end of the first day for 361. Their openers had faced the first two overs of their second innings before play finished on the second day, after sending back Sri Lanka for 321. South Africa's second innings ended on the fourth day at 311, which left Sri Lanka to make a massive 352 in their second innings on a pitch which was, by now, worn and was giving the bowlers a certain amount of help.

Sri Lanka lost their first wicket almost at once when Upul Tharanga followed one from Ntini which left him with his bat away from his body and Gibbs held a straightforward catch at second slip. Sangakkara joined Sanath Jayasuriya and they put on 82 in even time before Sangakkara came forward to drive a ball of full length outside the off stump from Shaun Pollock. He also played away from his body and the ball flew low down towards cover and Hashim Amla threw himself forward and took a good catch close to the ground.

Delighted as the South Africans were to see the back of Sangakkara, the sight of Mahela Jayawardene emerging from the pavilion will hardly have helped to settle their nerves. He began to bat as only he can and, with Jayasuriya going for his strokes at the other end in his usual busy left-handed way, Sri Lanka appeared to be in control. Then, at 121, left-arm spinner Nicky Boje had a bit of help from the pitch. Jayasuriya went back to a ball just short of a length which jumped awkwardly and hit him on the glove. The ball looped away on the leg side and Amla again, at short leg, dived forward and took a fine one-handed catch about an inch from the ground. Sri Lanka were now 121–3, the game had undergone a definite shift and suddenly there was rather more spring in the steps of the South African fielders.

Tillakaratne Dilshan settled in and helped Jayawardene put on 43 without much trouble. Then, suddenly, Dilshan's concentration went. He came down the pitch to one which Boje pitched on middle and off and, although he was not quite to the pitch of the ball, drove and the ball flicked the edge and Gibbs held the catch, diving to his right at slip. Sri Lanka were 164–4 and South Africa now began to sense they were on top, as they would have been long before if Gibbs had been able to hold on to Jayawardene in the slips when he had made only two. The fluctuations were intriguing and the excitement was building up nicely.

Chamara Kapugedera stayed for 40 minutes and saw up the 200, but immediately afterwards he came forward to Boje, making some room for himself so he could drive a straight one through the covers. He did not manage to control the stroke and A.B. de Villiers, in the covers, dived full length to his left and held on to a wonderful catch. De Villiers was, for many years, such an important figure in South African cricket, although in the end it is probably fair for me to feel that his Test career was restricted because he enjoyed the greater financial returns that came from playing one-day cricket. He was so good he could have adapted his style to any form of the game, but Test cricket was surely his natural home. His splendid catch reduced Sri Lanka to 201–5 and their target of 352 was looking a long way off. The Sri Lankan captain, Prasanna Jayawardene, no relation, now made his namesake an extremely effective partner. They came together nearly an hour before the end of the fourth day and by the close they had taken Sri Lanka to 262–5, Mahela having reached 77 and Prasanna 27. They needed another 90.

Mahela, who never seemed nervous or fussed by the situation the match was in, began the last day with two wonderful strokes off Andrew Hall. A magnificent cover drive was followed by a flawless square cut when Boje pitched short. At the other end, Prasanna was soon undone by a reverse inswinger from Hall, by which time they had taken their sixth-wicket stand to 78 and South Africa were beginning to get notably anxious. Hall bowled at Prasanna's middle and off stumps and then, late in the flight, the reverse swing took the ball past the inside edge. It crashed into his pad and he seemed to be in front of all three stumps.

The South Africans were cock-a-hoop and the noise and bustle at the P. Saravanamuttu Stadium was beginning to boil over. The South Africans discovered that Farveez Maharoof was a better batsman than they may have thought, but that was entirely their own fault. He was let off close to the wicket off consecutive balls. First, when he had made two, he should have been stumped by Mark Boucher off one from Boje which turned and lifted. Then, the very next ball, Amla dropped a catch off bat and pad at silly point. Mahela was undeterred by any of this and went happily on, driving Hall to the straight boundary and then square-cutting him past cover for another. This took him to within two runs of his hundred, which arrived in the next over. Steyn and Pollock then took the new ball, but without making the breakthrough South Africa needed. In putting on 54, Mahela and Maharoof had steered Sri Lanka to 333–6 by lunch on the last day, when Sri Lanka appeared to be sitting pretty, needing only 19 more with four wickets in hand.

Having gone into lunch pretty deflated, the South Africans re-emerged looking surprisingly reinvigorated. Steyn and Boje shared the attack. They did not allow the batsmen room to play their strokes and only eight runs came from the first seven overs. Suddenly, the batsmen found themselves under pressure, but with Mahela still there, Sri Lanka seemed safe enough. The pressure got to Mahela, however, and he now came charging down the wicket to Boje and tried to play his faithful cover drive. Boje had beaten him in the air. He did not get to the pitch of the ball and the resulting edge flew to Gibbs, who this time made no mistake.

With Mahela out of the way, it really was game on for South Africa, even though, at 341–7, only 11 runs were now wanted. The next five overs produced seven anxious runs and when Chaminda Vaas tried to break the deadlock with an attempted blow on the off side, A.B. de Villiers held another remarkable catch, left-handed in the gully. It was 348–8 and Sri Lanka were just one stroke from victory. Muralitharan aimed a slog for the boundary, which brought him two runs. The next ball from Hall was straight. He had another swing, but missed and was bowled. It was 350–9.

The tension and excitement had to be seen to be believed, but Maharoof remained calm enough. He took a single which ensured that the scores were level and so the best South Africa could hope for was a tie, meaning that Sri Lanka were guaranteed victory in the two-match series. The last man, Lasith Malinga, was on strike and somehow he managed to shovel the ball past the bowler for the winning run, which the good crowd greeted with a mixture of ecstasy and relief. It had been a wonderful Test match in which the advantage had fluctuated this way and that, and it had come down to the slenderest margin of victory on the last afternoon.

SRI LANKA v SOUTH AFRICA (2nd Test)

At P. Saravanamuttu Stadium, Colombo, on 4–8 August 2006.

South Africa

H.H. Gibbs lbw b Vaas	0	c Jayasuriya b Muralitharan	92
A.J. Hall c Dilshan b Malinga	0	c H.A.P.W. Jayawardene b Maharoof	32
J.A. Rudolph b Malinga	13	run out (Kapugedera)	15
H.M. Amla lbw b Muralitharan	40	run out (Kapugedera)	8
*A.G. Prince c H.A.P.W. Jayawardene b Muralitharan	86	c and b Muralitharan	17
A.B. de Villiers c H.A.P.W. Jayawardene b Malinga	95	c Dilshan b Muralitharan	33
†M.V. Boucher b Muralitharan	32	c Dilshan b Muralitharan	65
S.M. Pollock not out	57	c Tharanga b Muralitharan	14
N. Boje c Sangakkara b Maharoof	11	c H.A.P.W. Jayawardene b Muralitharan	15
D.W. Steyn c Jayasuriya b Muralitharan	6	lbw b Muralitharan	0
M. Ntini c Maharoof b Muralitharan	13	not out	5
Extras (8 nb)	8	(9 b, 4 lb, 1 nb, 1 w)	15
Total (all out, 89.5 overs)	**361**	(all out, 107.5 overs)	**311**

1–0 2–4 3–31 4–70 5–231 6–256 7–273 8–307 9–327 10–361

1–76 2–119 3–131 4–161 5–206 6–207 7–235 8–280 9–282 10–311

Bowling, *1st innings*: Vaas 18–4–71–1; Malinga 18–4–81–3; Muralitharan 33.5–2–128–5; Maharoof 15–2–52–1; Jayasuriya 5–0–29–0. *2nd innings*: Vaas 19–4–53–0; Malinga 12–1–55–0; Maharoof 21–3–53–1; Muralitharan 46.5–12–97–7; Jayasuriya 9–0–40–0.

Sri Lanka

W.U. Tharanga c Boje b Ntini	2	c Gibbs b Ntini	0
S.T. Jayasuriya c Gibbs b Ntini	47	c Amla b Boje	73
K.C. Sangakkara c Amla b Ntini	14	c Amla b Pollock	39
*D.P.M.D. Jayawardene c Boucher b Steyn	13	c Gibbs b Boje	123
T.M. Dilshan b Ntini	4	c Gibbs b Boje	18
C.K. Kapugedera b Boje	63	c de Villiers b Boje	13
†H.A.P.W. Jayawardene b Steyn	42	lbw b Hall	30
M.F. Maharoof b Steyn	56	not out	29
W.P.U.J.C. Vaas c Boucher b Steyn	64	c de Villiers b Hall	4
S.L. Malinga not out	8 (11)	not out	1
M. Muralitharan c Hall b Steyn	0 (10)	b Hall	2
Extras (1 lb, 5 nb, 2 w)	8	(4 b, 8 lb, 4 nb, 4 w)	20
Total (all out, 85.1 overs)	**321**	(9 wkts, 113.3 overs)	**352**

1–16 2–43 3–74 4–85 5–86 6–191 7–191 8–308 9–317 10–321

1–12 2–94 3–121 4–164 5–201 6–279 7–341 8–348 9–350

Bowling, *1st innings*: Ntini 21–3–84–4; Steyn 13.1–1–82–5; Pollock 16–4–52–0; Hall 15–7–31–0; Boje 20–6–71–1. *2nd innings*: Ntini 7.2–2–13–1; Steyn 22.4–2–81–0; Boje 39.3–11–111–4; Pollock 19–2–60–1; Hall 25–3–75–3.

Close of play, *day 1*: South Africa (1) 361 all out; *day 2*: South Africa (2) 6–0 (Gibbs 4*, Hall 2*); *day 3*: South Africa (2) 257–7 (Boucher 28*, Boje 5*); *day 4*: Sri Lanka (2) 262–5 (D.P.M.D. Jayawardene 77*, H.A.P.W. Jayawardene 27*).

Toss: South Africa. Last-innings target: 352 runs.
Umpires: Aleem Dar (Pak), B.F. Bowden (NZ).
Man of the Match: D.P.M.D. Jayawardene.

SRI LANKA won by one wicket.

24

ONLY AN IRISHMAN . . . IN BANGALORE

England v Ireland (World Cup, Group B)

2 March 2011; M. Chinnaswamy Stadium, Bangalore

Ireland won by three wickets.

Results that are inconceivable are almost certain, therefore, to be dramatic, but are seldom more deliciously outrageous than this one. Six years before they were elevated to Test match status, Ireland were one of the Associate Members of the ICC who qualified for the World Cup finals in India and Pakistan in 2010–11. For the 15th game of the qualifying round, Ireland took on England in Bangalore and after England had won the toss, they watched them amass 327–8 in their 50 overs. To underline the apparent hopelessness of it all – 328 was a more difficult target then than it appears to have become these days – Ireland lost their captain to the first ball of their innings and then found themselves sinking fast at 111–5, four balls short of the halfway stage. Their target then was 217 in 25.4 overs with five wickets left and they seemed beyond salvation.

At this point, Kevin O'Brien was joined by Alex Cusack and, with a series of blistering strokes, it took O'Brien 50 balls to reach the quickest ever hundred in a World Cup match. Australia's Matthew Hayden had reached a hundred in 66 balls against

South Africa in 2007. After 31 overs, the two Irishmen took the second five overs of Powerplay, when fewer fielders are allowed in the deep, and hammered 62 runs from them. When Cusack was run out, 55 were needed from 8.3 overs, with four wickets in hand. O'Brien was run out in the penultimate over, when 11 were still wanted from 11 balls, having hit 113 in 63 balls with 13 fours and six sixes. By then, John Mooney had already taken over the leading role. In the last over, when three were needed, he played Jimmy Anderson's first ball through midwicket for four and Ireland had won an incredible victory by three wickets with five balls remaining.

Kevin O'Brien, who had started out in life as an electrician, comes from a great sporting family. His elder brother, Niall, also played cricket for Ireland and was a member of the side that beat England in Bangalore. Their father, Brendan, had represented Ireland on 52 occasions. Both the brothers have played county cricket. Kevin joined Nottinghamshire and then Gloucestershire, while Niall has turned out for Kent, Northamptonshire and Leicestershire. Cricket Ireland awarded both brothers central contracts when they began in 2010 and they have been crucial to the development of the country's cricket. Ireland made their way up the ladder to the point where they were elected Full Members of the ICC in 2017, which brings Test match status with it. Kevin went on to score Ireland's first Test hundred when he made 118 against Pakistan in 2018 and the following year he made their first international T20 hundred. He is a punishing right-handed strokemaker and there is a compelling and infectious enthusiasm in his character which has enabled him cheerfully to take on bowling attacks in such an entertaining and destructive manner. He is, too, a useful fast-medium seam bowler.

An Ireland victory was made to seem even more unlikely when the toss was won by England who, having tied with India in their previous match, will have been keen to get back on the winning trail. By the time they had amassed 327–8, it had appeared extremely unlikely that what was still effectively a team of not much more than part-timers might make the highest ever score to win a match in a World Cup. Victories like Ireland's are, of course, the life's blood of any sporting competition and they can lift not only the cricketing community but the whole country as well. This result came at a time of considerable economic stress in Ireland, and it will have given the whole country a much-needed uplift, especially as the victories the Irish love the most are those they notch up against England. For Ireland as well as Irish cricket, it was joy unconfined for the next two days in Bangalore and for a lot longer than that back at home. Enda Kenny, Fine Gael leader and Taoiseach elect, summed it up perfectly: 'Their supreme effort will lift the spirits of every single Irish person, no matter where they are in the world.' At Balbriggan Cricket Club in north Dublin, where John Mooney, who hit the winning runs, came from, there was mayhem in the bar as that night merged into the next one.

The effect on the losing side on these occasions goes from initial anger, through disbelief and then, of course, to blame. Fortunately, there are always those who will accept these results with a smile and a shrug of the shoulders, as just one of those things. After the immediate frenetic excitement has died down, these unexpected results make the world a better and more amusing place. Like many sides beaten in this way, England almost certainly paid the penalty for taking the view that it was going to be easy and then, with Ireland 111–5, thinking that it was all over and subconsciously letting up. They were guilty, first when batting and later with the ball, of playing some lazy cricket brought on by the seeming certainty of victory. Then, as O'Brien and Cusack piled on the runs for the sixth wicket, they were unable to pull it back. What a joy actually to have spent that day at the Chinnaswamy Stadium, unless, of course, you were the staunchest of England supporters, come what may.

When Andrew Strauss and Kevin Pietersen took 72 off ten rather gentle overs at the start, England looked on course for an even larger total. Both openers perished to casual strokes: Strauss missed a pull against left-arm spinner George Dockrell, and Pietersen, who was off balance, played an ill-judged reverse sweep at off-spinner Paul Stirling, and gave a simple catch off the top edge to the wicketkeeper. Jonathan Trott and Ian Bell now added 167 in 26 overs, before Bell pulled a full toss to midwicket and Trott, who until then had taken no chances, suddenly had an enormous heave at Mooney and was bowled. None of the main batsmen had been prepared to work for the big score which in limited-overs cricket brings victory with it, even though a total of 327 will have seemed large enough. Mooney, who was the fifth bowler used, finished with 4–63 in nine overs and benefited from bowling straight and to a full length, which is the best way in the closing overs. Mooney had played an important part with his fast-medium seam bowling, just as he was to do later with his batting.

Ireland made the worst possible start when their captain, William Porterfield, played the first ball of the innings, from Anderson, into his wicket. Paul Stirling, the other opener, Ed Joyce, who had played for Middlesex and Sussex and from whom great things were expected, and Niall O'Brien all settled in, but none went on to play an innings which made any significant difference in such a big run chase. Graeme Swann, with his usual vibrant off-spin and clever variations of flight and pace, then picked up the important wickets of Joyce, Niall O'Brien and Gary Wilson, reducing Ireland to 111–5, when Kevin O'Brien was joined by Cusack.

O'Brien made an improbable spectacle, for he had dyed his hair pink and a good deal of it hung down outside his loosely fitting helmet. It was done in support of the Irish Cancer Society. He began his innings by aiming to drive his second ball, from Graeme Swann, fiercely through the covers and picked up four runs off the edge through where slip would have been standing if there had been one, and after that Michael Yardy was twice despatched, off the middle of the bat, to the boundary. O'Brien swung Swann for two big sixes on the leg side, before pulling Anderson to square leg for another.

After this stroke, Anderson and O'Brien had a lively verbal exchange, with the Irishman not letting his country down in the slanging match either. In this respect, he would hold his end up in similar verbal encounters with wicketkeeper Matt Prior later on. His fifty came from only 30 balls and after that, his runs came faster still. When the last Powerplay was taken, he made room for himself and edged the first ball he faced from Tim Bresnan through the slips for four and then later in the over slashed a ball over cover for six. He drove Anderson over long on for what was reckoned to be the biggest six of the tournament and O'Brien had scored 31 off just nine balls. It is hard to say at exactly what point the situation changed from Ireland being a side that was going down with all guns firing, to one which suddenly realised it had the chance of an extraordinary victory, but it was in his period of play.

O'Brien moved from 60 to 70 in two balls and then from 80 to 90 in two more, which indicates that he did not feel an over-whelming need for caution as victory approached, although he quietened somewhat after reaching his hundred, at which point John Mooney took over. Everyone in the ground, players and spectators alike, were getting nervous and edgy. Were Ireland really going to pull off the biggest run chase in the history of the World Cup and beat England? The fielding, particularly the catching, had not been good and now when O'Brien had reached 91, Andrew Strauss dropped a difficult chance. O'Brien's hundred – his first since February 2007 – arrived with a crafty flick and it was only the third time he had run a two during his innings.

While all this was going on, Alex Cusack made O'Brien the perfect partner. He kept the other end going and gave his partner the strike when he could, at the same time as picking up the runs that came his way, scoring 47 in 58 balls. He played an extremely important innings and in the end he was run out making sure it was not his partner who was out. When the left-handed Mooney joined O'Brien, 55 runs were still needed and Mooney had the confidence to take over the leading role. He and O'Brien took the score along to 317, when O'Brien was run out in the penultimate over, trying to turn a single into a two. Eleven were now needed and the experienced Trent Johnston took O'Brien's place and coolly cover-drove his first ball for four. Four more runs accrued during the rest of that over and three were, therefore, needed from the last. Anderson was bowling to Mooney and, with confidence and panache, he played the first off his legs through midwicket for four. It would be impossible to praise Mooney's innings of 33 too highly. He took the pressure off the tiring O'Brien, he never let the pace slacken and he hit six fours from 30 balls.

When it was all over, a thrilled Kevin O'Brien said, 'I remember at one stage looking up and I was 80 off 40 balls and I was like, "Where did that come from?" It was pretty surreal. I didn't have any clue what the record was at the time. I didn't know until after the match. It's the best I've ever played. Everything came off. I had a bit of luck and just kept going.'

It was good, uncomplicated stuff. There was no conceit, just a genuine sense of surprise from a lovely man who put his country's cricket more firmly on the map than it had ever been.

ENGLAND v IRELAND
ICC 2011 World Cup (Group B)

At M. Chinnaswamy Stadium, Bangalore, on 2 March 2011 (day/night).

England

*A.J. Strauss b Dockrell	34
K.P. Pietersen c N.J. O'Brien b Stirling	59
I.J.L. Trott b Mooney	92
I.R. Bell c Stirling b Mooney	81
P.D. Collingwood c K.J. O'Brien b Mooney	16
†M.J. Prior b Johnston	6
T.T. Bresnan c Johnston b Mooney	4
M.H. Yardy b Johnston	3
G.P. Swann not out	9
S.C.J. Broad did not bat	
J.M. Anderson did not bat	
Extras (1 b, 2 lb, 20 w)	23
Total (8 wkts, innings closed, 50 overs)	**327**

1–91 2–111 3–278 4–288 5–299 6–312 7–317 8–327

Bowling: Rankin 7–0–51–0; Johnston 10–0–58–2; Cusack 4–0–39–0; Dockrell 10–0–68–1; Mooney 9–0–63–4; Stirling 10–0–45–1.

Ireland

*W.T.S. Porterfield b Anderson	0
P.R. Stirling c Pietersen b Bresnan	32
E.C. Joyce st Prior b Swann	32
†N.J. O'Brien b Swann	29
G.C. Wilson lbw b Swann	3
K.J. O'Brien run out (Bresnan→Prior)	113
A.R. Cusack run out (Collingwood→Broad)	47
J.F. Mooney not out	33
D.T. Johnston not out	7
G.H. Dockrell did not bat	
W.B. Rankin did not bat	
Extras (5 b, 16 lb, 12 w)	33
Total (7 wkts, 49.1 overs)	**329**

1–0 2–62 3–103 4–106 5–111 6–273 7–317

Bowling: Anderson 8.1–1–49–1; Broad 9–0–73–0; Bresnan 10–0–64–1; Yardy 7–0–49–0; Swann 10–0–47–3; Collingwood 5–0–26–0.

Toss: England.
Umpires: Aleem Dar (Pak), B.F. Bowden (NZ).
Man of the Match: K.J. O'Brien.

IRELAND won by three wickets.

25
BRACEWELL'S FINEST HOUR

Australia v New Zealand (2nd Test)
9–12 December 2011; Bellerive Oval, Hobart
New Zealand won by seven runs.

W HEN New Zealand came to Hobart's lovely Bellerive Oval in December 2011, they were having a bad time of it. They had just been massively outplayed by Australia and lost the first Test in Brisbane by nine wickets. New Zealand had not won a Test match in Australia since the days of Richard Hadlee and Martin Crowe back in 1985. Now, for five days in as close and fascinating a game as one could wish to see, a remarkable bowling performance at fast-medium by Doug Bracewell took them to a thrilling victory by just seven runs.

Bracewell, who was 21, comes from a family steeped in cricket. His father was fast bowler Brendon, who played six Test matches for New Zealand, while his uncle, John, a fierce competitor and a fine off-spinner with a Test match hundred against England under his belt as well, played 41. In Australia's second innings, when they needed 241 to win, Doug took 6–40 and in one extraordinary burst removed Ricky Ponting, Michael Clarke and Michael Hussey without conceding a run.

Sadly, Doug was unable to build on the excellent start he made to his Test career with two five-wicket hauls in his first three Test matches. He is a strong, good-looking chap, but with a self-destruct button he has found it difficult to resist. This has undoubtedly harmed his career and will not have endeared him to the authorities. He made his Test debut for New Zealand against Zimbabwe in Bulawayo in 2011 and took five wickets in Zimbabwe's second innings. It is impossible not to feel that he should have done much better than he has for New Zealand. He is one of those lively, likeable characters to whom self-discipline does not come easily and from a cricketing point of view, he has let himself down. He is not the first talented young sportsman to do that.

His finest hour came in only his third Test and this is something which can never be taken away from him. It was an absorbing game from the moment Michael Clarke won the toss and put New Zealand in to bat on a surface which was unusually green on the first morning. Although the bounce was lower than it had been in the first match in Brisbane and the temperature was less conducive to swing, the New Zealand batsmen had a torrid time. James Pattinson, Peter Siddle and Mitchell Starc bowled out New Zealand for 150, but the Australian batsmen then fared even worse. The four New Zealand seam bowlers revelled in conditions that they found were similar to theirs at home, and Australia were bowled out for 136. Although the New Zealand captain, Ross Taylor, fought hard for more than three and a half hours for 56, which gives a good indication of the conditions, New Zealand only managed 226 in their second innings, which left Australia to score 241 to win the match and the series. They will have fancied their chances, especially when at the end of the third day David Warner and Phillip Hughes had put on 72 and, with all ten wickets in hand, Australia needed 169 more. They were well on their way.

This was opening batsman Warner's second Test and he was to leave a considerable mark on it. He has always been a fearlessly competitive batsman, although with an irresistible urge to be involved in controversy, and he has a formidable ability as a sledger. He batted magnificently for his first Test hundred. He is a chunky player, with strong wrists and forearms, and he loves to throw his bat at the ball if he is allowed the room. He played some cracking strokes whenever the bowlers gave him the slightest chance. His partner, Phil Hughes, played an altogether quieter role at the other end. Hughes was the batsman who, three years later, was hit on the neck by a bouncer from Sean Abbott when New South Wales were playing South Australia in Sydney. Hughes tragically died two days later from a brain haemorrhage without coming round after the accident.

The fourth day in Hobart began with Hughes being out before a run had been added. He pushed at a good-length ball from Chris Martin which left the bat a fraction on pitching and Martin Guptill held a good catch swooping to his left at second slip. A useful stand now developed between Warner, who had been punching the ball away through the off side with power and timing, and Usman Khawaja. The score had reached 122 when the left-handed Khawaja drove at Trent Boult and was brilliantly caught, low down to his left at first slip, by Taylor, although partially obscured by Guptill at second.

It was now former captain and Tasmanian Ricky Ponting's turn in what was his last Test innings in Tasmania. He and Warner took the score carefully along to 159 when, with 82 more runs needed, Australia still seemed to be in comfortable control of the match. Ponting then tried to force Bracewell through the covers, but did not time the shot and was easily caught at cover. He left the ground to a standing ovation. By now, Warner was in some discomfort, having hurt his back while diving in for a short single. Doug Bracewell had been bowling with good rhythm as he moved the ball about in the air and off the seam. His well-concealed changes of pace were also causing problems. In his next over, he pitched one up and Michael Clarke went to drive it through the covers. The ball moved away off the seam and Ross Taylor took the catch at first slip. This made it 159–4 and Australia were beginning to fret, while the overjoyed New Zealanders started to think they might have a chance.

The game was firmly back in the melting pot when Bracewell's next ball, of full length swinging in to the left-handed Hussey, pitched on leg stump and straightened before hitting Hussey on the pad. Umpire Asad Rauf turned down the appeal, but the New Zealanders reviewed it and the replay showed the ball would have hit the leg stump. Umpire Rauf had to reverse his decision. It was 159–5. The New Zealanders were cock-a-hoop, while Australian heads were beginning to drop. This was the moment when the balance of the game noticeably shifted, even though Warner was still batting as well as ever.

Warner reached his hundred immediately after lunch and celebrated with those leaps and waves and extravagant gestures which have become so familiar over the years. Tim Southee now came into the attack and found some outswing. After an edge for four, Brad Haddin went forward to the next ball, which again left him and Taylor made no mistake at first slip. When Peter Siddle followed suit almost immediately afterwards, Australia were 194–7 and for the first time New Zealand actually seemed to be winning the match, in spite of Warner's brooding presence at the non-striker's end. Five runs later, James Pattinson reached out at another from Bracewell which left the bat and Guptill held the catch at second slip, which made it 199–8. Led by Ross Taylor, the New Zealand slip-catching on this fourth day had been exceptional.

By now, the crowd which had come to cheer the Australians had been reduced to silence and the noise from the ecstatic New Zealanders, who had probably come along more than anything out of a sense of duty, must have been stirring for their fellow countrymen. Before another run had been scored, Bracewell made short work of Starc. He bowled him a beauty which pitched just outside the off stump and came back enough to hit the middle and off stumps, with Starc nowhere. Now the tall, balding figure of Nathan Lyon, the most enigmatic of cricketers, strode out to join Warner.

Lyon has taken more Test wickets than Dennis Lillee and there can be no doubting his ability as an off-spinner. He is probably the best Australia have ever had. He obviously likes to come in at number eleven, although there are plenty who have gone in above him without having any right to do so. Lyon enjoys being a nuisance to the bowling side right at the end and for that he is well-equipped. There is no keener Australian patriot in the side and there are a number of his opponents who he has not endeared himself to. When he fumbled the ball in the Test match at Headingley in 2019 with Jack Leach, England's last man, yards out of his ground, and England and the Ashes at his mercy, there will have been many people who will have smiled at his discomfort. Now, he joined the like-minded Warner and no one will have enjoyed helping him add 34 runs for the last wicket more than Lyon, and he will also have relished the agony of the New Zealanders as Australia drew ever closer to their target. There is a lot to be said for having a Lyon in your dressing room, as well as having him bat at number eleven.

A few solid punches from Warner reduced the target to 25. Then Southee struck lyon on the pad with a ball of full length and umpire Nigel Llong gave him out. Lyon decided on what most people thought was a pointless review. Far from it: the camera showed the ball had pitched at most a millimetre outside the leg stump. New Zealand had to stop their extravagant celebrations and the game continued. In the very next over, wicketkeeper Reece Young persuaded his captain to go for another review when an inswinger from Bracewell hit Lyon on the pad. The New Zealanders discovered the umpire was right in thinking the ball had been swinging down the leg side. Lyon celebrated with a flick off his pads to the midwicket boundary which any batsman would have envied.

A mere eight were needed when Bracewell ran in again to bowl to Lyon. The ball was on a good length starting outside the off stump and coming in just enough to find its way between Lyon's bat and pad before crashing into the middle and off stumps. Now, at last, the New Zealanders were able to celebrate their first victory in Australia for 26 years and what was also Australia's first ever defeat at the Bellerive Oval, that lovely ground backing onto the estuary of the Derwent River where Australia have been playing since 1989.

Everyone needed strong nerves to get through this last day. Warner was left on 123 not out, having carried his bat through the innings. At the end, Lyon sank to his knees and for some time refused to accept the match was finished. I don't think Warner will have been that happy either. Test matches do not come much more exciting or dramatic than this, and New Zealanders probably enjoy beating Australia even more than the English – well, as much, at any rate.

AUSTRALIA v NEW ZEALAND (2nd Test)

At Bellerive Oval, Hobart, on 9–12 December 2011.

New Zealand

B.B. McCullum c Haddin b Pattinson	16	(2)	c Hughes b Pattinson	12
M.J. Guptill c Haddin b Siddle	3	(1)	c Haddin b Siddle	16
J.D. Ryder lbw b Pattinson	0		st Haddin b Hussey	16
*L.R.P.L. Taylor lbw b Siddle	6		c Clarke b Pattinson	56
K.S. Williamson c Haddin b Starc	19		c Ponting b Siddle	34
D.G. Brownlie b Pattinson	56		c Haddin b Pattinson	21
†R.A. Young b Pattinson	0		lbw b Siddle	9
D.A.J. Bracewell c Clarke b Siddle	12		b Lyon	4
T.G. Southee b Starc	18		c Hussey b Lyon	13
T.A. Boult not out	0		c Hussey b Lyon	21
C.S. Martin b Pattinson	0		not out	2
Extras (2 b, 12 lb, 5 nb, 1 w)	20		(4 b, 11 lb, 2 nb, 5 w)	22
Total (all out, 45.5 overs)	**150**		(all out, 78.3 overs)	**226**

1–10 2–11 3–25 4–56 5–60 6–60 7–105
8–146 9–150 10–150

1–36 2–36 3–73 4–139 5–171
6–178 7–190 8–203 9–203 10–226

Bowling, *1st innings*: Pattinson 13.5–3–51–5; Siddle 13–3–42–3; Starc 11–4–30–2; Lyon 8–4–13–0. *2nd innings*: Pattinson 21–7–54–3; Siddle 25–11–66–3; Starc 19–6–47–0; Hussey 5–0–15–1; Lyon 7.3–1–25–3; Ponting 1–0–4–0.

Australia

D.A. Warner c Taylor b Martin	15	(2)	not out	123
P.J. Hughes c Guptill b Martin	4	(1)	c Guptill b Martin	20
Usman Khawaja c Young b Martin	7		c Taylor b Boult	23
R.T. Ponting lbw b Southee	5		c Southee b Bracewell	16
*M.J. Clarke b Bracewell	22		c Taylor b Bracewell	0
M.E.K. Hussey c Young b Boult	8		lbw b Bracewell	0
†B.J. Haddin c McCullum b Bracewell	5		c Taylor b Southee	15
P.M. Siddle c Guptill b Bracewell	36		c Ryder b Southee	2
J.L. Pattinson c Williamson b Boult	17		c Guptill b Bracewell	4
M.A. Starc lbw b Boult	4		b Bracewell	0
N.M. Lyon not out	1		b Bracewell	9
Extras (1 b, 8 lb, 3 nb)	12		(3 b, 18 lb)	21
Total (all out, 51 overs)	**136**		(all out, 63.4 overs)	**233**

1–7 2–24 3–31 4–35 5–58 6–69 7–75
8–131 9–131 10–136

1–72 2–122 3–159 4–159 5–159
6–192 7–194 8–199 9–199 10–233

Bowling, *1st innings*: Martin 16–1–46–3; Boult 13–4–29–3; Southee 12–2–32–1; Bracewell 10–3–20–3. *2nd innings*: Martin 16–4–44–1; Boult 12–1–51–1; Southee 19–3–77–2; Bracewell 16.4–4–40–6.

Close of play, *day 1*: Australia (1) 12–1 (Warner 7*, Usman Khawaja 1*); *day 2*: New Zealand (2) 139–3 (Taylor 42*, Williamson 34*); *day 3*: Australia (2) 72–0 (Hughes 20*, Warner 47*).

Toss: Australia. Last-innings target: 241 runs.
Umpires: Asad Rauf (Pak), N.J. Llong (Eng).
Man of the Match: D.A.J. Bracewell.

NEW ZEALAND won by seven runs.

26
SHRUBSOLE LIGHTS UP LORD'S

England v India (ICC Women's World Cup final)
23 July 2017; Lord's Cricket Ground, London
England won by nine runs.

A T Lord's, at any rate, the modern era of cricket took a considerable step forward in July 2017 when Anya Shrubsole, in the end almost on her own, bowled England to a most dramatically exciting victory over India, by nine runs, in the women's World Cup final. In her last four overs, Shrubsole took 5–11 in 19 balls, the fifth after a badly dropped catch off the previous ball. It was a day which had begun with queues forming in the early hours of the morning all round the outside of the ground, including MCC members outside the Grace Gates. A packed crowd watched a match which for most of the time seemed to be progressing towards a comfortable and uneventful victory for India. With 7.2 overs left, they were 191–3, needing only 38 more to beat England's disappointing 228–7 in their 50 overs. It looked all over at that point, except that in one-innings cricket it never quite is.

Lord's was on its toes well before the start of a great game of cricket. The ticket touts were out in force engaging in a busy two-way trade, and perhaps that more than anything illustrated the advance women's cricket has made in recent years. It was sad that Rachael Heyhoe Flint, who, in England, had carried the women's game on her back for so many years, captaining the side in 1973 when England won their first World Cup, was not there to take part in this extraordinary day. She had died in January and a tribute was paid to her before the start. By then, the five-minute bell in front of the Bowler's Bar in the Pavilion had been vigorously rung by Eileen Ash, née Whelan, who was 105 and had first played for England in 1937, against Australia at Northampton. She claimed that it was a combination of yoga and wine that had kept her going in such fine fettle. It was disappointing and perhaps inevitable, because MCC members do not change their minds in a hurry, that there were many empty seats in the Pavilion in spite of the early queues. By now, members of the MCC had become accustomed to and enjoyed one-day cricket, but they were still not convinced by the distaff side of the game, although I shall be surprised if there are any empty seats in the Pavilion the next time a women's World Cup final is played at Lord's.

Heather Knight won the toss for England and decided to bat on a day for which afternoon rain had been forecast, although it did not arrive until the very end. Six of the first eight England batters made a good start to their innings, but only Natalie Sciver (51) passed fifty and none went on to play the big innings which can take control of a one-day game. The first ten overs, three of which were maidens, were especially disappointing, with the openers scoring only 43 runs without being parted. Then both got out, Lauren Winfield bowled round her legs sweeping, while Tammy Beaumont swung a full toss to deep square leg. It became 63–3 when Knight was lbw, also trying to sweep, and the advantage of winning the toss had been thrown away.

There was only one partnership of any significance, when Sarah Taylor and Sciver put on 83 for the fourth wicket, but Taylor was out just as they were beginning to accelerate and the lower middle order fell badly away. One of the reasons for this was a fine spell by India's fast bowler Jhulan Goswami, who took 3–23 in her ten overs. When she came back for her second spell, she took two important wickets and was extremely accurate, preventing any late acceleration. It took a few good strokes towards the end from Katherine Brunt and Jenny Gunn to propel England as far as 228, but the slow start had meant that the other batsmen were forced to try and make up for lost ground before they were ready and got themselves out as a result. The pitch, which had been used for England's one-day international against Ireland early in May, played well enough and England had only themselves to blame for their relatively modest total.

For most of their innings, India went calmly along like a side that was fully in control. They lost a wicket in the second over when Smriti Mandhana was bowled by Shrubsole. Their number three, Mithali Raj, was then run out in the 13th over when the score was 43, apparently unaware that she was in any danger of not beating Sciver's throw to Taylor. Then opener Punam Raut and Harmanpreet Kaur, whose 171 in 115 balls had enabled India to beat Australia in the semi-finals, put together the best partnership of the innings, adding 95 without being seriously troubled. Kaur was then well caught at square leg by Beaumont off left-arm spinner Alex Hartley, but India took it in their stride and Veda Krishnamurthy now made another good partner for Raut. They took the score to 191–3, when India needed only 38 more runs with 44 balls and seven wickets remaining.

But England had not given up and with eight overs left, Knight brought back Shrubsole at the Pavilion End to bowl her last four overs. She bowls at about medium pace and her great virtue was that she bowled straight, which is always sensible in the closing overs of a one-day match. Her face somehow contained all the splendid West Country virtues of determination and practised hard work combined with that all-important tinge of humour. She had originally learned her bowling when playing with her family in their small garden in Bath. She had taken only one wicket in the semi-final and was afraid she would be left out for the final. I hope a Women's Honours Board has been erected in both the dressing rooms at Lord's. After this performance, Anya Shrubsole deserves nothing less.

In her first over of this spell, Raut, who had batted so well and held the innings together, was lbw playing across the line. In the next over, the new batter, Sushma Verma, was bowled round her legs, sweeping at Hartley, and in her second over Shrubsole had Krishnamurthy caught at midwicket and then bowled Goswami two balls later. Shrubsole had taken three for three in eight balls and this really brought a crowd which had seemed to be settling for the inevitable back to life with a vengeance. India were 201–7 and, having seemed well beaten, England now had an excellent chance of pulling off a remarkable victory. Every ball was greeted with great excitement, the noise grew and women's cricket had come of age at Lord's in the best possible way.

The eighth-wicket pair scrambled 17 runs which were agonising for both sides. Shikha Pandey then played Jenny Gunn to Shrubsole at short cover, who had the ball back in a flash to wicket-keeper Taylor, who was able to beat Pandey's desperate attempt to get back into her crease. With twelve balls left India needed 11 more and, with Deepti Sharma on 14 and playing well, they also still had a good chance of winning. But this was not allowing for Shrubsole, who now ran in to bowl the last over but one.

Sharma played the first ball from across her front pad to midwicket, where Sciver held the catch. Two balls later, Poonam Yadav, the last batter, spooned the easiest possible catch to the normally reliable Gunn at mid off. The intense pressure and excitement of the moment proved too much for her and to the agonised groans of the crowd, she made an awful mess of a catch she would normally have held in her sleep. If ever a player wanted the ground to swallow her up, it must have been Jenny Gunn who, like South African Herschelle Gibbs at Headingley in 1999, must have felt she had dropped the World Cup.

The stalwart Shrubsole now gripped the ball, bit her lip and strode steadfastly back to her mark, turned and started in again.

True to herself, the next ball pitched on a good length and, above all, it was straight. Gayakwad played all round it and was bowled and England's celebrations began, with Anya Shrubsole of course collecting the Player of the Match award for her 6–46. In brilliant and most emphatic style, women's cricket had come of age in a World Cup final at Lord's which had been as fine a game of one-day cricket as any played there – until perhaps two years later, when England's men somehow managed to get their heads in front of New Zealand in the very last stride.

ENGLAND v INDIA
ICC 2017 Women's World Cup (final)

At Lord's Cricket Ground, London, on 23 July 2017.

England

L. Winfield b Gayakwad	24
T.T. Beaumont c Goswami b Yadav	23
†S.J. Taylor c Verma b Goswami	45
*H.C. Knight lbw b Yadav	1
N.R. Sciver lbw b Goswami	51
F.C. Wilson lbw b Goswami	0
K.H. Brunt run out (Sharma)	34
J.L. Gunn not out	25
L.A. Marsh not out	14
A. Shrubsole did not bat	
A. Hartley did not bat	
Extras (3 lb, 1 nb, 7 w)	11
Total (7 wkts, innings closed, 50 overs)	**228**

1–47 2–60 3–63 4–146 5–146 6–164 7–196

Bowling: Goswami 10–3–23–3; Pandey 7–0–53–0; Gayakwad 10–1–49–1; Sharma 9–0–39–0; Yadav 10–0–36–2; Kaur 4–0–25–0.

India

P.G. Raut lbw b Shrubsole	86
S.S. Mandhana b Shrubsole	0
*M.D. Raj run out (Sciver→Taylor)	17
H. Kaur c Beaumont b Hartley	51
V. Krishnamurthy c Sciver b Shrubsole	35
†S. Verma b Hartley	0
D.B. Sharma c Sciver b Shrubsole	14
J.N. Goswami b Shrubsole	0
S.S. Pandey run out (Shrubsole→Taylor)	4
P. Yadav not out	1
R.S. Gayakwad b Shrubsole	0
Extras (3 lb, 1 nb, 7 w)	11
Total (all out, 48.4 overs)	**219**

1–5 2–43 3–138 4–191 5–196 6–200 7–201 8–218 9–218 10–219

Bowling: Brunt 6–0–22–0; Shrubsole 9.4–0–46–6; Sciver 5–1–26–0; Gunn 7–2–17–0; Marsh 10–1–40–0; Hartley 10–0–58–2; Knight 1–0–7–0.

Toss: England.
Umpires: G.O. Brathwaite (WI), S. George (SA).
Player of the Match: A. Shrubsole.

ENGLAND won by nine runs.

27

OLD-FASHIONED
CAN BE THE BEST

Pakistan v New Zealand (1st Test)

16–19 November 2018; Sheikh Zayed Stadium, Abu Dhabi
New Zealand won by four runs.

THE threat of terrorist attacks on international cricket teams visiting Pakistan led directly to the introduction of Test cricket to the United Arab Emirates. Happily, Test cricket returned to be played inside Pakistan in 2019, ten years after gunmen had opened fire on the Sri Lankan touring team's bus in Lahore in 2009. As a result of that incident, sides from other countries had been understandably reluctant to visit Pakistan and so they started playing their 'home' matches in the United Arab Emirates. They were lucky to have found such splendid replacement venues so close to home, which may continue to be used, for not all countries may necessarily agree to resume touring Pakistan. The only disappointment for international cricket in the UAE is that the three magnificent stadiums, in Abu Dhabi, Dubai and Sharjah, are unable to draw in crowds of any size. The reason for this is that the price of tickets is too high for the huge number of Pakistani and Indian immigrants who would normally flock to these games, but who tend to live at the bottom end of the income scale. Meanwhile, the game still remains an unsolvable mystery to most Arabs, who still do not understand or enjoy the game, although it is, of course, their oil-based wealth which makes these splendid facilities possible.

This Test match against New Zealand was played on the pleasant, open Sheikh Zayed Stadium in Abu Dhabi. It was the first of the series, and produced a wonderfully exciting game of cricket which any ground in the world would have been proud to host. It was, in many ways, an old-fashioned Test match. Both batting sides found it hard work to score runs on a slow pitch, not unlike many of those in the Subcontinent, which helped the spinners increasingly as the match went on. Pakistan became the favourites after bowling out New Zealand for 153 runs on the first day, but thereafter the Kiwis never let their opponents pull significantly away from them. In the best traditions of Test cricket, the advantage went first one way and then the other.

The deciding factor in this game was the left-arm spin of the 30-year-old New Zealander Ajaz Patel, who was playing in his first Test match for his adopted country. He took 5–59 in Pakistan's second innings when they were chasing 176 and, at one point on the final afternoon, had reached 130–3. Patel came to New Zealand when his parents moved from Mumbai to Auckland when he was eight years old. He started his cricketing life bowling fast left arm over the wicket and then one day, while playing club cricket in Auckland when he was 21, he bowled a few spinners with enough success for him to decide that this was the way forward. He had to wait almost ten years for his chance in the Test arena and when it came along he grabbed it with both hands.

Ajaz is only five feet six inches tall, with a lovely beaming smile, usually wearing a floppy sun hat as well as a distinctive pair of dark glasses, which give him a mildly comic appearance. He has a cheerful round face and a good sense of humour to go with it. He worked hard to get into the New Zealand side and his mentor is the former Kiwi off-spinning all-rounder Dipak Patel, originally from Kenya, who played for Worcestershire before emigrating to New Zealand in 1986.

New Zealand could hardly have made a worse start to this Test in Abu Dhabi. After winning the toss their batting was inept and only their captain, Kane Williamson, made any sort of a show, reaching a good 63. Runs were never easy to come by on a slow pitch which made strokeplay a tricky business for any but the best. Leg-spinner Yasir Shah was the best of the Pakistan bowlers and he was unlucky only to take three wickets in this first innings.

On the second day, Pakistan did not fare a great deal better. Babar Azam batted well for 62 and several of the others made a start but had the same problems as the New Zealanders with the ball coming through so slowly onto the bat. Trent Boult, in unhelpful conditions, bowled, as he always does, with speed and hostility, and did more than anyone to prevent Pakistan building a big lead, taking 4–54. When New Zealand batted again, a fifth-wicket partnership of 112 between Henry Nicholls and B.J. Watling made sure Pakistan had something to go for in the final innings, even if 176 did not really seem that much of a target. Once again, the New Zealanders did not play Yasir Shah with any confidence. In 37 overs he picked up 5–110 and bowled well enough to have taken more wickets than he did.

At the close of the third day of hard-fought but not, as yet, especially glamorous or exciting cricket, Pakistan were 37 for no wicket, needing only another 139 to win. It looked straightforward enough for them to gain a regulation victory the next day. This is the sort of situation which tends to bring out the best in New Zealand cricketers, who are as determined as any. There is almost always an excellent team spirit in the New Zealand dressing room. On the fourth morning, Kane Williamson turned at once to Ajaz and with immediate success. He varied his pace cleverly and only three more runs had been scored before Imam-ul-Haq was beaten by the flight and played back to one which was well up and turned a long way, hitting him on the pad in front of middle and leg.

It became 44–2 when Mohammad Hafeez played too early at leg-spinner Ish Sodhi, who also hails from India, and gave a simple catch to cover. Four runs later, the third wicket went down when Haris Sohail could only hit a full toss straight back to Sodhi. The New Zealanders were now really on their toes, but they could only watch while Azhar Ali and Asad Shafiq put on 82 for the fourth wicket in good time and without any obvious difficulty. When, in the last over of the morning, Asad was caught on the crease pushing at Neil Wagner outside the off stump and got an edge, Pakistan still seemed on course for victory, needing 46 more with six wickets in hand.

After the interval, 17 runs came easily enough before the patient Babar Azam was run out, with Sodhi flicking the ball quickly back to Ajaz at the bowler's end. It was 147–5 with 29 needed and suddenly the whole atmosphere changed, with the Pakistanis now seeming to be full of doubts, while the New Zealanders began to look as if they knew they had a good chance. It was sad that there were so few spectators in the ground to see such an exciting finish. The tension really increased and seven runs later Sarfaraz Ahmed swept at Ajaz and was hit on the pad. There was a huge appeal and when it was given not out, the New Zealanders reviewed the decision. The replay showed the ball had hit Sarfaraz's glove before going through to Watling and he was caught behind. At this point you could almost feel the game slipping away from Pakistan. Azhar was fast running out of partners, but surprisingly made no real attempt to try and take control.

It became 154–7 when Bilal Asif had a huge swing at Ajaz and his middle stump went over. One run later, Yasir followed one from Wagner which he should have left alone and was caught at slip: 155–8. The force now was with New Zealand, even though only 21 were needed. Pakistan struggled on to 164 before Hasan Ali tried to slog Ajaz out of the ground, but found the safe hands of the substitute, Tim Southee, at deep midwicket, and Pakistan were 164–9. With everyone in a real state of excitement, seven more runs were somehow gleaned before Azhar, who really should have won the match for Pakistan before it had got to this, faced Ajaz, who was bowling round the wicket. Azhar pushed forward, the ball hit him on the front pad and every New Zealander in Abu Dhabi appealed. The umpire gave Azhar out and of course Pakistan reviewed the decision. The replay showed the ball had pitched in line with the stumps and would have hit the off bail: umpire's call and New Zealand had won by four runs and Ajaz had taken 5–59 in 23.4 overs and 7–123 in his first Test match.

PAKISTAN v NEW ZEALAND (1st Test)

At Sheikh Zayed Stadium, Abu Dhabi, on 16–19 November 2018.

New Zealand

J.A. Raval c Sarfraz Ahmed b Mohammad Abbas	7	c Sarfraz Ahmed b Hasan Ali	46
T.W.M. Latham c Mohammad Hafeez b Yasir Shah	13	b Hasan Ali	0
*K.S. Williamson c Sarfraz Ahmed b Hasan Ali	63	b Yasir Shah	37
L.R.P.L. Taylor c Sarfraz Ahmed b Yasir Shah	2	lbw b Hasan Ali	19
H.M. Nicholls c Sarfraz Ahmed b Mohammad Abbas	28	c Sarfraz Ahmed b Yasir Shah	55
†B.J. Watling lbw b Haris Sohail	10	lbw b Yasir Shah	59
C. de Grandhomme lbw b Hasan Ali	0	lbw b Yasir Shah	3
I.S. Sodhi lbw b Haris Sohail	4	b Hasan Ali	18
N. Wagner c Asad Shafiq b Bilal Asif	12	b Yasir Shah	0
A.Y. Patel lbw b Yasir Shah	6	not out	6
T.A. Boult not out	4	c Mohammad Hafeez b Hasan Ali	0
Extras (4 lb)	4	(4 b, 1 nb, 1 w)	6
Total (all out, 66.3 overs)	**153**	(all out, 100.4 overs)	**249**

1–20 2–35 3–39 4–111 5–123 6–123 7–128 8–133 9–149 10–153

1–0 2–86 3–105 4–108 5–220 6–224 7–227 8–227 9–249 10–249

Bowling, *1st innings*: Mohammad Abbas 12–7–13–2; Hasan Ali 16–6–38–2; Bilal Asif 13–1–33–1; Yasir Shah 16.3–2–54–3; Haris Sohail 8–2–11–2; Mohammad Hafeez 1–1–0–0. *2nd innings*: Mohammad Abbas 22–10–31–0; Hasan Ali 17.4–3–45–5; Yasir Shah 37–6–110–5; Haris Sohail 7–1–12–0; Bilal Asif 14–3–43–0; Mohammad Hafeez 3–1–4–0.

Pakistan

Imam-ul-Haq c Williamson b de Grandhomme	6	lbw b Patel	27
Mohammad Hafeez c Williamson b Boult	20	c de Grandhomme b Sodhi	10
Azhar Ali c Watling b Boult	22	lbw b Patel	65
Haris Sohail c Latham b Sodhi	38	c and b Patel	4
Asad Shafiq b Boult	43	c Watling b Wagner	45
Babar Azam c Watling b Boult	62	run out (Sodhi→Patel)	13
*†Sarfaraz Ahmed c Wagner b Patel	2	c Watling b Patel	3
Bilal Asif st Watling b Patel	11	b Patel	0
Yasir Shah c Watling b Wagner	9	c Taylor b Wagner	0
Hasan Ali c Taylor b de Grandhomme	4	c sub (T.G. Southee) b Patel	0
Mohammad Abbas not out	0	not out	0
Extras (4 b, 4 lb, 1 nb, 1 w)	10	(4 b)	4
Total (all out, 83.2 overs)	**227**	(all out, 58.4 overs)	**171**

1–27 2–27 3–91 4–91 5–174 6–177 7–195 8–220 9–227 10–227

1–40 2–44 3–48 4–130 5–147 6–154 7–154 8–155 9–164 10–171

Bowling, *1st innings*: Boult 18.2–6–54–4; de Grandhomme 13–6–30–2; Patel 24–4–64–2; Wagner 18–5–30–1; Sodhi 10–0–41–1. *2nd innings*: Boult 7–0–29–0; de Grandhomme 3–0–15–0; Patel 23.4–4–59–5; Sodhi 12–0–37–2; Wagner 13–4–27–2.

Close of play, *day 1*: Pakistan (1) 59–2 (Azhar Ali 10*, Haris Sohail 22*); *day 2*: New Zealand (2) 56–1 (Raval 26*, Williamson 27*); *day 3*: Pakistan (2) 37–0 (Imam-ul-Haq 25*, Mohammad Hafeez 8*).

Toss: New Zealand. Last-innings target: 176 runs.
Umpires: I.J. Gould (Eng), B.N.J. Oxenford (Aus).
Man of the Match: A.Y. Patel.

NEW ZEALAND won by four runs.

28

LAST-WICKET WONDER

South Africa v Sri Lanka (1st Test)

13–16 February 2019; Kingsmead, Durban

Sri Lanka won by one wicket.

B Y their very nature, successful last-wicket partnerships are almost invariably extremely tense and exciting. In 2019, the two highest ever last-wicket stands to win Test matches were made within six months of each other. The record of 78 was put together by two Sri Lankans, Kusal Perera and Vishwa Fernando, at Kingsmead in Durban. Then, later in the year, Ben Stokes and Jack Leach steered England home against Australia at Headingley with a stand of 76.

Sri Lanka's hero at Kingsmead, Kusal Perera, although a short man, has the sort of Falstaffian figure in miniature, with a barrel chest and a robust, look-'em-in-the-face appearance, that could surely never belong to a blocker. He has a big, cheerful, bearded look to him, a ready smile which never seems to leave his face and an irresistible urge to hit a cricket ball hard. Like most small men, he scores a lot of his runs off the back foot, hooking, pulling and cutting. Give him an inch of space and he puts his strong wrists to full use on both sides of the wicket. What makes the left-handed Perera, who is also a wicketkeeper, especially unusual is that he began his life as a right-handed batsman. Then, at the age of 13, he fell in love with the stance of his hero, the Sri Lankan opening batsman Sanath Jayasuriya, and turned himself into an almost equally exciting left-handed strokemaker. He went on to establish a fast-scoring record in first-class cricket in Sri Lanka when he made 336 in 270 balls. In this extraordinary match-winning innings, his style of batting was almost more Jayasuriya than Jayasuriya.

In 2018, South Africa visited Sri Lanka and after their hosts had comfortably won both Test matches, South Africa then went on to win the one-day series just as convincingly. The same happened when Sri Lanka journeyed to South Africa six months later and won both Tests. The first was played in Durban and, as so often seems to happen when these dramatic last-wicket stands come along, the storyline for the first three days was turned on its head on the last. Sri Lanka put the South Africans in to bat and bowled them out for 235, which they must have thought was a good result. They were then failed lamentably by their batsmen and bowled out for 191, with only Perera passing 50. Thanks to their captain, Faf du Plessis, and Quinton de Kock, South Africa reached 259 in their second innings and with Sri Lanka needing 304 to win, South Africa seemed assured of victory.

This was underlined when both Sri Lankan openers and Kusal Mendis had departed with the score standing at 52–3, when Perera joined Oshada Fernando. They took the score carefully to 110 before Fernando's patient innings ended when he pushed at one from Dale Steyn which flicked the outside edge and flew to Du Plessis's safe hands in the slips. Two balls later, Niroshan Dickwella chipped a return catch back to Steyn. This brought in Dhananjaya de Silva and he and Perera put on 96. With both batsmen striking the ball well, Sri Lanka were beginning to feel that victory was a possibility, especially as South Africa were without Vernon Philander, who had pulled a hamstring the day before.

De Silva was two runs short of his fifty when he tried to sweep off-spinner Keshav Maharaj, who had pushed one through a little quicker, and was leg before. The innings now fell in a heap. Suranga Lakmal played inside the line of the next ball and Du Plessis did the rest at slip. Nine runs later, Lasith Embuldeniya was bounced out and when Kasun Rajitha was lbw pushing out at Maharaj, Sri Lanka were 226–9 and 78 runs short of their target. Perera, who had been playing some fine strokes, had now reached 86. Knowing that all he could hope for from Vishwa Fernando was that he would somehow keep his wicket intact, Perera had to score the runs on his own and he immediately stepped up a gear.

He began by pull-driving Maharaj over wide long on for six and this was followed by a lovely reverse sweep which took him to 99. A single brought him to his hundred when Sri Lanka needed 64 to win and victory looked only a remote possibility. Perera proceeded to farm the bowling with great skill and without wasting any opportunity to free those strong arms of his. One disappointment was that the cost of Test match tickets was out of range for such a large part of the South African population, so that the stands were largely empty, although there will have been a big television audience.

A beautifully hit six off Olivier onto those lovely grass banks at Kingsmead took him past his previous highest Test score of 110. The new ball was now due, but Perera managed to get the target down to below 50 before it was taken. Du Plessis waited for Steyn to bowl five balls with the old one before he got Vishwa on strike, when he took the new one, but a fast outswinger was too good for Vishwa and missed everything. Most sensibly, Perera now realised that the hardness of the new ball meant it would go quicker off the bat and he played a succession of strokes that were as powerful as they were magnificent.

It was when they saw that the new ball was not providing the answer that the South Africans began to lose their nerve and became extremely tense. They tried too hard, which is often the way in these circumstances. They were not helped when Dean Elgar's throw missed the stumps when Vishwa was comfortably out of his ground. The fifty partnership came up when Perera took his life in his hands and swung violently into Steyn and clubbed the ball miles over midwicket and deep into the stands.

It was a thrilling blow which really sapped the energy and the will out of the South Africans. It also brought the target down to 23 runs. A big swing and a top edge to third man off Kagiso Rabada brought him his fourth six and then another off Steyn and victory was only seven runs away. Three more runs were scampered and then, as calmly as anything, Perera steered a good-length ball from Rabada past slip to the third-man boundary and Sri Lanka had won a remarkable victory. There is often an element of humour in these last-wicket partnerships and here it was provided by a combination of Perera's mildly comical figure and his enthusiastic strokeplay, not that it will necessarily have been appreciated by the South Africans.

Perera had batted for just over five hours for 153. He had faced 200 balls and hit five sixes and twelve fours. His partner, Vishwa Fernando, hung in somehow against 27 balls and for 73 minutes and also made his highest score in Test cricket. It had been an amazing fourth afternoon which has never received the attention it deserves.

SOUTH AFRICA v SRI LANKA (1st Test)

At Kingsmead, Durban on 13–16 February 2019.

South Africa

A.K. Markram b M.V.T. Fernando	11	(2)	c Mendis b Rajitha	28
D. Elgar c Dickwella b M.V.T. Fernando	0	(1)	c and b Ambuldeniya	35
H.M. Amla c Mendis b Lakmal	3		c Thirimanne b M.V.T. Fernando	16
T. Bavuma run out (M.V.T. Fernando)	47		lbw b Ambuldeniya	3
*F. du Plessis c Dickwella b Rajitha	35		lbw b M.V.T. Fernando	90
†Q. de Kock c M.V.T. Fernando b Rajitha	80		lbw b Ambuldeniya	55
V.D. Philander c and b Rajitha	4		b Ambuldeniya	18
K.A. Maharaj c Dickwella b M.V.T. Fernando	29		b M.V.T. Fernando	4
K. Rabada c B.O.P. Fernando b M.V.T. Fernando	3		c Dickwella b Ambuldeniya	0
D.W. Steyn b Ambuldeniya	15		b M.V.T. Fernando	1
D. Olivier not out	0		not out	2
Extras (6 lb, 2 nb)	8		(2 lb, 3 nb, 2 w)	7
Total (all out, 59.4 overs)	**235**		(all out, 79.1 overs)	**259**

1–0 2–9 3–17 4–89 5–110 6–131 7–178
8–186 9–219 10–235

1–36 2–70 3–77 4–95 5–191 6–251
7–255 8–256 9–256 10–259

Bowling *1st innings*: Lakmal 14–3–29–1; M.V.T. Fernando 17–1–62–4; Rajitha 14.4–0–68–3; Karunaratne 3–0–9–0; Ambuldeniya 10–1–51–1; B.O.P. Fernando 1–0–10–0.
2nd innings: Lakmal 20–5–52–0; MVT Fernando 17.1–2–71–4; Rajitha 13–1–54–1; Ambuldeniya 26–3–66–5; de Silva 2–0–8–0; BOP Fernando 1–0–6–0.

Sri Lanka

*F.D.M. Karunaratne lbw b Philander	30		lbw b Philander	20
H.D.R.L. Thirimanne c de Kock b Steyn	0		c du Plessis b Rabada	21
B.O.P. Fernando lbw b Steyn	19		c du Plessis b Steyn	37
B.K.G. Mendis c du Plessis b Philander	12		c de Kock b Olivier	0
M.D.K.J. Perera c sub (Hamza) b Steyn	51		not out	153
†D.P.D.N. Dickwella c Steyn b Olivier	8		c and b Steyn	0
D.M. de Silva c Olivier b Rabada	23		lbw b Maharaj	48
R.A.S. Lakmal c Markram b Steyn	4		c du Plessis b Maharaj	0
L. Ambuldeniya c Steyn b Rabada	24		c Markram b Olivier	4
C.A.K. Rajitha run out (Markram)	12		lbw b Maharaj	1
M.V.T. Fernando not out	1		not out	6
Extras (3 b, 3 lb, 1 w)	7		(13 lb, 1 w)	14
Total (all out, 59.2 overs)	**191**		(9 wkts, 85.3 overs)	**304**

1–19 2–51 3–53 4–76 5–90 6–133 7–142
8–152 9–184 10–191

1–42 2–42 3–52 4–110 5–110
6–206 7–206 8–215 9–226

Bowling *1st innings*: Steyn 20–7–48–4; Philander 10–2–32–2; Rabada 12.2–2–48–2; Olivier 13–2–36–1; Maharaj 3–0–16–0; Elgar 1–0–5–0. *2nd innings*: Steyn 18–1–71–2; Philander 8–3–13–1; Maharaj 20–1–71–3; Rabada 22.3–3–97–1; Olivier 16–3–35–2; Markram 1–0–4–0.

Close of play, *day 1*: Sri Lanka (1) 49–1 (Karunaratne 28*, B.O.P. Fernando 17*);
day 2: South Africa (2) 126–4 (du Plessis 25*, de Kock 15*); *day 3*: Sri Lanka (2) 83–3
(B.O.P. Fernando 28*, Perera 12*).

Toss: Sri Lanka. Last-innings target: 304 runs.
Umpires: Aleem Dar (Pak), R.A. Kettleborough (Eng).
Man of the Match: M.D.K.J. Perera.

SRI LANKA won by one wicket.

29

THE SUPER OVER

England v New Zealand (ICC World Cup final)
14 July 2019; Lord's Cricket Ground, London
Match tied, Super Over tied. England won having hit more boundaries.

EVEN the most diehard supporter of Test cricket and severest critic of the limited-overs game would be hard-pressed to deny this was just about the best cricket match ever to have been played. The fact that it was a World Cup final, and at Lord's, only heightened the perception. After facing their 50 overs, England and New Zealand finished level, with 241 runs each, England profiting near the end from a huge piece of luck. This brought into play for the first time the Super Over, at the end of which we had another tie, with both sides scoring 15. After all this unprece-dented drama and excitement, the rules stated that the winner would be decided, not by a further contest, but by an intensely prosaic countback of the boundaries scored during the match. England had it by 26 to 17. World Cups apparently cannot be shared. The circumstances of this final surely should have led to a sudden and imaginative decision from somewhere within the Lord's Pavilion that the 2019 World Cup should, indeed, have been shared. Not only did New Zealand not deserve to lose the match, but also, of overwhelming importance in this, they did *not* lose it.

England's luckiest break could not have been more cruel or unfair to New Zealand, even though what happened was within the Laws of the game. Through this extraordinary day, the New Zealanders had arguably played the better cricket at the tightest moments before Ben Stokes took over. This most crucial moment of all came in the final over of the main match. Halfway through the previous over, when England needed 22 from nine balls and New Zealand were more than fancying their chances, Stokes had sent the ball soaring away towards the midwicket boundary where Trent Boult was fielding. He judged the catch well, but as he took it, his foot trod on the boundary rope: it was six runs. Fifteen were needed from the last over, bowled by Boult. Stokes refused runs off the first two balls to keep the strike. Somehow, these two dot balls made it all seem even more unreal, even if it was not allowing for the genius of Stokes. The third ball was bowled and Stokes, down on one knee, swung it into the Mound Stand for six. His previous inactivity was immediately forgiven. Now it was nine from three balls as Stokes pummelled the next to deep midwicket and came back for a despairing second run. His dive for the crease coincided with the arrival of Martin Guptill's throw to wicket-keeper Tom Latham. The ball deflected off Stokes's outstretched bat, reaching desperately for the crease. The convention is that batsmen do not run when this happens and it was clear that Stokes and Adil Rashid were not going to. But it was out of their control. The ball sped away to the Pavilion boundary. It was all a complete accident and Stokes, on his knees, raised both hands in apology, for the Laws of cricket dictated that the boundary had to be allowed.

That was not quite the end of it either. Six runs were given, two off the bat and four overthrows. Technically, the overthrows start from the moment the throw leaves the fielder's hand. At that precise moment the batsmen did not appear to have crossed for their second run and therefore it looked as if only a single should have been added to the four overthrows, making a total of five and not six from that delivery. Even more important, Stokes would no longer have been on strike. It would have needed huge technical resources to conclusively prove this and the relevant replays may well not have existed. If they had, the third umpire would probably still be looking at the screen and trying to make up his mind. It was the cruellest of blows for New Zealand, and it was to their huge and everlasting credit that when it was all over, they accepted the incident as just 'one of those things'. Even so, I dare say strong words were spoken in the visitors' dressing room at Lord's that evening. And who can blame them if they were?

In all the years I have been watching cricket, I can think of no other situation which has produced the tension, the tumultuous excitement and the drama as these last few minutes played themselves out on cricket's most famous ground. England strove with everything they had for the biggest trophy of all, which they had never been able to win, and this was their twelfth attempt. As we have seen, Stokes was still on strike and three were now wanted from the last two balls. From the first, Adil Rashid sacrificed himself going for an impossible second run in order to keep Stokes on strike. Two were needed from the last ball, which Stokes pushed gently down the ground, hoping they would have time to run two. They did not: Mark Wood was run out trying for another improbable second run and the scores were level.

Now it was all down to the Super Over, which had never before been needed. First, Trent Boult was going to bowl six balls to Ben Stokes and Jos Buttler, and then it would be Jofra Archer's turn to bowl at Jimmy Neesham and Martin Guptill. This was cricket's first ever penalty shoot-out, but it was better than a penalty shoot-out. The electric atmosphere now had to be seen and felt to be believed. It was midsummer madness, pure and simple. We were all of us out of our depth; this was new territory for everyone. It had never before come to this.

Stokes sliced Boult's first ball over short third man for three. A single to square leg by Buttler brought Stokes back into strike and the third ball, an inswinger, Stokes dispatched to the midwicket boundary. He then sliced a full toss to cover for one and Buttler dug out a yorker on the off side for two more before coolly placing the last ball, a full toss, to the midwicket boundary, and England had ended up with 15.

Was captain Eoin Morgan right to entrust the colossal task of bowling England's one over to the inexperienced Archer? Probably, because he had earlier bowled five good overs at the end of New Zealand's innings, although it already seemed a long time ago. When his first ball produced an off-side wide, most people will have felt that Morgan had got it wrong. The next ball, Neesham drove to long off for two and when he swung the third ball for six to the short boundary in front of the Tavern Stand at square leg, it looked as if it was going to be New Zealand's game. Neesham played the next ball to leg for two runs, thanks to a misfield by Jason Roy, and the one after it for two more, again on the leg side.

This meant that three more were needed from the last two balls. It was not the moment to go and buy a drink; the crowd did not know whether to yell or to watch in silence. The fifth legitimate ball brought Neesham a scrambled single and with two now needed, Guptill took guard for the first time. The World Cup was down to the last ball and New Zealand were well aware that a tie would give the match to England, who had hit more boundaries – we had already had one tie that afternoon which had been a sort of a cricketing miracle for this occasion, but now it was more than possible that we were going to have another, which was even more unthinkable, but a tie was not enough for New Zealand.

Guptill played a firm stroke off his legs towards the midwicket boundary on the Grandstand side of the ground, raced a single, turned and came back for the second, but this time Roy watched the ball into his hands and his flat throw, although a little way off course, allowed Buttler to collect the ball and dive at the stumps, with Guptill a couple of yards short of his ground. England's celebrations began, while it would be difficult to imagine two more lonely and forlorn figures than Neesham and Guptill, on the fringe of a party to which they had not been invited. They plodded back to the Pavilion on what must have seemed the longest and most sorrowful journey of their lives. After a day like this, there surely should not have been a loser.

It had been an incredible day's cricket and by the end, I found it difficult to remember exactly what had happened in the first half of it. It all now seemed such a long way away and almost irrelevant, which was exactly what it was not. England were at last able to celebrate the considerable and long-awaited hat-trick of Wembley 1966, Sydney 2003 and Lord's 2019 – Bobby Moore, Martin Johnson and now Eoin Morgan, and what a journey he had had from Rush in County Dublin, where he was born on 10 September 1986.

I think everyone watching at Lord's or on television will have felt dreadfully sorry for New Zealand. They had competed brilliantly, they had had the better of some important moments and yet they had been undone right at the end by the cruellest piece of misfortune. My own heart bled for their captain, Kane Williamson, an inspiring leader. His form in this World Cup had been extraordinary. In ten matches he had made 578 runs for an average of 82.57, a larger total than any captain had made before in the World Cup finals, beating Mahela Jayawardene's 548 for Sri Lanka in 2007. Williamson's captaincy had contributed substantially to New Zealand's success. He was always a splendidly unflappable character, as we saw now at Lord's. Unlike many captains, he never shirked or put off an awkward or uncomfortable decision. He has a good tactical awareness and his players have the greatest respect for him.

His first decision at Lord's was not the most straightforward. When Williamson won the toss, he had no hesitation in batting on a slow pitch which was at best uncertain. Morgan, another outstanding captain, would probably have fielded first, although he would not have done it for negative reasons. In a match as important as this, some captains would have felt it safer to field first. Having made his decision, New Zealand only lost one wicket early on. Guptill, after a splendid uppercut off Archer which flew over third man for six and a searing drive back just over the bowler's head for four, had been lbw to a ball of full length from Chris Woakes, who had used the new ball well.

The left-handed Henry Nicholls and Williamson added 74 for the second wicket and made it look perhaps a little easier than it was. One of the most important of England's bowlers at this form of the game in the last few years has been Liam Plunkett and this was his moment. At fast-medium he has become a past master at removing the middle order, as he now showed. Plunkett is a big man and hits the pitch a little harder than batsmen anticipate and this, allied to good control and just a little movement, obtained by holding the ball across the seam, makes him more dangerous than he may look, especially if batsmen try to get after him.

At 103, Williamson drove at one from Plunkett which slid down the hill at the Pavilion End and was caught behind. Fifteen runs later, Nicholls drove at another which may also have gone a fraction down the slope and the inside edge went into his stumps. Ross Taylor was soon lbw to Mark Wood and Plunkett then picked up his third wicket when Neesham drove at one which seemed to stop on him and gave an easy catch to mid on. New Zealand were now 173–5 and it was only some robust left-handed strokes from wicketkeeper Latham that enabled them to get to 241 which, after a good start, will have been at least 20 runs fewer than they will have hoped for.

It was sad that the recent weather had dictated that the pitch for this game did not encourage batsmen to play their strokes. As so often happens, though, these low-scoring matches can produce the most exciting cricket. At the halfway point, England will probably have felt the more confident of victory. They had an anxious moment with the first ball of the innings, when Roy survived a big appeal for lbw. It was reviewed by the New Zealanders and the verdict of 'umpire's call' saved Roy. England had reached 28 when Roy was caught behind, driving at one from Matt Henry which swung in and straightened on pitching.

Joe Root now had a most uncomfortable few minutes trying to work out this lifeless pitch before being caught behind driving at one of Colin de Grandhomme's niggling medium-pacers. At 71, Jonny Bairstow tried to square-cut a ball from Lockie Ferguson that was too close to him and edged it into his stumps. Fifteen runs later, Morgan slapped a short one from Neesham away on the off side and was brilliantly caught low down by Ferguson sprinting in from deep cover and diving forward at the last moment. England were 86–4 and struggling, but Stokes and Buttler restored order with a fine stand of 110. Buttler was in great form, playing his shots easily enough and going along at a run a ball, while Stokes found it more difficult and was content for the time being to make the other end safe.

These two appeared to be winning the match for England, but at 196 Buttler mistimed his stroke against a slower ball from Ferguson and, after misjudging the catch, Tim Southee – who we saw substituting with equally good effect when New Zealand beat Pakistan in Abu Dhabi – recovered and held a really good one falling forward as he came in from deep cover. Once more the game was wide open, with England needing 46 from 31 balls. Stokes now began to bat more confidently and with wickets falling regularly at the other end and only Plunkett making any sort of contribution, it all built up beautifully to the high drama that was enacted in the last two overs of the innings.

It is impossible to pay Stokes too much credit for his magnificent innings of 84 not out which gave England the chance of victory. What more can one say about this complex character who is the most uncomplicated cricketer? It is a measure of his ability that he will be endlessly compared to Ian Botham. So far, I think it is fair to say that he may be an even better batsman than Botham, but not nearly as good a bowler, although an equally good catcher in the slips. When Stokes came off after this innings, he said that he was completely exhausted and there is no doubt that he puts everything he has into every moment of the game. The second he knew he was going to have to go straight back for the Super Over and do it all again, if only for one over, he will have summoned up the effort and his whole being will have been ready for the final battle. He was more than prepared to go out with Buttler for this last Super Over joust with Trent Boult when the moment came.

It was only a week or two later that the extraordinary Stokes played another equally astonishing innings, in the third Test against Australia – an account of which begins in a moment. Now at Lord's, he will have been especially happy to put the record straight after Carlos Brathwaite of the West Indies had hit him for four successive sixes to win the Twenty20 World Cup final in Kolkata in 2016. Part of Stokes will also have been apologising to his team-mates for what had gone on near the end of the season in 2017 outside that nightclub in Bristol. It was an apology made on a grand scale and, like the day on which it was made, it will never be forgotten.

ENGLAND v NEW ZEALAND
ICC 2019 World Cup (final)

At Lord's Cricket Ground, London, on 14 July 2019.

New Zealand

M.J. Guptill lbw b Woakes	19
H.M. Nicholls b Plunkett	55
*K.S. Williamson c Buttler b Plunkett	30
L.R.P.L. Taylor lbw b Wood	15
†T.W.M. Latham c sub (Vince) b Woakes	47
J.D.S. Neesham c Root b Plunkett	19
C. de Grandhomme c sub (Vince) b Woakes	16
M.J. Santner not out	5
M.J. Henry b Archer	4
T.A. Boult not out	1
L.H. Ferguson did not bat	
Extras (12 lb, 1 nb, 17 w)	30
Total (8 wkts, innings closed, 50 overs)	**241**

1–29 2–103 3–118 4–141 5–173 6–219 7–232 8–240

Bowling, Woakes 9–0–37–3; Archer 10–0–42–1; Plunkett 10–0–42–3; Wood 10–1–49–1; Rashid 8–0–39–0; Stokes 3–0–20–0.

England

J.J. Roy c Latham b Henry	17
J.M. Bairstow b Ferguson	36
J.E. Root c Latham b de Grandhomme	7
*E.J.G. Morgan c Ferguson b Neesham	9
B.A. Stokes not out	84
†J.C. Buttler c sub (Southee) b Ferguson	59
C.R. Woakes c Latham b Ferguson	2
L.E. Plunkett c Boult b Neesham	10
J.C. Archer b Neesham	0
A.U. Rashid run out (Santner→Boult)	0
M.A. Wood run out (Neesham→Boult)	0
Extras (2 b, 3 lb, 12 w)	17
Total (all out, 50 overs)	**241**

1–28 2–59 3–71 4–86 5–196 6–203 7–220 8–227 9–240 10–241

Bowling, Boult 10–0–67–0; Henry 10–2–40–1; de Grandhomme 10–2–25–1; Ferguson 10–0–50–3; Neesham 7–0–43–3; Santner 3–0–11–0.

England – Super Over

B.A. Stokes not out	8
†J.C. Buttler not out	7
Extras	0
Total (no wicket, innings closed)	**15**

Bowling, Boult 1–0–15–0.

New Zealand – Super Over

J.D.S. Neesham not out	13
M.J. Guptill run out (Roy→Buttler)	1
Extras (1 w)	1
Total (1 wicket, innings closed)	**15**

Bowling, Archer 1–0–15–0.

Toss: New Zealand.
Umpires: H.D.P.K. Dharmasena (SL), M. Erasmus (SA)
Man of the Match: B.A. Stokes

MATCH TIED (England won in the Super Over).

30
STOKES OUT-JUMPS THE KANGAROOS

England v Australia (3rd Test)
22–25 August 2019; Headingley, Leeds
England won by one wicket.

IN 1981 it was the right-handed Ian Botham and England won by 18 runs, to bring the series level at one match all; in 2019 it was the left-handed Ben Stokes and England won by one wicket, which also brought the series level at one match all. In 1981, it was only the second time a side that had been made to follow on had won a Test match. In 2019, England made more runs than they have ever made before to win a Test match. Stokes and Leach's unbroken tenth-wicket stand of 76 was also the highest ever by England to win a Test match.

There was a remarkable similarity between the overall shape of the two matches as well. In 1981, England were being trounced rather than beaten by Australia until Graham Dilley joined Ian Botham late on the fourth day when, with three second-innings wickets left, they still needed 92 to avoid an innings defeat. In 2019, even when England's last-wicket pair came together with 73 more runs needed to win, Australia were still looking at the victory they had been expecting ever since they bowled out England for 67 in their first innings.

The first day was wet and gloomy and only 52 overs could be bowled. Not surprisingly, Joe Root put Australia in and on his first appearance in any cricket at Headingley, Jofra Archer, who hailed from Barbados, fresh from his triumph in the World Cup final at Lord's, was keen to show he was a force in Test cricket too. He took 6–45 in the innings, which were the best figures by an English bowler at Headingley since Bob Willis's 8–43 in that match in 1981. Archer bowled a fraction below his top pace and explained afterwards that, in the conditions, accuracy was more important than sheer pace. Archer and Stuart Broad both took an early wicket and the England bowlers were then frustrated by a stand of 111 in 23 overs. David Warner, who at times severely tested the spirit of the Laws of cricket and was perhaps not the most popular of the Australians, made 61, his only score above 11 in the series. He and Marnus Labuschagne, an Australian of South African origin, rode their luck at first and then took advantage of some poor bowling by Stokes and Chris Woakes until Archer returned and found the outside edge of Warner's bat. Australia's third wicket fell at 136 and they were all out 43 runs later, just before the close, for 179.

The sun shone the next day, but not for England, who shortly before lunch found themselves at 45–6. Josh Hazlewood bowled brilliantly, although he was helped by some lamentable English batting. Joe Denly was the only one to reach double figures and they were all out early in the afternoon for 67. At this point, just as had happened 38 years before, there was only one side in it – and that side was also Australia. By the close on the second day, Australia had reached 171–6, largely as the result of another solid display by Labuschagne, who had reached his second fifty of the match. They were 283 runs ahead, and already that seemed more than enough. They added another 75 the next day and England owed much to a long and extremely hostile spell by Stokes, who finished with 3–56. England had been left to score 359 in the fourth innings, which was by some way the biggest total of the match. Small wonder that Headingley had not been overpopulated so far, for it had been tough going for the spectators.

By the end of the third day England had reached 156–3, with Root, who was batting well, on 75, and Stokes together after a long and obdurate 50 from Denly. He and Root had put on 126 in 53 overs before Denly was bounced out by Hazlewood, leaving Stokes to see out the day with his captain. When the fourth day dawned there was just a glimmer of hope that Root and Stokes might inspire something remarkable. These hopes were soon shattered when, after scoring two more runs in five and a bit overs the next morning, Root came down the pitch to Nathan Lyon and was brilliantly caught by Warner at slip after edging the ball into his pad.

Root is undoubtedly the best of all England's recent batsmen and is close to becoming their best post-war batsman, although Peter May still sits on that particular pedestal. Root has one major failing as a Test match batsman. He consistently gets himself out when he has done all the hard work and played himself in. He has scored a huge number of fifties for England, but he does not convert anything like as many as he should into hundreds. It is easy to put this down to the demands of the one-day game and the constant moving from one-innings to two-innings cricket. It must surely come down to a lack of concentration, which is made all the more surprising by the number of big innings he has proved himself capable of playing, although sadly, to date, he has sometimes found runs hard to come by against Australia.

Stokes scored three singles from his first 73 balls on the third evening and fourth morning and appeared to be embarking on a form of self-denying ordinance. In the last part of the morning session, he began to bat more normally and at the other end Jonny Bairstow also played some fine strokes when the second new ball was taken. They put on 62 from the first ten overs, shared by Hazlewood, Pat Cummins and James Pattinson, whose line and length was as bad as it had been good on the first two days.

At lunch, England needed 121 more with six wickets in hand and were in with a real chance of reaching the highest total they had ever made in the fourth innings to win a Test match. After the interval, the game rapidly changed. Bairstow was caught at slip cutting at Hazlewood and Jos Buttler had only made one when Stokes called him for an impossible run. Chris Woakes immediately drove Hazlewood to short extra cover, Archer slogged three fours before holing out to deep square leg and when Broad was lbw to Pattinson, England were 286–9, five wickets having gone down for only 41 runs.

It was now that the improbable, bespectacled, Harry Potter-like figure of Jack Leach walked out to join Stokes. He looked like an innocent abroad who had just discovered he had come out of the wrong door. Headingley 2019 will go down as one of the great Test matches and yet here we were, with England needing 73 to win with the last pair together and not a single person in the ground reckoning they had even an outside chance. There was certainly no great sense of expectation buzzing around; more a resignation to the inevitability of defeat, although it was closer than at one time had been feared. No last-wicket pair had ever scored as many as 73 to win a Test match for England, let alone one against Australia. Sixty-three balls later, England had won a victory after the most dramatic and exciting last-wicket partnership in the history of cricket.

It would have been interesting to know what was going on in Stokes's mind as he watched the decidedly fragile figure of his final partner walk out to join him. Comparisons with Ian Botham 38 years before come flooding back. When Botham was joined by Graham Dilley in 1981, he is purported to have said to him, 'Come on, let's have some fun,' or something of that sort. Stokes has a hard, unrelenting facial expression and I think it would have been out of character if he had greeted Leach now with a smile and a similar suggestion. Instead, he turned his full attention to the Australian bowlers.

Good bowler that Nathan Lyon is – he had gone past Dennis Lillee's record of 355 Test wickets earlier in the match – his off-spin will have suited Stokes, who now cleared his throat, as it were, by driving him down the ground for sixes in successive overs. This will have made the crowd sit up. Normally, those two sixes would have been seen as providing welcome light relief rather than being regarded as the first serious steps towards another cricketing miracle. But the bat was in Stokes's hands and no one will have needed reminding of what he had done six weeks before in the World Cup final at Lord's. The crowd at Headingley was now a millimetre or two nearer the edge of their seats.

Shortly afterwards, Stokes played what one day might come to be called 'the stroke of the century', which surely must have changed the perception of the day. Lyon was again the bowler and with two slips waiting for the edge, he was aiming at the rough patch outside the left-handed Stokes's off stump. Over came his arm and in a movement which was quick and yet somehow unhurried, Stokes played a reverse sweep. The ball went out of the middle of the bat far over the heads of the two fielders on the boundary. They had been at deep cover and square-ish third man when the ball left Lyon's hand, but found themselves at deep forward and backward square leg when the ball left Stokes's bat. The most remarkable thing about the stroke was that Stokes was in complete control of it from start to finish. It was the most amazing stroke I have seen in all the years I have been watching cricket.

This must have been the moment that those watching realised another cricketing miracle was being played out in front of them. There was a long way still to go, but the Australians began to look rattled, tense and without any idea what to do next. Stokes said later he sensed a sudden change in the Australians: 'You could just feel their tension. You could just sense from their body language.' By now the crowd were in great voice as they cheered every England run to the echo. It is surprising how quickly a game can change. Only a few minutes before this, Australia were in complete charge and then suddenly, although England still had 50 runs to make, the batsmen were in control and Australia's bounce and excited anticipation had evaporated.

Now Stokes faced Cummins and played another stroke which has its origins in the one-day game. He scooped a short ball over his own head for six and reached his hundred when he thumped Hazlewood through midwicket for four. Stokes's determination and singleness of purpose were obvious from the way he stood there, head down, refusing to acknowledge the generous applause. His mind was on the greater goal and, at 326–9, England needed 33 more.

At the other end, Leach defended dourly when Stokes allowed him to face one and sometimes two balls at the end of an over. He may have looked fragile, but there was no way he was going to be blown over. His main trouble came from his glasses, which kept misting up from his sweat, and on a great number of occasions he held up play while he polished them furiously with a piece of black cloth. It made him look an even more fragile and unlikely figure.

Stokes faced Hazlewood. He paddled a low full toss round the corner for six and then pulled the next ball away for another which did not clear the two boundary fielders by all that much. The crowd greeted each stroke with frenzied cheering and Headingley came to resemble the Headingley of 1981 when Willis was destroying Australia's second innings. The certainty of Stokes's strokeplay was bewildering and so too was the imperturbability of his partner, spectacles apart. Then, with 17 wanted, Stokes heaved at Cummins and the ball flew off the edge over the slips. Marcus Harris came racing in from third man and dropped a horribly difficult diving catch low down in front of him. Stokes's immediate retort was a pull through midwicket for four, which was followed by a magnificent drive off the back foot which sped to the straight boundary for four more.

The crowd, which had grown during the day, was beside itself with excitement. Nine more were needed. Stokes ran a single to long off, leaving Leach to negotiate the last two balls of the over. The first was a bouncer which Leach dutifully avoided, the second was well up to the bat and hit him on the pad. There was a frantic appeal which was turned down. There was now a fevered discussion among the Australians. Cummins apparently thought Leach had edged a ball which had pitched in line with the stumps. Paine, behind the wicket, had not spotted an edge, but felt the ball had pitched outside the leg stump. In spite of these negative thoughts, the Australians, grasping for anything they could, decided to review the decision. The crowd held its breath and soon everyone saw the ball had pitched outside the leg stump. Most significantly, Australia were now out of reviews.

Stokes's reaction was to drive Lyon down the ground for another six which was only just out of Labuschagne's reach on the boundary. Only two more runs were wanted and the fielders all came in to save the single. Lyon bowled again and Stokes played another reverse sweep, which went straight to Cummins at short third man. Stokes instinctively started for a run and Leach, arms and legs flying, set off at speed from the non striker's end. By the time Stokes sent him back and returned to his own crease, Leach was almost three-quarters of the way down the pitch. He started on the return journey as fast as he could, knowing that if it was a good throw to the bowler he would be well short of his crease. The throw from Cummins was a good one, coming right over the stumps and at a comfortable height for Lyon. Although an extremely experienced Test cricketer, Lyon had looked to be one of the tensest of the Australians in these closing stages. With the stumps at his mercy and the Ashes within his grasp, he must have taken his eye off the ball at the crucial moment, for it went through his hands and Leach scampered home. There was a sort of strangulated sigh of relief from the crowd, but it was far from over yet.

Stokes tried to sweep the next ball, which thumped into his pad. The appeal was earth-shattering and umpire Joel Wilson, after a moment's pause, shook his head. The Australians could not believe it, but of course they had no reviews left. They had no right of appeal. The replay suggested the ball would have hit the stumps, although, not surprisingly, Stokes sprang to the umpire's defence when the match was over.

England still needed two to win and now for the first time in his innings, Leach had to face the first ball of an over. He survived Cummins's first two balls. Then he turned the third off his hip and they scampered the single which got him off the mark and brought the scores level. This was the 17th ball Leach had faced and seldom can a single have been greeted so enthusiastically by the crowd. The most important part of it all for England was that Stokes was now on strike.

Cummins's next ball was slightly short and gave Stokes a bit of room to play a square cut for four, which gave England victory by one wicket after they had scored more runs than ever before in the fourth innings to win a Test match. Stokes and Leach had put on 76 runs from 63 balls and Stokes had made 74 of them. It is a moot point whether the screams of joy that greeted this final stroke were louder than the yells of triumph when Bob Willis removed Ray Bright's middle stump 38 years before.

Which was the more remarkable game of cricket? It is an argument which will run for ever and maybe it is a generational thing. I shall show my age by voting for 1981, when Ian Botham and Bob Willis turned in performances no less incredible than that of Ben Stokes. The pre-match dramas in 1981 were greater and victory in that match led to the return of the Ashes. But was there anything to beat Stokes's extraordinary reverse sweep for six off Lyon? Probably not. And would the odds against England's last pair putting on 76 to win the match have been longer or shorter than 500–1?

ENGLAND v AUSTRALIA (3rd Test)

At Headingley, Leeds, 22–25 August 2019.

Australia

D.A. Warner c Bairstow b Archer	61	(2)	lbw b Broad		0
M.S. Harris c Bairstow b Archer	8	(1)	b Leach		19
Usman Khawaja c Bairstow b Broad	8		c Roy b Woakes		23
M. Labuschagne lbw b Stokes	74		run out (Denly→Bairstow)		80
T.M. Head b Broad	0		b Stokes		25
M.S. Wade b Archer	0		c Bairstow b Stokes		33
*†T.D. Paine lbw b Woakes	11		c Denly b Broad		0
J.L. Pattinson c Root b Archer	2		c Root b Archer		20
P.J. Cummins c Bairstow b Archer	0		c Burns b Stokes		6
N.M. Lyon lbw b Archer	1		b Archer		9
J.R. Hazlewood not out	1		not out		4
Extras (4 b, 2 lb, 2 nb, 5 w)	13		(5 b, 13 lb, 7 nb, 2 w)		27
Total (all out, 52.1 overs)	**179**		(all out, 75.2 overs)		**246**

1–12 2–25 3–136 4–138 5–139 6–162
7–173 8–174 9–177 10–179

1–10 2–36 3–52 4–97 5–163 6–164
7–215 8–226 9–237 10–246

Bowling, *1st innings*: Broad 14–4–32–2; Archer 17.1–3–45–6; Woakes 12–4–51–1;
Stokes 9–0–45–1. *2nd innings*: Archer 14–2–40–2; Broad 16–2–52–2; Woakes 10–1–34–1;
Leach 11–0–46–1; Stokes 24.2–7–56–3.

England

R.J. Burns c Paine b Cummins	9		c Warner b Hazlewood	7
J.J. Roy c Warner b Hazlewood	9		b Cummins	8
*J.E. Root c Warner b Hazlewood	0		c Warner b Lyon	77
J.L. Denly c Paine b Pattinson	12		c Paine b Hazlewood	50
B.A. Stokes c Warner b Pattinson	8		not out	135
†J.M. Bairstow c Warner b Hazlewood	4		c Labuschagne b Hazlewood	36
J.C. Buttler c Usman Khawaja b Hazlewood	5		run out (Head)	1
C.R. Woakes c Paine b Cummins	5		c Wade b Hazlewood	1
J.C. Archer c Paine b Cummins	7		c Head b Lyon	15
S.C.J. Broad not out	4		lbw b Pattinson	0
M.J. Leach b Hazlewood	1		not out	1
Extras (3 lb)	3		(5 b, 15 lb, 1 nb, 10 w)	31
Total (all out, 27.5 overs)	**67**		(9 wkts, 125.4 overs)	**362**

1–10 2–10 3–20 4–34 5–45 6–45 7–54
8–56 9–66 10–67

1–15 2–15 3–141 4–159 5–245
6–253 7–261 8–286 9–286

Bowling, *1st innings*: Cummins 9–4–23–3; Hazlewood 12.5–2–30–5; Lyon 1–0–2–0;
Pattinson 5–2–9–2. *2nd innings*: Cummins 24.4–5–80–1; Hazlewood 31–11–85–4;
Lyon 39–5–114–2; Pattinson 25–9–47–1; Labuschagne 6–0–16–0.

Close of play *day 1*: Australia (1) 179 all out; *day 2*: Australia (2) 171–6 (Labuschagne 53*,
Pattinson 2*); *day 3*: England (2) 156–3 (Root 75*, Stokes 2*).

Toss: England. Last-innings target: 359 runs.
Umpires: C.B. Gaffaney (NZ), J.S. Wilson (WI).
Man of the Match: B.A. Stokes.

ENGLAND won by one wicket.

ACKNOWLEDGEMENTS

I would like to say a huge thank you to my editor, Roddy Bloomfield of Hodder & Stoughton, who has masterminded this book with his usual skill and his unfailing good humour which, I am ashamed to say, I must frequently have brought almost to breaking point. In a variety of publishing incarnations, this is the ninth book of mine he has presided over. I would like to thank that supreme *Test Match Special* scorer and statistician, Andrew Samson, for putting me right on a couple of things, and also my long-term, old *TMS* producer, great friend and stage partner, Peter Baxter, for continuing – with some success – to keep me on the straight and narrow when it came to the Botham Test at Headingley and England's three-run victory in Melbourne. And finally I would like to thank John Woodcock, the famous Cricket Correspondent of *The Times*, with whom I once drove in a 1921 Rolls-Royce from London to Bombay, for cheerfully confirming a few important details from the depths of Longparish. Sadly, Johnny Woodcock died at the age of ninety-four as I was putting the finishing touches to this book. He was the dearest of men and, in my view, the most respected and revered cricket writer of them all.

PICTURE ACKNOWLEDGEMENTS

The author and publisher would like to thank the following for permission to reproduce photographs:

Section One: George Beldam/Popperfoto via Getty Images/ Getty Images; TopFoto; George Beldam/Popperfoto via Getty Images/Getty Images; Popperfoto via Getty Images/Getty Images; Illustrated London News Ltd/Mary Evans; Public Domain/from *Great Bowlers and Fielders: Their Methods at a Glance*, Beldam, George W and Fry, Charles B.; George Beldam/ Popperfoto via Getty Images/Getty Images; Public Domain/*The Cricketer*, London The Cricketer Ltd: 13. 10 September 1921; Topical Press Agency/Getty Images; PA Images/Alamy Stock Photo; Central Press/Hulton Archive/Getty Images; Ted Abell/ Mirrorpix/Getty Images; Getty Images/Fairfax Media via Getty Images via Getty Images; News Ltd/Newspix; PA Images/Alamy Stock Photo.

Section Two: TopFoto; Patrick Eagar/Popperfoto via Getty Images; Paul Popper/Popperfoto via Getty Images; Patrick Eagar/ Popperfoto via Getty Images; Ben Radford/Allsport/Getty Images; Getty Images; Patrick Eagar/Popperfoto via Getty Images; AFP/Getty Images; Stu Forster/Allsport/Getty Images; John MacDougall/AFP via Getty Images; Patrick Eagar/ Popperfoto via Getty Images; Back Page Images/Shutterstock; Ross Kinnaird/Allsport/Getty Images; Quinn Rooney/Getty

INDEX